COLOSSIANS

THE

TEACHER'S

OUTLINE & STUDY

BIBLE

COLOSSIANS

THE

TEACHER'S

OUTLINE & STUDY

BIBLE

NEW TESTAMENT

KING JAMES VERSION

Leadership Ministries Worldwide
PO Box 21310
Chattanooga, TN 37424-0310

Please address all requests for information or permission to:
    Leadership Ministries Worldwide
    PO Box 21310
    Chattanooga TN 37424-0310
    Ph.# 615-855-2181 FAX # 615-855-8616 CompuServe # 74152,616

Library of Congress Catalog Card Number: 94-073070
International Standard Book Number: 0-945863-39-X

PRINTED IN THE U.S.A.

PUBLISHED BY LEADERSHIP MINISTRIES WORLDWIDE

HOW TO USE
THE TEACHER'S OUTLINE AND STUDY BIBLE (TOSB)

To gain maximum benefit, here is all you do. Follow these easy steps, using the sample outline below.

1 STUDY TITLE

2 MAJOR POINTS

3 SUB-POINTS

4 COMMENTARY, QUESTIONS, APPLICATION, ILLUSTRATIONS
(Follows Scripture)

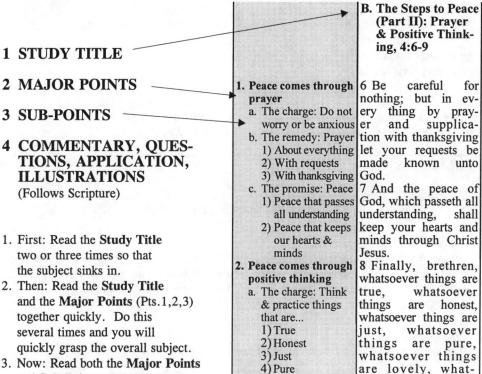

B. The Steps to Peace (Part II): Prayer & Positive Thinking, 4:6-9

1. Peace comes through prayer
  a. The charge: Do not worry or be anxious
  b. The remedy: Prayer
    1) About everything
    2) With requests
    3) With thanksgiving
  c. The promise: Peace
    1) Peace that passes all understanding
    2) Peace that keeps our hearts & minds
2. Peace comes through positive thinking
  a. The charge: Think & practice things that are...
    1) True
    2) Honest
    3) Just
    4) Pure

6 Be careful for nothing; but in every thing by prayer and supplication with thanksgiving let your requests be made known unto God.
7 And the peace of God, which passeth all understanding, shall keep your hearts and minds through Christ Jesus.
8 Finally, brethren, whatsoever things are true, whatsoever things are honest, whatsoever things are just, whatsoever things are pure, whatsoever things are lovely, what-

1. First: Read the **Study Title** two or three times so that the subject sinks in.
2. Then: Read the **Study Title** and the **Major Points** (Pts.1,2,3) together quickly. Do this several times and you will quickly grasp the overall subject.
3. Now: Read both the **Major Points** and **Sub-Points**. Do this slower than Step 2. Note how the points are beside the applicable verse, and simply state what the Scripture is saying—in Outline form.
4. Read the **Commentary**. As you read and re-read, pray that the Holy Spirit will bring to your attention exactly what you should study and teach. It's all there, outlined and fully developed, just waiting for you to study and teach.

TEACHERS, PLEASE NOTE:

⇒ Cover the **Scripture** and the **Major Points** with your students. Drive the **Scripture** and **Major Points** into their hearts and minds.

(Please continue on next page)

⇒ Cover *only some of the commentary* with your students, not all (unless of course you have plenty of time). Cover only as much commentary as is needed to get the major points across.

⇒ Do NOT feel that you must...
- cover all the commentary under each point
- share every illustration
- ask all the questions

An abundance of commentary is given so you can find just what you need for...
- your own style of teaching
- your own emphasis
- your own class needs

PLEASE NOTE: It is of utmost importance that you (and your study group) grasp the Scripture, the Study Title, and Major Points. It is this that the Holy Spirit will make alive to your heart and that you will more likely remember and use day by day.

MAJOR POINTS include:

APPLICATIONS:
Use these to show how the Scripture applies to everyday life.

ILLUSTRATIONS:
Simply a window that allows enough light in the lesson so a point can be more clearly seen. A suggestion: Do not just "read" through an illustration if the illustration is a story, but learn it and make it your own. Then give the illustration life by communicating it with *excitement & energy*.

QUESTIONS:
These are designed to stimulate thought and discussion.

A CLOSER LOOK:
In some of the studies, you will see a portion boxed in and entitled: "A Closer Look." This discussion will be a closer study on a particular point. It is generally too detailed for a Sunday School class session, but more adaptable for personal study or an indepth Bible Study class.

PERSONAL JOURNAL:
At the close of every lesson there is space for you to record brief thoughts regarding the impact of the lesson on your life. As you study through the Bible, you will find these comments invaluable as you look back upon them.

Now, may our wonderful Lord bless you mightily as you study and teach His Holy Word. And may our Lord grant you much fruit: many who will become greater servants and witnesses for Him.

REMEMBER!

The Teacher's Outline & Study Bible is the only study material that actually outlines the Bible verse by verse for you right beside the Scripture. As you accumulate the various books of The Teacher's Outline & Study Bible for your study and teaching, you will have the Bible outlined book by book, passage by passage, and verse by verse.

The outlines alone makes saving every book a must! (Also encourage your students, if you are teaching, to keep their student edition. They also have the unique verse by verse outline of Scripture in their version.)

Just think for a moment. Over the course of your life, you will have your very own personalized commentary of the Bible. No other book besides the Bible will mean as much to you because it will contain your insights, your struggles, your victories, and your recorded moments with the Lord.

> **"Study to show thyself approved unto God, a workman that needeth not to be ashamed, rightly dividing the word of truth" (2 Tim.2:15).**

> **"All scripture is given by inspiration of God, and is profitable for doctrine, for reproof, for correction, for instruction in righteousness: that the man of God may be perfect, throughly furnished unto all good works" (2 Tim.3:16-17).**

*** All direct quotes are followed by a Superscript Endnote number. The credit information for each Endnote is listed at the end of the individual study session for your reference.

MISCELLANEOUS ABBREVIATIONS

&	=	And
Bckgrd.	=	Background
Bc.	=	Because
Circ.	=	Circumstance
Concl.	=	Conclusion
Cp.	=	Compare
Ct.	=	Contrast
Dif.	=	Different
e.g.	=	For example
Et.	=	Eternal
Govt.	=	Government
Id.	=	Identity or Identification
Illust.	=	Illustration
K.	=	Kingdom, K. of God, K. of Heaven, etc.
No.	=	Number
N.T.	=	New Testament
O.T.	=	Old Testament
Pt.	=	Point
Quest.	=	Question
Rel.	=	Religion
Resp.	=	Responsibility
Rev.	=	Revelation
Rgt.	=	Righteousness
Thru	=	Through
V.	=	Verse
Vs.	=	Verses

Publisher &
Distributer

DEDICATED:

To all the men and women of the world
who preach and teach the Gospel of our
Lord Jesus Christ
and
To the Mercy and Grace of God.

─────────────── *&* ───────────────

- Demonstrated to us in Christ Jesus our Lord.

  "In whom we have redemption through His
  blood, the forgiveness of sins, according to the
  riches of His grace." (Eph. 1:7)

- Out of the mercy and grace of God His Word has
  flowed. Let every person know that God will have
  mercy upon him, forgiving and using him to fulfill
  His glorious plan of salvation.

  "For God so loved the world, that he gave his only
  begotten Son, that whosoever believeth in him should
  not perish, but have everlasting life. For God sent not
  his Son into the world to condemn the world; but that
  the world through him might be saved." (Jn 3:16-17)

  "For this is good and acceptable in the sight of God
  our Saviour; who will have all men to be saved, and to
  come unto the knowledge of the truth." (I Tim. 2:3-4)

─────────────── *&* ───────────────

The Teacher's Outline and Study Bible™
is written for God's people to use
in their study and teaching of God's Holy Word.

9/98

LEADERSHIP MINISTRIES WORLDWIDE

OUR FIVEFOLD MISSION & PURPOSE:

- To share the Word of God with the world.
- To help the believer, both minister and layman alike, in his understanding, preaching, and teaching of God's Word.
- To do everything we possibly can to lead men, women, boys, and girls to give their hearts and lives to Jesus Christ and to secure the eternal life which He offers.
- To do all we can to minister to the needy of the world.
- To give Jesus Christ His proper place, the place which the Word gives Him. Therefore — No work of Leadership Ministries Worldwide will ever be personalized.

This material, like similar works, has come from imperfect man and is thus susceptible to human error. We are nevertheless grateful to God for both calling us and empowering us through His Holy Spirit to undertake this task. Because of His goodness and grace, *The Preacher's Outline & Sermon Bible®* - New Testament is complete in 14 volumes as well as the single volume of **The Minister's Handbook**.

God has given the strength and stamina to bring us this far. Our confidence is that, as we keep our eyes on Him and grounded in the undeniable truths of the Word, we will continue working through the Old Testament Volumes and introduce a new series known as *The Teacher's Outline & Study Bible.* Future materials will include CD-ROM, The Believer's *Outline* Bible, and similar *Outline* and **Handbook** materials.

To everyone, everywhere who preaches and teaches the Word, we offer this material firstly to Him in whose name we labor and serve, and for whose glory it has been produced.

Our daily prayer is that each volume will lead thousands, millions, yes even billions, into a better understanding of the Holy Scriptures and a fuller knowledge of Jesus Christ the incarnate Word, of whom the Scriptures so faithfully testify.

As you have purchased this volume, you will be pleased to know that a portion of the price you paid goes to underwrite providing similar volumes at affordable prices in other languages (Russian, Korean, Spanish and others yet to come) to a preacher, pastor, church leader, or Bible student somewhere around the world, who will present God's message with clarity, authority, and understanding beyond their own. *Amen.*

• *Equipping God's Servants Worldwide with OUTLINE Bible Materials* •
— LMW is a 501(c)3 nonprofit, international nondenominational mission agency —   8/97

LEADERSHIP MINISTRIES WORLDWIDE
P.O. Box 21310, 515 Airport Road, Suite 107
Chattanooga, TN 37424-0310
(423) 855-2181 FAX (423) 855-87616
E-Mail - outlinebible@compuserve.com
www.outlinebible.org [Free download samples]

ACKNOWLEDGMENTS

Every child of God is precious to the Lord and deeply loved. And every child as a servant of the Lord touches the lives of those who come in contact with him or his ministry. The writing ministry of the following servants have touched this work, and we are grateful that God brought their writings our way. We hereby acknowledge their ministry to us, being fully aware that there are so many others down through the years whose writings have touched our lives and who deserve mention, but the weaknesses of our minds have caused them to fade from memory. May our wonderful Lord continue to bless the ministry of these dear servants, and the ministry of us all as we diligently labor to reach the world for Christ and to meet the desperate needs of those who suffer so much.

THE GREEK SOURCES

1   Expositor's Greek Testament, Edited by W. Robertson Nicoll. Grand Rapids, MI: Eerdmans Publishing Co., 1970

2.   Robertson, A.T. Word Pictures in the New Testament. Nashville, TN: Broadman Press, 1930.

3.   Thayer, Joseph Henry. Greek-English Lexicon of the New Testament. New York: American Book Co.

4.   Vincent, Marvin R. Word Studies in the New Testament. Grand Rapids, MI: Eerdmans Publishing Co., 1969.

5.   Vine, W.E. Expository Dictionary of New Testament Words. Old Tappan, NJ: Fleming H. Revell Co.

6.   Wuest, Kenneth S. Word Studies in the Greek New Testament. Grand Rapids, MI: Eerdmans Publishing Co., 1953.

THE REFERENCE WORKS

7.   Cruden's Complete Concordance of the Old & New Testament. Philadelphia, PA: The John C. Winston Co., 1930.

8.   Josephus' Complete Works. Grand Rapids, MI: Kregel Publications, 1981.

9.   Lockyer, Herbert, Series of Books, including his Books on All the Men, Women, Miracles, and Parables of the Bible. Grand Rapids, MI: Zondervan Publishing House.

10.   Nave's Topical Bible. Nashville, TN: The Southewstern Co.

11.   The Amplified New Testament. (Scripture Quotations are from the Amplified New Testament, Copyright 1954, 1958, 1987 by the Lockman Foundation. Used by permission.)

12.   The Four Translation New Testament (Including King James, New American Standard, Williams - New Testament In the Language of the People, Beck - New Testament In the Language of Today.) Minneapolis, MN: World Wide Publications.

13.   The New Compact Bible Dictionary, Edited by T. Alton Bryant. Grand Rapids, MI: Zondervan Publishing House, 1967.

14.   The New Thompson Chain Reference Bible. Indianapolis, IN: B.B. Kirkbride Bible Co., 1964.

THE COMMENTARIES

15.   Barclay, William. Daily Study Bible Series. Philadelphia, PA: Westminster Press.

16.   Bruce, F.F. The Epistle to the Colossians. Westwood, NJ: Fleming H. Revell Co., 1968.

17.   Bruce, F.F. Epistle to the Hebrews.Grand Rapids, MI: Eerdmans Publishing Co., 1964.

18.   Bruce, F.F. The Epistles of John. Old Tappan, NJ: Fleming H. Revell Co., 1970.

19.   Criswell, W.A. Expository Sermons on Revelation. Grand Rapids, MI: Zondervan Publishing House, 1962-66.

20.   Greene, Oliver. The Epistles of John. Greenville, SC: The Gospel Hour, Inc., 1966.

21.   Greene, Oliver. The Epistles of Paul the Apostle to the Hebrews. Greenville, SC: The Gospel Hour, Inc., 1965.

22.   Greene, Oliver. The Epistles of Paul the Apostle to Timothy & Titus. Greenville, SC: The Gospel Hour, Inc., 1964.

23.   Greene, Oliver. The Revelation Verse by Verse Study. Greenville, SC: The Gospel Hour, Inc., 1963.

24.   Henry, Matthew. Commentary on the Whole Bible. Old Tappan, NJ: Fleming H. Revell Co.

25.   Hodge, Charles. Exposition on Romans & on Corinthians. Grand Rapids, MI: Eerdmans Publishing Co., 1972-1973.

26.   Ladd, George Eldon. A Commentary On the Revelation of John. Grand Rapids, MI: Eerdmans Publishing Co., 1972-1973.

27.   Leupold, H.C. Exposition of Daniel. Grand Rapids, MI: Baker Book House, 1969.

28. Newell, William R. <u>Hebrews, Verse by Verse</u>. Chicago, IL: Moody Press.

29. Strauss, Lehman. <u>Devotional Studies in Philippians</u>. Neptune, NJ: Loizeaux Brothers.

30. Strauss, Lehman. <u>Galatians & Colossians</u>. Neptune, NJ: Loizeaux Brothers.

31. Strauss, Lehman. <u>The Book of the Revelation</u>. Neptune, NJ: Loizeaux Brothers.

32. <u>The New Testament & Wycliffe Bible Commentary</u>, Edited by Charles F. Pfeiffer & Everett F. Harrison. New York: The Iverson Associates, 1971. Produced for Moody Monthly. Chicago Moody Press, 1962.

33. <u>The Pulpit Commentary</u>, Edited by H.D.M. Spence & Joseph S. Exell. Grand Rapids, MI: Eerdmans's Publishing Co., 1950.

34. Thomas, W.H. Griffith. <u>Hebrews, A Devotional Commentary</u>. Grand Rapids, MI: Eerdman's Publishing Co., 1970.

35. Thomas, W.H. Griffith. <u>Studies in Colossians & Philemon</u>. Grand Rapids, MI: Baker Book House, 1973.

36. <u>Tyndale New Testament Commentaries</u>. Grand Rapids, MI: Eerdman's Publishing Co., Began in 1958.

37. Walker, Thomas. <u>Acts of the Apostles</u>. Chicago, IL: Moody Press, 1965.

38. Walvoord, John. <u>The Thessalonian Epistles</u>. Grand Rapids, MI: Zondervan Publishing House, 1973.

OTHER SOURCES

39. Barnhouse, Donald Grey. <u>Let Me Illustrate</u>.Grand Rapids, MI: Fleming H. Revell Co., A Division of Baker Book House,1967.

40. Cymbala, Jim. <u>How To Light The Fire</u>. Brooklyn, NY, 1994.

41. Doan, Eleanor. <u>The New Speaker's Source Book</u>. Grand Rapids, MI: Zondervan Publishing House, 1968.

42. Jenkins, Jerry. <u>Hedges--Loving Your Marriage Enough to Protect It</u>. Chicago, IL: Moody Press, 1989.

43. Knight, Walter B. <u>Knight's Master Book of 4,000 Illustrations</u>. Grand Rapids, MI: Eerdmans Publishing Company, 1956.

44.   Knight, Walter B. Knight's Treasury of 2000 Illustrations. Grand Rapids, MI: Eerdmans Publishing Company, 1963.

45.   Knight, Walter B. Three Thousand Illustrations for Christian Service. Grand Rapids, MI: Eerdmans Publishing Company, 1947.

46.   Larson, Craig B., Editor. Illustrations for Preaching and Teaching. Grand Rapids, MI: Baker Books, 1993.

47.   Leadership Journal. Carol Stream, IL: Christianity Today Inc., 1994.

48.   McGee, J. Vernon. Thru The Bible, 5 Vols. Nashville, TN: Thomas Nelson Publishers, 1983.

49.   Morley, Patrick. I Surrender: Submitting to Christ in the Details of Life. Dallas, TX: Word Publishing, 1990.

50.   Morley, Patrick. The Man in the Mirror. Dallas, TX: Word Publishing, 1989.

51.   Tan, Paul Lee. Encyclopedia of 7,700 Illustrations: Signs of the Times. Rockville, MD: Assurance Publishers, 1985.

52.   Warren W. Wiersbe. The Bible Exposition Commentary, Vol.2. Wheaton, IL: Victor Books, 1989.

PUBLISHER & DISTRIBUTOR OF OUTLINE BIBLE MATERIALS

Currently Available Materials, with New Volumes Releasing Regularly

- **THE PREACHER'S OUTLINE & SERMON BIBLE® — DELUXE EDITION**

  Volume 1 . . . . St. Matthew I (chapters 1-15)   3-Ring, looseleaf binder
  Volume 2 . . . . St. Matthew II (chapters 16-28)
  Volume 3 . . . . St. Mark
  Volume 4 . . . . St. Luke
  Volume 5 . . . . St. John
  Volume 6 . . . . Acts
  Volume 7 . . . . Romans
  Volume 8 . . . . 1, 2 Corinthians (1 volume)
  Volume 9 . . . . Galatians, Ephesians, Philippians, Colossians (1 volume)
  Volume 10 . . . . 1,2 Thessalonians, 1,2 Timothy, Titus, Philemon (1 volume)
  Volume 11 . . . . Hebrews -James (1 volume)
  Volume 12 . . . . 1,2 Peter, 1,2,3 John, Jude (1 volume)
  Volume 13 . . . . Revelation
  Volume 14 . . . . Master Outline & Subject Index
                   FULL SET — 14 Volumes

- **THE PREACHER'S OUTLINE & SERMON BIBLE® — OLD TESTAMENT**

  Volume 1 . . . . Genesis I (chapters 1-11)
  Volume 2 . . . . Genesis II (chapters 12-50)
  Volume 3 . . . . Exodus I (chapters 1-18)
  Volume 4 . . . . Exodus II (chapters 19-40)
  Volume 5 . . . . Leviticus   **New volumes release periodically**

- **THE PREACHER'S OUTLINE & SERMON BIBLE® — SOFTBOUND EDITION**
  Identical content as Deluxe above. Lightweight, compact, and affordable for overseas & traveling

- **THE PREACHER'S OUTLINE & SERMON BIBLE® — 3 VOL HARDCOVER w/CD**

- **THE PREACHER'S OUTLINE & SERMON BIBLE® — NIV SOFTBOUND EDITION**

- **The Minister's Personal Handbook** - What the Bible Says...to the Minister
  12 Chapters - 127 Subjects - 400 Verses *OUTLINED* - Paperback, Leatherette, 3-ring

- **THE TEACHER'S OUTLINE & STUDY BIBLE™** • New Testament Books •
  Complete 45 minute lessons - 4 months of studies/book; 200± pages - Student Journal Guides

- **OUTLINE Bible Studies series: 10 Commandments - The Tabernacle**

- **Practical Word Studies: New Testament - 2,000 Key Words Made Easy**

- **CD-ROM: Preacher, Teacher, and Handbook-** (Windows/STEP) - **WORD**Search

- **Translations of Preacher, Teacher, and Minister's Handbook: <u>Limited Quantities</u>**
  Russian — Spanish — Korean Future: French, Portuguese, Hindi, Chinese
       — Contact us for Specific Language Availability and Prices —

For quantity orders and information, please contact either:

LEADERSHIP MINISTRIES WORLDWIDE   *Your OUTLINE Bible Bookseller*
PO Box 21310
Chattanooga, TN 37424-0310
(423) 855-2181 (9am - 5pm Eastern) • FAX (423) 855-8616 (24 hours)
E•Mail - outlinebible@compuserve.com.
     → FREE Download Sample Pages — www.outlinebible.org

• *Equipping God's Servants Worldwide with OUTLINE Bible Materials* •
LMW is a nonprofit, international, nondenominational mission agency   9/98

> **"**
> *Go ye therefore, and
> teach all nations*
> **"** *(Mt. 28:19)*

OUTLINE OF COLOSSIANS

THE TEACHER'S OUTLINE & STUDY BIBLE™ is *unique*. It differs from all other Study Bibles & Sermon Resource Materials in that every Passage and Subject is outlined right beside the Scripture. When you choose any *Subject* below and turn to the reference, you have not only the Scripture, but you discover the Scripture and Subject *already outlined for you--verse by verse*.

For a quick example, choose one of the subjects below and turn over to the Scripture, and you will find this marvelous help for faster, easier, and more accurate use.

In addition, every point of the Scripture and Subject is *fully developed in a Commentary with supporting Scripture* at the bottom of the page. Again, this arrangement makes sermon preparation much easier and faster.

Note something else: The Subjects of Colossians have titles that are both Biblical and *practical*. The practical titles sometimes have more appeal to people. This *benefit* is clearly seen for use on billboards, bulletins, church newsletters, etc.

A suggestion: For the quickest overview of Colossians, first read *all the major titles* (I, II, III, etc.), then come back and read the subtitles.

OUTLINE OF COLOSSIANS

THE EPISTLE OF PAUL THE APOSTLE TO THE

COLOSSIANS

INTRODUCTION

AUTHOR: Paul, the Apostle.

Paul's authorship is disputed by some commentators, but the majority still hold that Paul was the author. The strongest argument for Paul's authorship is seen in the great similarity between Colossians, Philemon, and Ephesians (See Ephesians, Introductory Notes, To Whom Written, point 4). Philemon definitely comes from Paul's hand. Note five other facts as well:

1.   Paul's son in the faith, Timothy, was his companion in both letters (Col.1:1; Phile.1).

2.   Paul's companions in Philemon were also present at the writing of Colossians: Epaphras, Mark, Aristarchus, Demas, and Luke (Col.4:12f; Phile.22-23).

3.   Paul was in prison while writing both letters (Col.4:7f; Phile.1).

4.   Paul sent a message to the same man in both letters--Archippus (Col.4:17; Phile.2).

5.   Paul had Onesimus to travel with Tychicus in taking the letter to the church of Colosse. Onesimus was the slave or the subject of the Philemon letter (Col.4:7-9; Phile.10).

DATE: Uncertain. Probably between A.D. 60-63.

Colossians was probably written during Paul's imprisonment at Rome. But this too is disputed by some. Some hold that the letter was written from Caesarea (A.D. 58-60) or Ephesus (A.D. 55-56).

TO WHOM WRITTEN: To the believers and faithful brothers in Christ which are at Colosse (Col.1:2).

PURPOSE: To combat an extremely dangerous and threatening heresy that was arising in the Colosse church.

There have been several suggestions as to what the heresy was. But the value in identifying the name of the heresy is questionable, since few if any ever hold to a belief in its entirety or in its pure form. The Christian believer and carnal church can, however, benefit from a study of its characteristics. (See notes--Col.1:15; 2:8-10; 2:11-12; 2:13-15; 2:16-19; 2:20-23 for more discussion.)

1.   It stressed astrology, the signs and spirits of the stars and planets. Paul warns, "Beware lest any man spoil you...after the rudiments [elementary signs and spirits] of the world, and not after Christ" (Col.2:8). Then Paul asks, "If ye be dead with Christ from the rudiments of the world, why, as though living in the world, are ye subject to ordinances?" (Col.2:20).

2.   It stressed philosophy. The heresy attacked the simplicity of the gospel. It prided itself in being original and in its ability to rationalize. Paul warns, "Beware lest any man spoil you through philosophy and vain deceit" (Col.2:8).

3.   It stressed "enlightenment." It had a strong emphasis upon wisdom and knowledge (Col.2:3); philosophy and tradition (Col.2:8); delving into the unknown and using one's fleshly mind (Col.2:18); and worshipping man's own ability and will to control and discipline himself (Col.2:23).

4.   It stressed soul over body. The body was considered evil, a prison house that imprisoned the soul. The consequences were twofold. First, some said the way to release or take care of the soul was to subdue the body, discipline and control it. Therefore, asceticism became the inevitable result: "Touch not, taste not, handle not" (Col.2:21). Second, some said that since the soul is what is important, the body does not matter. One can do what he wishes with his body just so he takes care of his soul by

(Col.2:21). Second, some said that since the soul is what is important, the body does not matter. One can do what he wishes with his body just so he takes care of his soul by participating in religious worship and ordinances. Therefore, loose living became acceptable. One could be worldly so long as he was also religious. This is what is so strongly attacked by Paul in passages such as Col.3:5-8 and by John in 1 Jn.1:6-2:2.

5. It stressed ritual and tradition. Special foods and drinks, days and festivals, traditions and man-made rules were insisted upon (Col.2:16, 22).

6. It stressed other mediators between God and man: elementary spirits (Col.2:8, 20) and angels (Col.2:18).

7. It stressed spiritual humility. Man was considered to be so unworthy that he was unable to approach God himself. Man had to submit to other mediators to approach God for him. This evidently resulted in a great spiritual pride and snobbishness and in false humility (Col.2:23. Note also the stress upon "every man" of Col.1:28. Paul is pointing out that salvation is not limited to a special few.)

The heresy attacked Jesus Christ at every point.

1. It attacked His supremacy, His deity, His messiahship and His incarnation. The heresy said this: if the world and its material, including man's body, is evil and imprisons the soul, then God would never take human flesh upon Himself. Why? Human flesh is evil. And God would become evil by taking man's flesh upon Himself. This argument took two directions.

    a. There was Docetism. Docetism said that Christ was not really human; He only appeared human. The word "Docetism" means *to seem*. Jesus only seemed to have a body. He was never really flesh and blood. He came to earth only as a pure spiritual being.

    b. There was Cerinthinism. Cerinthinism said that there was a clear distinction between the human and the divine Christ. This just had to be, for God could never suffer and die. He could not really be God if He suffered and died. Thus it was claimed that the Spirit of God Himself did not enter Jesus until His baptism, and He left Jesus right before His death.

Paul has to insist that Jesus is "the image of the invisible God, the firstborn of every creature" (Col.1:15): that "it pleased the Father that in Him should all fulness dwell" (Col.1:19); that "in Him are hid all the treasures of wisdom and knowledge" (Col.2:3); that "in Him dwelleth all the fulness of the Godhead bodily" (Col.2:9). John combated the same heresy by saying that the eternal God has come to earth and entered time and space (1 Jn.1:1-4; see Outline). He asks, "Who is a liar but he that denieth that Jesus is the Christ" (1 Jn.22). He pointedly says, "Every spirit that confesseth not that Jesus is come in the flesh is not of God, and this is that spirit of antichrist" (1 Jn.4:3). In answer to Cerinthus John says, "This is He that came by water and blood, even by Jesus Christ; not water [baptism] only, but by water and blood [death]" (1 Jn.5:6).

2. It attacked the creative power and supreme role of Jesus Christ in creation. Paul has to insist that "by Him were all things created, that are in heaven, and that are in earth, visible and invisible, whether they be thrones, or dominions, or principalities, or power; all things were created by Him, and for Him; and He is before all things and by Him all things consist" (Col.1:16-17).

3. It attacked the humanity of Jesus Christ. Paul says it was "in the body of His flesh" that He redeemed man (Col.1:22); that "in Him [His body] dwelleth all the fulness of the Godhead bodily [in His bodily form]" (Col.2:9).

4. It attacked the redemptive power of Jesus Christ. The heresy was claiming that something more than Christ was needed to defeat the powers that oppose man. Christ has His place, but only as one among others. He is one way to God, but there are other ways as well. Paul insists that "you...hath He reconciled in the body of His death" (Col.1:21-22); that "ye are complete in Him, which is the head of all principality and power" (Col.2:10); that "having spoiled principalities and powers, He made a show of them openly, triumphing over them in it" (Col.2:15).

Laodicea, the chief city of the area, were only six miles apart. Colosse was twelve miles away and was the least important of the three. The city was about one hundred miles east of Ephesus. The area was a fertile land providing a feast for flocks. It was also one of the clothing and dye centers of the world.

2. The Church at Colosse. Paul never visited Colosse so far as is known. The church had never seen his face (Col.2:1), and the book of Acts does not record a mission to the area. He was writing the city to combat the heresy discussed in the Purpose above. Paul mentions both Laodicea and Hierapolis (Col.2:1; 4:13, 16). Apparently some of Paul's converts founded the church. While in Ephesus for three years, Paul saw to it that "all they which dwelt in Asia heard the word of the Lord Jesus" (Acts 19:10). Epaphras, who was the fellow servant of Paul, was the pastor of the Colosse church. Apparently, he was also the area pastor of Laodicea and Hierapolis (Col.1:7; 4:12-13; Phile.23). The church met in Philemon's home, a convert of Paul (Phile.10). The church was primarily Gentile in membership, for they were aliens from God's promises to Israel (Col.1:21). He speaks of making known the "mystery of God to the Gentiles" (Col.1:27). And he gives a list of sins that were viewed as common to the Gentiles (Col.3:5-7).

The church showed some strengths despite the heresy. They held "faith in Christ Jesus" and showed "love to all the saints" (Col.1:4). They were bearing evangelistic fruit, reaching people for Christ (Col.1:6). They were stedfast in their faith (Col.2:5). This seems to indicate that the heresy was just beginning to seep into the church and had not yet become a major problem. Paul's task was to stop it dead in its tracks.

3. Colossians is "The Epistle Similar to Ephesians" (see Ephesians, Introductory Notes, To Whom Written, point 4). In Ephesians, the church is seen as the body of Christ. In Colossians, Christ is seen as the Head of the church (cp. Col.1:15f).

COLOSSIANS

	CHAPTER 1	Jesus Christ by the will of God, and Timotheus our brother.	fession: The will of God
	I. THE FOUNDA-TIONS OF THE BELIEVER'S LIFE, 1:1-11		2. Life has one essential relationship: Broth-erhood
		2 To the saints and faithful brethren in Christ which are at Colosse: Grace be unto you, and peace, from God our Father and the Lord Jesus Christ.	3. Life has two levels of spiritual maturity: A carnal person vs. a faithful believer
	A. The Great Beliefs of a True Chris-tian, 1:1-2		4. Life has two dimensions
			5. Life has two basic spiritual needs: Grace & peace
1. Life has one basic pro-	Paul, an apostle of		

Section I
THE FOUNDATIONS OF THE BELIEVER'S LIFE,
Colossians 1:1-11

Study 1:   **THE GREAT BELIEFS OF A TRUE CHRISTIAN**

Text: **Colossians 1:1-2**

Aim: To firmly root your life in the great beliefs of Christianity.

Memory Verse:
> "Not every one that saith unto me, Lord, Lord, shall enter into the kingdom of heaven; but he that doeth the will of my Father which is in heaven" (Mt.7:21).

INTRODUCTION:
You've heard the expression that a picture is worth a thousand words. That may be true in many instances, but in Scripture, a few words are worth a thousand pictures! No person could ever pack so much in so little space as the Word of God does. This is one of the proofs of the inspiration of Scripture. These two single verses which open the Book of Colossians are a prime example. In just a few words, the great beliefs of a true Christian are covered.

OUTLINE:
1. Life has one basic profession: the will of God (v.1).
2. Life has one essential relationship: brotherhood (v.1).
3. Life has two levels of spiritual maturity: a carnal person or a faithful believer (v.2).
4. Life has two dimensions of being: physical and spiritual (v.2).
5. Life has two basic spiritual needs: grace and peace (v.2).

1. LIFE HAS ONE BASIC AND UNDERLYING PROFESSION: THE WILL OF GOD (v.1).

Two things are stressed.
1. What Paul did was "by the will of God"; that is, his profession and work were exactly what God wanted him to do. Paul did not dare choose his life's work without the direction of God; for he knew he could make a mistake, and he did not want to waste his life. He did not want to come to the end of his life and be counted a failure by God. To Paul, there was only one

work or profession for him: the job God wanted him to do. The profession he wanted did not matter; only God's will for his life mattered.

APPLICATION:

There is only one profession for any believer: the work God wants him to do. God has put every believer upon the earth for a specific task. If the believer chooses some profession or job other than the work God wants him to do, then he is out of the will of God. He is not fulfilling his purpose for being upon the earth.

> **"Ye have not chosen me, but I have chosen you, and ordained you, that ye should go and bring forth fruit, and that your fruit should remain: that whatsoever ye shall ask of the Father in my name, he may give it you" (Jn.15:16, cp. Heb.13:21).**

2. The profession chosen by God for Paul was that of being a minister, in particular, an apostle. The word "apostle" means a person who is especially sent to go among men as an ambassador or messenger. The key thought is this:

⇒ He is sent forth by God. He does not go forth on his own nor by the authority of other men. His profession and authority are both of God.

⇒ He is the messenger of God. In fact, his very call or profession exists only to deliver the message of God. He has no right to proclaim his own message and thoughts nor the message and thoughts of others.

> **"Now then we are ambassadors for Christ, as though God did beseech you by us: we pray you in Christ's stead, be ye reconciled to God" (2 Cor.5:20).**

ILLUSTRATION:

When God calls you to a task, He always equips you with the abilities to accomplish His will. Do you ever worry about not having the "right credentials" needed to share Christ? Listen to this story:

A speaker was presenting Christ to a large audience on one of the great university campuses. One of the professors in the audience was stricken by the power of the message and the calm and peaceful appearance of the speaker. Leaving the auditorium the professor said to a fellow professor walking beside him, "I suppose that preacher spends most of his time in study and preparation of sermons, away from the tension and strain of this busy world of ours."

"Would you like to meet the speaker?" the fellow professor asked. *"I know him well."* The professor said he would, so a meeting was scheduled for lunch the next day.

How shocked the professor was when he was taken to a snack room in one of the local factories. Sitting there at the table with the speaker, he asked the speaker about his profession. *"My occupation is to do the will of God and to love people while I wait for Christ to return to earth,"* the speaker replied. *"Meanwhile, I operate one of the machines here at the factory."*[1]

The point is this: a person does not have to be a great preacher to be in the will of God. Your profession is to do the will of God and to be a strong witness for Christ no matter where God places you.

> **"Faithful is He that calleth you, who also will do it" (1 Th.5:24).**

2. LIFE HAS ONLY ONE ESSENTIAL RELATIONSHIP, THAT OF BROTHERHOOD (v.1).

Paul mentions Timothy, a young disciple or student of his. Timothy had joined Paul to learn all he could about the ministry and to serve right along beside Paul. But note that the relationship mentioned by Paul was not that of a student or disciple. It was not even that of a fellow preacher, teacher, or administrator. It was that of being a *brother in Christ*. And note the word "our." The basic relationship between Timothy and the believers at Colosse was that of being brothers. Note also that he calls the Colossians *brothers* (v.2).

APPLICATION 1:
There are many different relationships in life. There are relationships between...

*   family members
*   employer and employee
*   worker and co-worker
*   teacher and student
*   merchant and customer
*   minister and parishioner
*   one neighbor to another
*   one friend to another

All the relationships of life are important and have their place in the welfare of society, but there is one relationship that is essential: that of brotherhood. A man does not walk as a solitary figure upon this earth. He walks *among* people—people just like himself. Thus, a man who walks alone does not understand that brotherly relationships are essential in life. Paul knew this: wherever he went, he initiated and nourished relationships. Here he calls Timothy *brother* and the Colossians *brothers* (v.2). One of the most valuable qualities in all the world is knowing how to properly relate to people.

One essential for believers is to walk as brothers to other believers. Within the church there is not to be any sense of...

*   superiority
*   pride
*   arrogance
*   super-spirituality
*   criticism
*   grumbling
*   judging
*   censoring
*   envy
*   cliqueishness
*   divisiveness
*   self-seeking

APPLICATION 2:
A true brotherhood is to be the fundamental relationship within the church and with believers. Treating one another as brothers and sisters is the secret to peace in both the world and the church.

> **"So we, being many, are one body in Christ, and every one members one of another" (Ro.12:5).**

Even in a healthy, loving family there can occasionally be strife, tension, and disagreements. But because of our genuine love for one another and desire to resume a right relationship, we strive to work things out.

Our relationships with our Christian brothers and sisters should be no less important. (In fact, the tie is even more permanent!) We should strive to resolve all conflicts with the spirit of Christ—one of peace, love, and forgiveness. And it is only through Christ that we have the power to do this!

QUESTIONS:
1. Based on the scale below, rate your *current* commitment to each relationship:
   a) My most important relationship, an intense commitment.
   b) A significant relationship, a strong commitment.
   c) An acquaintance, a moderate commitment.

RELATIONSHIPS:

_____Immediate family members
_____A fellow employee
_____Christian friends
_____My neighbors
_____Jesus Christ
Are you comfortable with these ratings? Why or why not?

2. Do you initiate and nourish relationships or do you avoid involvement to protect your time and privacy?
3. How would you describe the basic relationship that exists within your church as a whole? What can you do to help build the one essential relationship within your church, the relationship of brotherhood?

3. LIFE HAS TWO LEVELS OF SPIRITUAL MATURITY, THAT OF BEING A CARNAL PERSON OR OF BEING A FAITHFUL BELIEVER (v.2).

Paul addresses his letter to the *saints* (believers) and faithful brothers in the church. Paul is making a clear distinction between two classes of believers.

1.   There are the "saints," that is, the *carnal* believers within the church. This refers to those who in the past had set their lives apart to follow the Lord Jesus. They *had separated* themselves from the world and *had turned* to the Lord Jesus to save them. However, a saint or believer may or may not *continue on* with the Lord Jesus. Some in the Colossian church *were not continuing on*. They were not fully committed. Their commitment to the Lord Jesus Christ was lacking. Therefore, they were running the risk of falling into the error of false teaching and turning away from Christ.

APPLICATION:
A person can be a carnal believer or carnal "saint" within the church. Just because a person has made a profession and given some semblance of following Christ does not mean he is safe and secure forever—that he is automatically mature in Christ. When a person truly comes to know Christ, he is just beginning a journey with Christ, a journey that has a much higher level of spiritual growth to reach.

"Wherefore come out from among them, and be ye separate, saith the Lord, and touch not the unclean thing; and I will receive you, and will be a Father unto you, and ye shall be my sons and daughters, saith the Lord Almighty" (2 Cor.6:17-18, cp. Ro.6:12-13).

2.   There are *faithful saints* or believers in the church. This refers to those who had set their lives apart to Christ and *had continued on*. They were loyal and stedfast in their allegiance, and they held firm against the attacks of worldliness and false teaching. They were not shaken by the temptations of the devil nor by the urges of the flesh. They were faithful against all foes.

APPLICATION 1:
Once a person has become a saint, that is, set his life apart to follow Christ, he is to be faithful. And he is to grow in his faithfulness. In fact, the highest level of spiritual

maturity is that of faithfulness. Being faithful or obedient to Christ is the one thing that pleases Christ above all else.

"He that hath my commandments, and keepeth them, he it is that loveth me: and he that loveth me shall be loved of my Father, and I will love him, and will manifest myself to him" (Jn.14:21).

APPLICATION 2:

Note something that needs to be stressed about the church: the church is people; it is not a building. It is men, women, boys, and girls. It is saints, genuine believers, and faithful brothers. Weak members make a weak church; strong members make a strong church.

QUESTIONS:
1. In which category do you fall—a faithful saint or a carnal saint? What kinds of things can you do in order to mature in your spiritual growth and relationship with the Lord?
2. How can you guard against becoming a carnal believer?
3. What practical things can you do in order to minister to church members who are carnal believers?

4. LIFE HAS TWO DIMENSIONS OF BEING, THE PHYSICAL DIMENSION AND THE SPIRITUAL DIMENSION (v.2).

Note that believers are said to be both *in Christ* and *at Colosse*. The believer is a citizen of the city or place where he happens to live upon earth, but he is also a citizen of the kingdom of Christ, that is, of heaven.

William Barclay has an excellent description of this point that is well worth quoting.

"[Paul] writes to the Christians who are in Colosse and who are in Christ. A Christian always moves in two spheres. He is in the town, the place, the society where he happens to stay in this world; but he is also in Christ. The Christian lives in two dimensions. He lives in this world, and he does not take the duties and relationships of this world lightly; he fulfils his every obligation to the world in which he lives. But above and beyond that he lives in Christ. In this world he may move from place to place, so that now he is in one place and now in another; but wherever he is, he is in Christ. That is why outward circumstances will make very little difference to the Christian; his happiness and his peace and his joy are not dependent on them; these things can change, but the fact that he is in Christ can never change. That is why the Christian will do any job and any task with all his heart. It may be menial; it may be unpleasant; it may be painful; it may be far less distinguished than he might expect to have; its rewards may be small, and its praise may be non-existent; nevertheless the Christian does it diligently, uncomplainingly and cheerfully, for he is in Christ and does all things as to the Lord. We are all in our own Colosse, wherever that Colosse may be, but we are all in Christ, and it is Christ who sets the tone of our life and our living."[2]

QUESTIONS:
1. Why is it important for you to live in Christ as well as in your community?
2. Can you be so "heavenly-minded" that you are no earthly good?
3. Is the reverse true of you: Are you so "earthly-minded" that you are no heavenly good?
4. What is the secret to keeping a balance in this area of your life?

5. LIFE HAS TWO BASIC SPIRITUAL NEEDS, THAT OF GRACE AND PEACE (v.2).

A person may wish a man wealth, pleasure, fame, or even health. But there is really only one necessary blessing, the blessing of God's grace and peace. If a person possesses God's grace and peace, he possesses all the inner strength and confidence that are needed to overcome and to walk joyfully in the world, regardless of circumstances.

1.   Grace means the *undeserved favor and blessings* of God. The word *undeserved* is the key to understanding grace. Man does not deserve God's favor; he cannot earn God's approval and blessings. God is too high and man is too low for man to deserve anything from God. Man is imperfect and God is perfect; therefore, man cannot expect anything from God. Man has reacted against God too much. Man has...

- rejected God
- rebelled against God
- ignored God
- neglected God
- cursed God
- sinned against God
- disobeyed God
- denied God
- questioned God

APPLICATION:
Man deserves nothing from God except judgment, condemnation, and punishment. But God is love—perfect and absolute love. Therefore, God makes it possible for man to experience His grace, in particular the favor and blessing of salvation which is in His Son, Jesus Christ.

> **"For by grace are ye saved through faith; and that not of yourselves: it is the gift of God: not of works, lest any man should boast" (Eph.2:8-9).**

2.   Peace means to be bound and joined together with God and with everyone else. It means to be confident and secure in the love and care of God. It means to have a knowledge that God will...

- provide
- guide
- strengthen
- sustain
- deliver
- encourage
- save
- give true life both now and forever

APPLICATION:
A person can experience true peace only as he comes to know Jesus Christ. Only Christ can bring peace to the human heart, the kind of peace that brings deliverance and assurance to the human soul.

> **"These things I have spoken unto you, that in me ye might have peace. In the world ye shall have tribulation: but be of good cheer; I have overcome the world" (Jn.16:33).**

ILLUSTRATION:
How many of us take on heavy burdens that weigh us down? Somehow, a warped sense of personal strength and obligation makes us turn away from God's grace. Instead, we would rather work things out ourselves. In carrying around all these burdens, is it any wonder we get frustrated and "crabby"?

The little red-headed girl's attention was fixed on the hermit crab. She noticed that when he wanted to move, his shell went along for the ride. Her conclusion expressed the frustration that many Christians face: *"Daddy, every time that crab moved, he had to carry his house with him.*

COLOSSIANS 1:1-2

Just imagine! What if we had to lift <u>our house</u> whenever we wanted to move! It would be too heavy!

Doing things in our own strength will crush us and make us crabby to everyone we know. Are you like the hermit crab: carrying the weight of the world?

QUESTIONS:

1. Can a good person earn his own salvation? Why or why not? How can it be obtained?
2. Do you ever miss out on the peace offered by Christ when you take matters into your own hands? Share a recent example.
3. How would you explain the grace of God to a non-believer? What important things need to be considered so they can understand what you share?
4. What burden is weighing you down right now? What is God's promise to you?

SUMMARY:

Have you ever wanted to know the rules of a game before you began to play? Sure you have. So why is it that so many Christians play the game of life without knowing all the rules? For Christians, ignorance is no longer an excuse. We must become spiritual believers. We must remember:

1. Life has one basic profession: the will of God.
2. Life has one essential relationship: brotherhood.
3. Life has two levels of spiritual maturity: a carnal person or a faithful believer.
4. Life has two dimensions of being: physical and spiritual.
5. Life has two basic spiritual needs: grace and peace.

PERSONAL JOURNAL NOTES
(Reflection & Response)

1. The most important thing that I learned from this lesson was:

2. The area that I need to work on the most is:

3. I can apply this lesson to my life by:

4. Closing Statement of Commitment:

---

[1] Unknown.

[2] William Barclay *The Letters to the Philippians, Colossians, and Thessalonians* "<u>Daily Study Bible</u>" (Philadelphia, PA: Westminister Press, Began in 1953), *p.125.*

	B. The Great Pillars of the Christian Life, 1:3-8	word of the truth of the gospel; 6 Which is come unto you, as it is in all the world; and bringeth forth fruit, as it doth also in you, since the day ye heard of it, and knew the grace of God in truth:	4. The believer's hope has one great source: The gospel
1. The great pillars are good reasons for giving thanks to God	3 We give thanks to God and the Father of our Lord Jesus Christ, praying always for you,		a. It is truth, v.5 b. It is for individuals c. It is for all men d. It produces fruit e. It comes by hearing
2. The great pillars are faith & love	4 Since we heard of your faith in Christ Jesus, and of the love which ye have to all the saints,	7 As ye also learned of Epaphras our dear fellowservant, who is for you a faithful minister of Christ;	f. It is God's grace g. It is shared by men
3. The great pillars have one great basis: The believer's hope	5 For the hope which is laid up for you in heaven, whereof ye heard before in the	8 Who also declared unto us your love in the Spirit.	h. It results in love

Section I
THE FOUNDATIONS OF THE BELIEVER'S LIFE,
Colossians 1:1-11

Study 2: **THE GREAT PILLARS OF THE CHRISTIAN LIFE**

Text: Colossians 1:3-8

Aim: To build your life upon the great pillars of faith, love, and hope.

Memory Verse:
"And now abideth faith, hope, love, these three; but the greatest of these is love" (1 Cor.13:13).

INTRODUCTION:
"A Hindu student said to Billy Graham in Madras, 'I would become a Christian if I could see one!' Said Graham, 'And when he said that, he was looking at me! That was one of the greatest sermons ever preached to me!'"[1]

When we claim to be a follower of Christ, we must assume that our lives will be closely examined by the lost. People will inspect our lives for any flaws and failures. How then can we be strong in the Lord? How can we keep from collapsing and from being a poor testimony before the world?

This is the discussion of this power-packed passage, a passage that covers the great pillars of the Christian life—the pillars of faith and love. It also covers the great hope of the Christian and the source of hope which is the Word of God. As stated, this is a power-packed study! Note how it lays a solid foundation against false teaching, the great threat which the Colossian church was facing and which churches of every generation face.

OUTLINE:
1. The great pillars are good reasons for giving thanks to God (v.3).
2. The great pillars are faith and love (v.4).
3. The pillars have one great foundation: the believer's hope (v.5).
4. The believer's hope has one great source: the gospel (v.5-8).

1. THE GREAT PILLARS ARE GOOD REASONS FOR GIVING THANKS TO GOD (v.3).

The pillars will be identified in just a moment in the next point. But first of all, what is a pillar? A pillar is a "firm upright support for a superstructure" (Webster's Dictionary. Springfield, MA: G. & C. Merriam Co., 1969). Pillars are vital to the support of a building. How much more important are the pillars of the Christian life? They are so great, such wonderful qualities of life, that they stirred Paul to thank God that the pillars existed in the lives of the Colossian believers. The pillars are the very supports that hold together the lives of believers. The Colossian believers could not exist as a church without the foundational support of the pillars.

Note one other fact: Paul gives thanks to the only living and true God, the Father of our Lord Jesus Christ. There is no God except the Father of our Lord Jesus Christ. This stresses something of critical importance: Jesus Christ is the Son of God; He is exactly whom He claimed to be.

QUESTIONS:
1. What are some things that happen to a building that is without strong pillars?
2. What are some pillars upon which unbelievers build their lives? Some pillars that unbelievers choose to support their lives?
3. What kinds of things actually hold life together?
4. What are some things that happen to a Christian without strong support?
5. Why do you think some Christians settle for a life without pillars?

2. THE GREAT PILLARS OF THE CHRISTIAN LIFE ARE FAITH AND LOVE (v.4).

Faith and love are the two basic qualities of life for true Christians. In fact, they form the one great commandment of God Himself.

> **"And this is his commandment, That we should believe on the name of his Son Jesus Christ, and love one another, as he gave us commandment"** (1 Jn.3:23).

1. There is the great pillar of faith. But note: the faith being spoken about...
    * is not the faith needed to plow through life.
    * is not the faith in self or others that is needed to live successfully as a human being.

The great pillar of faith is faith in a particular person: the person of our Lord Jesus Christ. What is there about Jesus Christ that makes faith in Him so superior to faith in other great leaders? Stated as simply as possible, Jesus Christ is the Son of God, so He brings us in touch with His Father. He makes it possible for God to adopt us as His sons and daughters. Jesus Christ has the right to ask His Father to adopt a *fatherless person*. Jesus Christ makes a Father-son relationship possible between God and the believer. But we must always remember: the Father-son relationship with God does not automatically exist. The only natural relationship between God and man is that of Creator and subject. Jesus Christ alone brings about the Father-son relationship between God and man.

The point is this: faith in Jesus Christ assures a person of God's wonderful presence and blessings. It means...
* that God looks after the believer as a father looks after his child.
* that God helps and directs the believer through all the trials and temptations of life.
* that the believer has the very strength of God at his disposal as he faces life day by day.
* that the believer is assured of living with God forever and ever.

The believer lives by his *faith in Christ*. He believes in Christ; therefore, he lives by his belief. He governs his life by Christ. He strives to do nothing that his faith in Christ forbids. His faith in Christ becomes one of the great pillars of his life.

> "For God so loved the world, that he gave his only begotten Son, that whosoever believeth in him should not perish, but have everlasting life" (Jn.3:16).
> "But as many as received him, to them gave he power to become the sons of God, even to them that believe on his name" (Jn.1:12).

2.   There is the great pillar of love. But note: the love being spoken about is not the natural love which all men *should* have for one another. We are fellow members of the human race; therefore, all men *should* love one another with a natural love. But, as stated, this is not the love being spoken about in this passage. The great pillar of love is the love which believers hold for each other. Why is the love of believers for one another greater than the natural love of men for fellow men? There are two reasons.

    a)   The love of believers is based upon the love of Jesus Christ, and the love of Jesus Christ is the summit of love. This is seen in His sacrificial death for men. He paid the ultimate price for man: He sacrificed His life to bear the sins of men—men who opposed Him and stood against Him. No greater love could ever be demonstrated. Therefore, when a man gives his life to follow Christ, he is giving himself to love as Christ loved. He is proclaiming that he will love to the ultimate degree: he will sacrifice himself for men even as Christ sacrificed Himself.

    b)   The love of believers is stirred by the Holy Spirit; that is, the believer's love is a supernatural love. The Holy Spirit, who lives within the believer, arouses the love of God within the heart of the believer. The believer is actually stirred to love others by the Spirit of God.

APPLICATION:

Believers possess a great love for all men: the very love of Christ. But they possess a very special love for fellow believers. Why? Because they have their faith in Christ in common. Because they have all committed themselves to follow the same Lord. Because the same Holy Spirit dwells in all believers. There is bound to be a very special bond among all who are filled with a common faith and by the same Spirit of God.

This is a striking point. It means that there is no room within the church or among believers for...

- division
- cliques
- grumbling
- envy
- criticism
- argument
- strife
- hard feeling

> "A new commandment I give unto you, That ye love one another; as I have loved you, that ye also love one another. By this shall all men know that ye are my disciples, if ye have love one to another" (Jn.13:34-35).

In conclusion, faith and love are the two great pillars of the Christian life. A person who has faith in Jesus Christ and loves as Christ loves is the person who possesses the two basic pillars of Christian life. Without these two qualities, it is impossible for a person to be given the privilege of living forever.

1. Do you know someone who thinks he is a child of God *automatically by birth*, that is, simply because God created him? That he has to do nothing to share the inheritance with Jesus Christ? That he can live any way he chooses and still be a *child of God*?
2. Have *you* taken the step of faith that takes you from being the "subject" of God's creation over to being God's child?
3. What is the believer's source of faith? What barriers do you have to overcome in order for your faith to grow?
4. How can Christian believers show a true love for all believers? How does trusting God help you to love believers who are hard to love?

3. THE PILLARS OF FAITH AND LOVE HAVE ONE GREAT FOUNDATION: THE BELIEVER'S HOPE (v.5).

Hope, the hope that God gives, is the reason we surrender our lives to Jesus Christ and go to such limits to love one another. Only one thing could make a man love to such a point that he would sacrifice himself for another man, especially when the man is attacking or trying to destroy him. That one thing is the hope of some great promise, the hope of some great reward. Note what the hope or reward is: it is the hope that is *laid up* for us in heaven. What is that hope?

- It is the hope of being raised from the dead and being given a new, perfect, and glorious body, a body just like Jesus Christ.

    "And have hope toward God, which they themselves also allow, that there shall be a resurrection of the dead, both of the just and unjust" (Acts 24:15).

- It is the hope of the Lord's return and of being with the Lord Himself forever.

    "For the Lord himself shall descend from heaven with a shout, with the voice of the archangel, and with the trump of God: and the dead in Christ shall rise first: then we which are alive and remain shall be caught up together with them in the clouds, to meet the Lord in the air: and so shall we ever be with the Lord" (1 Th.4:16-17).

- It is the hope of entering heaven and of living there forever.

    "In my Father's house are many mansions: if it were not so, I would have told you. I go to prepare a place for you. And if I go and prepare a place for you, I will come again, and receive you unto myself; that where I am, there ye may be also" (Jn.14:2-3).

- It is the hope of the glorious inheritance we are to receive from God as sons and daughters of His.

    "Blessed be the God and Father of our Lord Jesus Christ, which according to his abundant mercy hath begotten us again unto a lively hope by the resurrection of Jesus Christ from the dead, to an inheritance incorruptible, and undefiled, and that fadeth not away, reserved in heaven for you" (1 Pt.1:3-4).

APPLICATION:

People hope for various things. What are your greatest hopes? Are you hoping for...

- health
- friends
- acceptance
- success

- wealth
- position
- security
- love

Some of these hopes are very important, but no hope compares with the glorious hope of living forever with God. Think about it: you can actually live forever. You do not have to die. You can live eternally in heaven, live in a perfect body and perfect world; free from all the pain, suffering, corruption, trouble, insecurity, loneliness, emptiness; free from all the terrible problems, heartaches, and failures—of this world. This is the great hope that God gives, the hope of living forever in a perfect body and perfect hope.

> **"And God shall wipe away all tears from their eyes; and there shall be no more death, neither sorrow, nor crying, neither shall there be any more pain: for the former things are passed away" (Rev.21:4).**

ILLUSTRATION:

God loves you! Think of what God has provided for you in Jesus Christ and how Christianity differs from other religions in what it offers. A major distinction is pointed out by Donald Barnhouse in this story:

> *"In the lobby of the Imperial Hotel in Tokyo, Japan, the girl at one of the airline desks spoke Chinese, Japanese and English; she was obviously from a cultured background. I asked her if she was a Christian. She replied that she was a Buddhist. Further questions elicited the information that she had heard of Christ and knew that there was a sacred book, the Bible; but she had never read it and knew nothing of Christian truth. I then asked her, 'Do you love Buddha?' She was startled and said, 'Love? I never thought about love in connection with religion.' I said to her, 'Do you know that in the whole world no God is truly loved except the Lord Jesus Christ? Other gods are hated and feared. You have statues of fierce monsters to guard the gates of your temples, and the people stand at a distance and try to awaken their gods by clapping their hands. They burn incense and offer sacrifices to them as though they were gods who had to be appeased. But Jesus Christ loves us; He came to die for us, and those of us who truly know Him have learned to love Him in return...Mohammedans do not love Allah; Hindus do not love their gods, and neither do you love Buddha. But we love the Lord Jesus because He died for us."[2]*

What a hope! What a powerful reason to follow the Lord Jesus Christ!

QUESTIONS:

1. What are your greatest hopes? Are you hoping for...

- health
- friends
- acceptance
- success

- wealth
- position
- security
- love

2. How does this verse help you to focus your hope (v.5)? Upon what should you focus?
3. Share a time when your hopes were dashed. What lessons did you learn from that experience? How would you handle it differently now?
4. What is the secret to keeping your hope alive?

COLOSSIANS 1:3-8

4. THE BELIEVER'S HOPE HAS ONE GREAT SOURCE: THE GOSPEL, THE WORD OF GOD (v.5-8).

Note that both "the Word" and "the gospel" are mentioned in verse 5. It is the Word of God that reveals the great hope for man. Man cannot find hope—not a permanent or eternal hope, not a hope that lasts forever—anyplace else. The only lasting hope ever offered to man is found in the Word of God, in the glorious message of its gospel (good news). Note what is said about the Word of God or the gospel in these four verses. (These verses provide an excellent study of the gospel or of the Word of God.)

1. The gospel or Word is truth. It is not false. Neither is it just a wish or guess that its message is true. The gospel is the truth of God, the very Word and promise of the Sovereign Majesty of the universe. This means a most wonderful thing: the hope offered to man is true. It is not a *desire* or guess that *may* or *may not* be true. The hope promised in the gospel is the very truth of God Himself.

> **APPLICATION:**
> What more assuring thought can we have than to know that everything God tells us is the truth! Every word, every promise ever made by Him will be fulfilled. Can we make that claim about anyone else? No, for despite our best intentions, we all fail from time to time. But God never fails!

"Sanctify them through thy truth: thy word is truth" (Jn.17:17).

2. The gospel or Word is for individuals. Paul says that it has come to *you*. He is addressing all the believers together, but he is saying that the gospel is for *every one of them*—for every individual. It is the individual who has to respond to the gospel; no one can respond for him. The hope laid up in heaven is for the individual, and the individual has to give his heart to pursue the hope.

> **"Also I [Christ] say unto you, Whosoever shall confess me before men, him shall the Son of man also confess before the angels of God: but he that denieth me before men shall be denied before the angels of God" (Lk.12:8-9).**

3. The gospel or Word is for the world: it is universal as well as individual. The gospel is...

- not for a particular body of people.
- not for a particular nation or nationality.
- not for a particular religion, denomination, or church.
- not for a particular social class.
- not for a particular intelligence.

The gospel is not to be limited in any sense of the word: it is to be proclaimed to the whole world. The hope offered by God is for every human being who lives and ever will live on the earth. There is to be no discrimination, partiality, or favoritism shown whatsoever, not to anyone.

"God is no respecter of persons" (Acts 10:34).

4. The gospel or Word produces fruit. It produced fruit in the Colossians, and it will produce fruit within any person who surrenders his life to follow the gospel. What fruit?

⇒ There is the fruit of the Spirit.

> **"But the fruit of the Spirit is love, joy, peace, longsuffering, gentleness, goodness, faith, meekness, temperance: against such there is no law" (Gal.2:22-23).**

⇒ There is the fruit of bearing converts, of reaching others for Christ.

> **"Now I would not have you ignorant, brethren, that oftentimes I purposed to come unto you, (but was let [hindered] hitherto,) that I might have some fruit among you also, even as among other Gentiles" (Ro.1:13).**

⇒ There is the fruit of sanctification, that is, of purity and cleanliness of life.

> **"Every branch in me that beareth not fruit he taketh away: and every branch that beareth fruit, he purgeth it, that it may bring forth more fruit. Now ye are <u>clean through the word</u> which I have spoken unto you" (Jn.15:2-3).**

APPLICATION:

The gospel gives us hope, hope for a life of love, joy, and peace, a life that works to change society by converting *individuals*. The gospel alone offers the hope of such a life to man.

5. The gospel or Word comes by hearing. This is common sense, yet it is seldom thought about. Men will sit under the gospel and never listen. They allow their minds to wander or to focus upon other subjects, or they close their ears lest they hear the gospel. Yet, no person can ever hear the gospel until he opens his ears and willingly receives the message. The power of the ear is in the hands of man: he can either open or shut his ears. The decision is his.

> **"So then faith cometh by hearing, and hearing by the word of God" (Ro.10:17).**

6. The gospel or Word is the message of God's grace. There is no greater message than the gospel of God. The grace of God is the great hope which He offers man—the great gifts and blessings which He extends to men.

> **"For the grace of God that bringeth salvation hath appeared to all men, teaching us that, denying ungodliness and worldly lusts, we should live soberly, righteously, and godly, in this present world" (Tit.2:11-12).**

7. The gospel or Word is shared by men. The Colossians learned the hope of the gospel from their minister, Epaphras. God has not committed the gospel to angels, but to men. He has chosen man and holds man accountable for sharing His Word. It is our privilege and our responsibility to spread His Word. If we do not do it, it will not be done.

> **"Ye have not chosen me, but I have chosen you, and ordained you, that ye should go and bring forth fruit, and that your fruit should remain: that whatsoever ye shall ask of the Father in my name, he may give it you" (Jn.15:16).**

8. The gospel or Word results in love. The Colossian believers were true believers, so they were filled with love *in the Spirit of God*. They had given their hearts over to the hope of the gospel. Therefore, the love of Christ was generated in their hearts by the Holy Spirit.

APPLICATION:

How many believers today are only half-committed to the Lord, to the mission of spreading the gospel to the whole world? Unfortunately, the majority do not take the commission seriously. But when we give our hearts over totally to the Lord, to the great hope that He gives us in the gospel, we will have our hearts filled with love and will be constrained and compelled to share the good news.

> **"And hope maketh not ashamed; because the love of God is shed abroad in our hearts by the Holy Ghost which is given unto us"**
> **(Ro.5:5, cp. Gal.5:22).**

ILLUSTRATION:

There are a lot of different ideas in the marketplaces of the world that attempt to fill the "God-void" in the hearts of people. Man is prone to put his hope in a variety of things. The Scriptures tell us that our hope must have a certain focus in order to have eternal life. Warren Wiersbe shares this story:

> *"When I was a young pastor, one of my favorite preachers was Dr. Walter Wilson of Kansas City. He had a unique way of making old truths seem new and exciting. I once heard him quote John 3:16 and ask, 'If you were to give a gift that would be suitable for the whole world, what would you give?'*
> *"He then listed several possibilities and showed how those gifts could not suit everybody: books (many people cannot read); foods (people eat different things in different parts of the world); clothing (climates are different); money (not every culture makes use of money). He came to the logical conclusion that only the Gospel, with its gift of eternal life, was suitable for the whole world; and he was right."[3]*

Are you offering the gospel of Jesus Christ to the lost?

QUESTIONS:
1. How do these verses help you better understand the contents of the gospel?
2. What are some ways you can share the Gospel at work or school? What barriers do you need to overcome in order to be more courageous in sharing the gospel?
3. What are the characteristics of the gospel?
4. What is the ultimate goal of the gospel according to verse eight? Are you failing to experience this in your life? What do you need to do in order to mature in this area?

SUMMARY:

We must build our lives upon the great pillars of faith, love, and hope:
1. The great pillars are good reasons for giving thanks to God.
2. The great pillars are faith and love.
3. The pillars have one great foundation: the believer's hope.
4. The believer's hope has one great source: the Gospel.

PERSONAL JOURNAL NOTES
(Reflection & Response)

1. The most important thing that I learned from this lesson was:

2. The area that I need to work on the most is:

3. I can apply this lesson to my life by:

4. Closing Statement of Commitment:

---

[1] Walter B. Knight. *Knight's Treasury of 2,000 Illustrations* (Grand Rapids, MI: Eerdman's Publishing Company, 1963), p.34.

[2] Donald Grey Barnhouse. *Let Me Illustrate* (Grand Rapids, MI: Fleming H. Revell, 1967), p.163-164.

[3] Warren W. Wiersbe. *The Bible Exposition Commentary, Vol.2* (Wheaton, IL: Victor Books, 1989), p.107.

COLOSSIANS 1:9-11

	C. The Great Requests of Prayer, 1:9-11	10 That ye might walk worthy of the Lord unto all pleasing, being fruitful in every	2. Request 2: To walk worthy of Christ a. By being fruitful in good works
1. Request 1: To know God's will—to be filled with the knowledge of God's will a. In all wisdom b. In all spiritual understanding	9 For this cause we also, since the day we heard it, do not cease to pray for you, and to desire that ye might be filled with the knowledge of his will in all wisdom and spiritual understanding;	good work, and increasing in the knowledge of God; 11 Strengthened with all might, according to his glorious power, unto all patience and longsuffering with joyfulness;	b. By increasing in the knowledge of God 3. Request 3: To possess the power of God a. To make us stedfast b. To make us longsuffering c. To give us joy

Section I
THE FOUNDATIONS OF THE BELIEVER'S LIFE,
Colossians 1:1-11

Study 3: **THE GREAT REQUESTS OF PRAYER**

Text: Colossians 1:9-11

Aim: To learn to pray daily for three great things: God's will, a worthy life, and the power of God.

Memory Verse:
"That ye might walk worthy of the Lord unto all pleasing, being fruitful in every good work, and increasing in the knowledge of God" (Col.1:10).

INTRODUCTION:
Our faith must be real, and faith becomes real when we commit ourselves to prayer. Pastor Jim Cymbala shares his experience with us:

"After I had been pastor of Brooklyn Tabernacle for about a year, the church had grown to fifty people, but we were facing problems: little money, few people coming to faith in Christ. One Tuesday afternoon I sat in my cubbyhole office on Atlantic Avenue, depressed. I knew that later that day, fifteen people, at most, would come to church to pray. How could God call me and my wife to this city not to make a difference? I wondered.

"I walked into our empty, little sanctuary and recited to God a list of my problems: "Look at this building, this neighborhood...Our offerings are laughable...I can't trust So-and-so...There's so little to work with."

"Then the Holy Spirit impressed upon me, 'I will show you the biggest problem in the church. It's you.'

"In that moment I saw with excruciating clarity that I didn't really love the people as God wanted me to. I prepared sermons just to get through another Sunday. I was basically prayerless. I was proud.

"I fell on my face before God and began to weep. 'God, whatever it takes, please change me. I would rather die than live out some useless ministry of catch phrases.'

"The Brooklyn Tabernacle began to turn around, and twenty years later, we are still learning about the tremendous power of prayer. Every Tuesday evening many hundreds of people come together simply to pray."[1]

How often we go through life expecting God to meet our needs! And we never grasp the critical importance of our own involvement—that of prayer, constant prayer.

Paul was in prison in Rome when writing to the Colossian believers. At some point he had been visited by Epaphras, the pastor of the great Colossian church. Apparently Epaphras had felt a need for some advice on how to handle the false teaching that had seeped into the church. Paul, God's chosen apostle to the Gentiles, was the natural person to ask for advice. This was the purpose for writing the letter to the Colossians: to encourage the church to get rid of the false teaching and to continue on with Christ.

Remember: Paul had never visited the Colossian church. The believers had never seen him face to face, and he was unable to visit them now because of being in prison. They needed him, for the false teaching was extremely dangerous, threatening the very ministry of the church. Being in prison and unable to reach them, what could he do? Only two things:

⇒ He could write them to share the Word of God in a letter.

⇒ He could pray for them.

Paul did both. The present passage covers his prayer: what he asked God to do for the Colossian believers. He asked three things; he made three great requests. All three requests are needed by every church and all believers, in particular those who face false teaching. Note how these three requests lead to a deeper experience with the Lord, a much stronger walk than most believers experience. Every believer should covet these three things and covet them diligently.

OUTLINE:
1. Request 1: to know God's will—to be filled with the knowledge of God's will (v.9).
2. Request 2: to walk worthy of Christ (v.10).
3. Request 3: to possess the power of God (v.11).

1. THE FIRST GREAT REQUEST IS TO KNOW GOD'S WILL (v.9).

Note exactly what Scripture says: we are to be filled with the knowledge of God's will. It is not enough to just know God's will; we are to be *filled* with the knowledge of His will. What is being talked about is not God's will for a particular thing nor for a few things. God's will involves *all of life*, everything we do every moment of every day. The will of God involves what we do, say, and even think. Briefly stated, God's will for us involves all behavior and all conduct, even our imaginations and thoughts. Imagine! Even *every thought* is to be controlled by God's will.

> **"Casting down imaginations, and every high thing that exalteth itself against the knowledge of God, and bringing into captivity every thought to the obedience of Christ" (2 Cor.10:5).**

The point is this: God tells us how to live, and what He tells us is His will. Therefore, we are to study God's Word: we are to study to gain all the knowledge we can about His will, about how to live. We are to study to learn until the knowledge of His will just floods our conduct and behavior.

> **"Teach me to do thy will; for thou art my God: thy spirit is good; lead me into the land of uprightness" (Ps.143:10, cp. Jn.4:34; Ro.12:1-2; 2 Cor.10:5; 1 Jn.2:17).**

Note a wonderful thing: the person who is filled with God's will possesses spiritual wisdom and spiritual understanding.

⇒ "Wisdom" means that a person knows the first principles or basic principles of life.

⇒ "Understanding" means that a person has the ability to apply the basic principles to everyday life, to the circumstances and decisions of life.

The believer needs both wisdom and understanding. One without the other is useless. He must learn all the basic principles of life, and he must learn how to apply them to everyday life. But how can he secure wisdom and understanding?

- By studying God's Word.

> **"All scripture is given by inspiration of God, and is profitable for doctrine, for reproof, for correction, for instruction in righteousness" (2 Tim.3:16).**

- By prayer—praying to be filled with the knowledge of God's will

> **"If any of you lack wisdom, let him ask of God, that giveth to all men liberally, and upbraideth not; and it shall be given him" (Jas.1:5).**

APPLICATION:

Think about the shallow lives of so many people, going from day to day being concerned only with the moment: working, eating, sleeping, playing, and relaxing. Think about how little most people know about God's will. Compare this tragic fact with the kind of life God wills man to live. Is it any wonder...

- that so many have been deceived by false teaching?
- that so much of our ministry is superficial and formal?

QUESTIONS:
1. Are you living for God, really living for Him in every area of life? Living like He tells you to live? In which areas do you need a change of attitude?
2. Are you consistently experiencing the fulness of God's will? What kinds of things can you do in order to be filled with the knowledge of God's will?
3. What "short-cuts" do some people take in trying to know God's will? What are some of the natural results of missing the fulness of God's will?

2. THE SECOND GREAT REQUEST IS TO WALK WORTHY OF CHRIST (v.10).

This is a critical point for the believer, a point that must be taught constantly. This truth must be hammered into the minds and hearts of believers:

⇒ It is not enough *to know* God's will.
⇒ It is not enough *to possess* wisdom: to possess the basic principles of life.
⇒ It is not even enough *to possess* understanding: to have the ability to apply the basic principles of life to everyday living.

Knowing something and having the ability to do something are important, but they involve only head knowledge. The critical point is putting what we know into practice. We are to live out the will of God; we are to practice doing the will of God. Knowing the will of God is of no value until we have committed our lives to doing it.

⇒ The word "walk" means that we *set* our lives—our behavior and conduct—after Christ.
⇒ The word "worthy" means to have the weight of something else or to weigh as much as something else.[2]

This means an amazing thing: our walk is to weigh as much as the walk of Christ. Our conduct is to conform to the will of God as much as the conduct of Christ. We are to live a life just as worthy as the life of Christ. The will of God is to control our behavior as much as it did the behavior of Christ.

⇒ Christ is the pattern, and we are the copy. The copy is to be just like the pattern.[3]

How is such a walk possible? We must be totally committed to do two things.

COLOSSIANS 1:9-11

1.   We must be fruitful in every good work; that is, we must do every good work. Note the word "every." Everything that God says is to be done. Dealing with God is just like dealing with any other person. No person is pleased when he does only half of what he says. To please a person, we have to do all that he says. How much more true with God! If we are to please Him, we must do every good work; and we must do it faithfully, bearing as much fruit as possible.

"Let your light so shine before men, that they may see your good works, and glorify your Father which is in heaven" (Mt.5:16).

2.   We must grow in the knowledge of God. But how do we get to know God; how do we gain a personal knowledge and relationship with God?
⇒ We do not know God just because we know *about* God. Just knowing the Word of God does not mean that we know God Himself—not in a personal and intimate way.

Note exactly what the verse says: "that ye might walk worthy of the Lord...increasing in the knowledge of God." The way we get to know God is the same way we get to know anyone. We walk with the person: associate, fellowship, and share with the person. So it is with God, and the more we walk with Him, the more we increase in the knowledge of Him.

"But if we walk in the light, as he is in the light, we have fellowship one with another, and the blood of Jesus Christ his Son cleanseth us from all sin" (1 Jn.1:7).

ILLUSTRATION:
Do the things of God consume your life? Listen for a moment to this example:

Aunt Vertie, one of the godliest women I have ever heard about, was once asked the meaning of "praying without ceasing." She replied: "Well, it means what it says:
⇒ "When I put on my clothes in the morning, I thank God for clothing me in the righteousness of Christ.
⇒ "When I wash in the morning, I ask God to cleanse me from my sin.
⇒ "When I eat breakfast, I thank Christ for being the bread of life.
⇒ "When I clean house, I ask God to be merciful and cleanse the houses of the world from sin.
⇒ "When I talk with people throughout the day, I ask God to save and grow them in Christ and to meet their particular needs.
⇒ "When I see strangers or crowds of people on the streets, I pray for the salvation of the people of the world."

On and on the list could go. Aunt Vertie prayed all day, using the events of the day to remind her of the prayer that was needed to reach the world for Christ. What a walk! A life totally lived for Christ! A life worthy of Christ! A life worthy to be called Christian!

QUESTIONS:
1.   How do you know for sure that you are in God's will?
2.   What kinds of things must you do in order to grow in the knowledge of God?
3.   How would you describe your fruitfulness in what you do?
        Abundant
        Lasting (eternal)
        Unpicked
        Bruised
        Spoiled
4.   Explain what you can do in order to be more fruitful.

3. THE THIRD GREAT REQUEST IS FOR THE POWER OF GOD (v.11).

God's power is an absolute essential for the believer. This is easily seen by asking two questions.

⇒ What good is it if the believer knows God's will, but he does not have the power to do God's will?

⇒ How can the believer walk worthy of Christ if he does not have the power to walk worthy?

Many in the world believe that man has the strength within himself to become spiritually strong; that it is a matter of the will and discipline; that man can apply himself and conquer the circumstances of life. And, to some degree, this is true. But man's flesh fails in three critical areas.

⇒ The flesh cannot become perfect, neither can it do anything about perfection. Therefore, no matter what the flesh becomes or does, it is still unacceptable to God. Why? Because God is perfect; thus God can accept only perfection.

⇒ The flesh cannot conquer death. No matter what the flesh does, it all ends up as dead matter. One thing is certain: death has no part with God.

⇒ The flesh cannot do what this verse says: it cannot be patient and longsuffering against all the traumatic trials and temptations of life and *be joyful at the same time*.

It is for these three reasons that we need the power of God. Man's power can overcome some of the problems of life, but his power cannot overcome all the problems, especially the three mentioned in this Scripture.

⇒ Only God's power can make us acceptable (perfect) before Him.

⇒ Only God's power can conquer death, that is, raise us up to live eternally.

⇒ Only God's power can infuse enough strength in us to make us endure any and all trials with a spirit of joy.

Imagine some of the trials we have to face: disease, accident, poverty, loss, death. There is no way for the flesh to *work up a joyful spirit* through some of the traumas of life. But God has the power...

• to give us understanding and peace.
• to strengthen and settle us.
• to give us hope and security.

Where does such power come from? From God. And we secure His power through prayer. This is the point of this great request of Paul. Now, note the results of God's power.

1. God's power gives us a spirit of patience: endurance, fortitude, stedfastness, constancy, perseverance. The word *patience* is not passive; it is active. It is not the spirit that just sits back, putting up with the trials of life and taking whatever may come. Rather, it is the spirit that stands up and faces the trials of life, that actively goes about conquering and overcoming them. The believer knows that God is allowing the trials in order to teach him more and more patience (endurance).

> "Rejoicing in hope; patient in tribulation; continuing instant in prayer" (Ro.12:12).

2. God's power gives us a spirit of longsuffering: patience, bearing and suffering a long time, perseverance. Long-suffering never gives in.

⇒ Pressure and hard work may fall upon us, but the Spirit of God helps us suffer long under it.

⇒ Disease or accident or old age may afflict us, but the Spirit of God helps us to suffer long under it.

⇒ Discouragement and disappointment may attack us, but the Spirit of God helps us to suffer long under it.

⇒ Men may do us wrong, abuse, slander, and injure us; but the Spirit of God helps us to suffer long under it.

Note: longsuffering never strikes back! The Christian believer is given the power of longsuffering—the power to suffer the situation or person for a long, long time. And longsuffering is one of the great traits of God. As Gal.5:22 says, it is a fruit of God's very own Spirit.

3.   God's power gives us a spirit of joy through all the trials and tribulations of life. Joy means an inner gladness, a deep-seated pleasure that gives the believer a rejoicing heart regardless of circumstances.

The joy of the Lord is not the same as the joy of the world. The world's joy is always nagged by some incompleteness, some lack, some unfulfilling thing or missing ingredient. The world's joy always knows that something can go wrong. But the believer's joy is divine; it is given only by God. It is the joy of the Holy Spirit. It does not depend on circumstances or happiness but instead springs from faith. The joy of future reward, despite the sufferings of this world, fills the believer with joy, keeping him faithful.

> **"Whom having not seen, ye love; in whom, though now ye see him not, yet believing, ye rejoice with joy unspeakable and full of glory" (1 Pt.1:8).**

ILLUSTRATION:
God has designed us so that we can possess His power. Unfortunately, many of us tend to run out of gas.

> *"On New Year's Day in the Tournament of Roses parade, a beautiful float suddenly sputtered and quit. It was out of gas. The whole parade was held up until someone could get a can of gas.*
> *"The amusing thing was this float represented the Standard Oil Company. With its vast oil resources, its truck was out of gas.*
> *"Often Christians neglect their spiritual maintenance, and though they are 'clothed with power' (Luke 24:49) [they] find themselves out of gas.'"*[4]

QUESTIONS:
1.   What is the source of the Christian's power? What are the supernatural results of this power at work in you?
2.   Have you ever heard it said that "7 days without prayer makes 1 weak"? What do you need to do in order to strengthen your prayer life?
3.   Share a time when you sensed God's power. What impact did it make on how you live today?

SUMMARY:

Are you trying to live the Christian life in your own power? If so, you should diligently pray and covet these three things:

1.   To know God's will—to be filled with the knowledge of God's will.
2.   To walk worthy of Christ.
3.   To possess the power of God.

PERSONAL JOURNAL NOTES
(Reflection & Response)

1. The most important thing that I learned from this lesson was:

2. The area that I need to work on the most is:

3. I can apply this lesson to my life by:

4. Closing Statement of Commitment:

---

[1] Jim Cymbala. Selected from the article *"How To Light The Fire,"* _Leadership Journal_ (Carol Stream, IL, Fall 1994), p.57.

[2] Kenneth S. Wuest. *Word Studies in the Greek New Testament,* Vol.1 (Grand Rapids, MI: Eerdmans Publishing Co., 1953), p.176.

[3] Ibid., p.176.

[4] Craig B. Larson, Editor. *Illustration's for Preaching & Teaching.* Grand Rapids, MI: Baker Books, 1993), p.181.

	II. THE PREEMI-NENT CHRIST: GOD'S DEAR SON, 1:12-23 A. God & Man: What God Has Done for Man, 1:12-14	takers of the inheritance of the saints in light: 13 Who hath delivered us from the power of darkness, and hath translated us into the kingdom of his dear Son:	2. God has delivered us from the power of darkness
1. God has given us an inheritance	12 Giving thanks unto the Father, which hath made us meet to be par-	14 In whom we have redemption through his blood, even the forgiveness of sins:	3. God has saved us and forgiven our sins

SECTION II
THE PREEMINENT CHRIST: GOD'S DEAR SON,
Colossians 1:12-23

Study 1:   GOD AND MAN: WHAT GOD HAS DONE FOR MAN

Text: Colossians 1:12-14

Aim: To grasp the great things God has done for us.

Memory Verse:
> **"Giving thanks unto the Father, which hath made us meet [fit, qualified] to be partakers of the inheritance of the saints in light" (Colossians 1:12).**

SECTION OVERVIEW

This is one of the greatest passages of Scripture ever written. Its importance cannot be overstressed. It is a passage that reveals the supremacy of the Lord Jesus Christ. Who He is and what He has done for man can never be matched. This is the purpose of this great passage, a passage that covers so much in twelve brief verses: to show to the world just who Jesus Christ is and what He has done. Here is a list of the great lessons coming up:

Session 1: God and Man: What God Has Done for Man, 1:12-14
Session 2: God and Christ (Part I): The Person of Christ, 1:15
Session 3: God and Christ (Part II): Christ the Creator, 1:16-17
Session 4: God and Christ (Part III): Christ the Head of the Church, 1:18-19
Session 5: God and Christ (Part IV): Christ the Reconciler of All things, 1:20-23

INTRODUCTION:
Have you ever attempted to count the stars on a clear night? Or have you tried to count the number of waves that roll in from the sea? On that same sea shore, how long would it take you to count the grains of sand that lie before you? Obviously, an attempt to try any of these tasks would frustrate you to no end. In the same sense, when we attempt to count the total number of God's blessings, we discover there is no end. But what a wonderful frustration! Go ahead and try to count all of His blessings. You will discover what King David did:

> **"Many, O Lord my God, are the wonders which Thou hast done, and Thy thoughts toward us; there is none to compare with Thee; if I would declare and speak of them, they would be too numerous (many) to count" (Ps.40:5).**

Three of the things God has done for man are so great that they just explode human imagination. If we diligently concentrate upon these three things, the depth of what God has done will erupt in our lives for good. We will never be the same. What has God done for man?

OUTLINE:
1. God has given us an inheritance (v.12).
2. God has delivered us from the power of darkness (v.13).
3. God has saved us and forgiven our sins (v.14).

1. GOD HAS GIVEN US AN INHERITANCE (v.12).

Before we proceed to discuss the inheritance, note two other points.
1. We have to be *prepared*, that is, qualified and made fit, before we can receive the inheritance. Man is not qualified to receive anything from God, especially an inheritance, not in his present sinful and corruptible state. If he is to ever receive an inheritance from God, he first has to be made acceptable to God. Scripture says God has made us acceptable. It does not yet say what He did to qualify us; what He did to make us qualified will be discussed in verses 13-14.
2. We share the inheritance with all other saints in light. Remember, the word *saints* simply means those who have set their lives apart to live for God. God is Light; therefore, when a person turns his life over to God, he is turning his life over to Light. He is to walk in the *light of God Himself*, so much so that he, the believer, is called the light of the world. This is what is meant by "saints in light." They are people who have committed their lives to walk in the light of God.
The point is this: every saint who lives and moves in the light of God is to receive the inheritance of God. But note: since God is light, only those *set apart in light* can live with God. Any person who sets his life apart *in darkness* can never receive the inheritance of God, for darkness can never dwell in light. The light destroys and eliminates the darkness.

Now note the inheritance God has given to believers. What is the inheritance? Scripture describes the inheritance in the following ways.
⇒ We are heirs of eternal life.

> **"That being justified by his grace, we should be made heirs according to the hope of eternal life" (Tit.3:7).**

⇒ We are heirs of salvation.

> **"Are they not all ministering spirits, sent forth to minister for them who shall be heirs of salvation?" (Heb.1:14).**

⇒ We are heirs of the promises made to Abraham, that is, the promises to inherit the world and to be a citizen of a great nation of people.

> **"For the promise, that he should be the heir of the world, was not to Abraham, or to his seed, through the law, but through the righteousness of faith" (Ro.4:13).**

⇒ We are heirs of glory.

> **"And if children, then heirs; heirs of God, and joint-heirs with Christ; if so be that we suffer with him, that we may be also glorified together" (Ro.8:17).**

⇒ We are heirs of righteousness.

"By faith Noah, being warned of God of things not seen as yet, moved with fear, prepared an ark to the saving of his house; by the which he condemned the world, and became heir of the righteousness which is by faith" (Heb.11:7).

⇒ We are heirs of the grace of life.

"Likewise, ye husbands, dwell with them according to knowledge, giving honour unto the wife, as unto the weaker vessel, and as being heirs together of the grace of life; that your prayers be not hindered" (1 Pt.3:7).

⇒ We are heirs of God's very special favor, heirs that shall stir the praise of His glory.

"In whom [Christ] also we have obtained an inheritance....that we should be to the praise of his glory, who first trusted in Christ" (Eph.1:11-12).

⇒ We are heirs of the reward, of the inheritance and all that it includes.

"Knowing that of the Lord ye shall receive the reward of the inheritance: for ye serve the Lord Christ" (Col.3:24).

⇒ We are heirs of the eternal inheritance.

"And for this cause he is the mediator of the new testament, that by means of death, for the redemption of the transgressions that were under the first testament, they which are called might receive the promise of eternal inheritance" (Heb.9:15).

⇒ We are heirs of an immortal and perfected body that shall be given us when Christ returns.

"Now this I say, brethren, that flesh and blood cannot inherit the kingdom of God; neither doth corruption inherit incorruption. Behold, I show you a mystery; We shall not all sleep, but we shall all be changed, in a moment, in the twinkling of an eye, at the last trump: for the trumpet shall sound, and the dead shall be raised incorruptible, and we shall be changed. For this corruptible must put on incorruption, and this mortal must put on immortality. So when this corruptible shall have put on incorruption, and this mortal shall have put on immortality, then shall be brought to pass the saying that is written, Death is swallowed up in victory" (1 Cor.15:50-54).

APPLICATION:

Who is the richest man you know upon earth? Suppose you were the heir of his wealth. Think how excited you would be! But note: his wealth is nothing in comparison to the inheritance promised by God. In fact, everything that we inherit from our earthly parents passes away. Even if it exists when we leave this earth, someone else gets it. We cannot take it with us. But not so with the inheritance offered by God. It is eternal!

How desperately we need to learn the stark difference between the false, fleeting riches of this earth and the true, eternal riches of God.

QUESTIONS:
1. According to this verse, who initiated the action of giving you an inheritance? What type of response is required on your part?
2. What thoughts come to your mind when you hear the word *inheritance*?
3. What is the difference between an earthly and a heavenly inheritance?

2. GOD HAS DELIVERED US FROM THE POWER OF DARKNESS AND TRANS-FERRED US INTO THE KINGDOM OF HIS DEAR SON (v.13).

1. Note two things about the "power of darkness."
   a. The "power of *darkness*" indicates there is a kingdom, a realm, a world of darkness. Darkness means just what is indicated: a person is unable to see, understand, or know. Picture a person trying to walk but stumbling through a world of darkness. He cannot see or understand:
      ⇒ who he really is.
      ⇒ where he has come from.
      ⇒ where he is.
      ⇒ where he is going.

   This is the very situation of natural man, the man who has not been delivered from the world of darkness by God. The man in darkness does not know...
   - who he is: why God created him nor what God has planned for man.
   - where he has come from: that his origin is God; that God created him.
   - where he is: that the world was made by God and that it has an eternal purpose in the plan of God.
   - where he is going: that he is an eternal being who is to either live forever in the light of God's presence or in the darkness away from God's presence.

   The point to see is that darkness is a realm or a world in which the unbeliever lives and moves. He never knows these things, never knows the truth of his world and life nor of God. He walks in a life and world of darkness, blinded from the truth.
   b. The "*power* of darkness" also indicates that the darkness is not only a realm or world, but a *power*—an active power that enslaves people and stands in opposition to the light of God. The *world of darkness* is a kingdom in rebellion against God. This is the very reason people struggle against God so much. It is difficult to imagine the antagonism of most people against God, yet it is true. Just imagine how contradictory it is to see a *rational creature*...
   - cursing God.
   - denying God.
   - rejecting God.
   - hurting people.
   - damaging himself.
   - ridiculing, persecuting, and killing those who profess God.

   There is no way a rational creature would act like this unless he was enslaved by the power of darkness.

   > **"But if thine eye be evil, thy whole body shall be full of darkness. If therefore the light that is in thee be darkness, how great is that darkness!" (Mt.6:23).**

ILLUSTRATION:
"A man asked an old Christian woman, 'Does the Devil ever trouble you about your past sins?' She said, 'Yes.' 'What do you do then?' 'Oh, I just send him [the devil] to the east.' 'Does he come back after that?' 'Aye.' 'And what do you do then?' 'I just send him away to the west.' 'And when he comes back from the west what do you do?' 'Man, I just keep him going between the east and the west.'"[1]

"As far as the east is from the west, so far hath he removed our transgressions from us" (Ps.103:12).

Just like the Christian woman, you have to constantly be on guard against the devil. The devil will never quit trying to lure you into the power of darkness!

2. Note that it is God Himself who has delivered believers from darkness. The word "delivered" means to *rescue* or *snatch* from darkness. A person lost in total darkness is hopeless unless someone rescues him. And note: he cannot be rescued by those who are lost in the same darkness as he is. No person who is in the world of darkness has light, or else he would use the light to get out of the darkness. This is the very reason God had to rescue man. He alone is light; therefore, He alone could reach down and snatch man from the darkness. How did He do this? The answer is given in the next point.

3. God has transferred believers into the kingdom of His dear Son, into the kingdom of the Lord Jesus Christ. We must always remember that the kingdom of Christ already exists.
   ⇒ His rule and reign already exist in the spiritual world or spiritual dimension of being, that is, in heaven.
   ⇒ His rule and reign already exist in the hearts and lives of believers in this physical world or physical dimension of being.
The message of the glorious gospel is that God has transferred the believer from the power of darkness into the kingdom of His dear Son.

> **"Jesus answered, My kingdom is not of this world: if my kingdom were of this world, then would my servants fight, that I should not be delivered to the Jews: but now is my kingdom not from hence. Pilate therefore said unto him, Art thou a king then? Jesus answered, Thou sayest that I am a king. To this end was I born, and for this cause came I into the world, that I should bear witness unto truth. Every one that is of the truth heareth my voice" (Jn.18:36-37, cp. Jn.3:3; Acts 14:22; Ro.14:17; 1 Cor.15:25; Heb.1:8; Rev.11:15; Is.9:7; Jer.23:5).**

APPLICATION:
There are many religions, cults, and organizations today who claim to know the way to God and His kingdom. But there is only one way to God: through Jesus Christ our Lord. Jesus Christ alone is the way to God. A person has to believe in Jesus Christ, believe that Jesus Christ can make him acceptable to God. When a person really believes that Jesus Christ can save him, that Jesus Christ can make him acceptable to God, then God transfers that person out of darkness into the kingdom of His dear Son.

ILLUSTRATION:
The Bible tells us that before Christ came into our lives, our existence was spent in the darkness. Thankfully, God had a plan:

> Bob Woods, in *Pulpit Digest*, tells the story of a couple who took their son, 11, and daughter, 7, to Carlsbad Caverns. As always, when the tour reached the deepest point in the cavern, the guide turned off all the lights to dramatize how completely dark and silent it is below the earth's surface.
> The little girl, suddenly enveloped in utter darkness, was frightened and began to cry.
> Immediately [she] heard the voice of her brother: "Don't cry. Somebody here knows how to turn on the lights."
> In a real sense, that is the message of the gospel: light is available, even when darkness seems overwhelming."[2]

1. Do you ever walk and live in the power of darkness? Do you curse God, use His name in vain? Do you ignore God? Reject Him? Question Him? Deny Him? If so, what do you need to do to be freed from the power of darkness? To move out of darkness into the light? If you are a believer, what do you need to do to live a more consistent life in the light?
2. What is your role in freeing the lost from a life of darkness?
3. How do you treat unbelievers? Do you hurt them? By-pass them? Ignore them?
4. How do you treat other believers? Do you ridicule them? Persecute them? Or do you have a reputation of encouragement? What kinds of things can you do to bring Christ's light into other Christian relationships?

3. GOD HAS SAVED US AND FORGIVEN OUR SINS (v.14).

The word "forgiveness" means to send away, to release, to let go. The word for "sin" means transgression, trespass, a falling away. All men have broken the law of God and fallen away from God, and the penalty for breaking the law is death. But the blood of Jesus Christ brings forgiveness to us. How? Jesus Christ died *for man*, as our substitute. He took the penalty of sins, bearing the punishment Himself. He could do this because He was the Perfect and Ideal Man, and His sacrifice was perfectly acceptable to God. All of us who really believe that Jesus Christ died for us are forgiven our sins. God takes our faith and counts it as the death of Jesus Christ. Therefore, the guilt and penalty for breaking God's laws are completely removed. Our sins and guilt are sent away or washed away by the blood of Jesus Christ.

APPLICATION:
Consider a ledger of accounts. Our sin is a debit, a liability, a debt owed. Christ's sacrifice is a credit, an asset, a payment. The sacrifice completely wipes out the debt of our sin. It is paid in full—but we have to accept the gift of Christ's sacrifice in order to have a clean slate.

> "My little children, these things write I unto you, that ye sin not. And if any man sin, we have an advocate with the Father, Jesus Christ the righteous: and he is the propitiation [sacrifice, covering] for our sins: and not for ours only, but also for the sins of the whole world" (1 Jn.2:1-2).

QUESTIONS:
1. Have you committed any sins that have been forgiven by God, but not by you? Why do some believers have a hard time forgiving themselves? What kind of encouragement could you offer someone who was burdened with this kind of guilt and condemnation?
2. Do you believe that God has taken care of your *future* sins? What is your Scriptural basis for believing this?
3. What does this verse tell you about God's promise to forgive you of your sins?

SUMMARY:

We must see the depths of what God has done for us: God has offered us an inheritance, deliverance from the power of darkness, salvation, and the forgiveness of our sins. It is up to us to receive what God has offered, to make absolutely sure...

- that we *receive* the future inheritance of God.
- that we are *delivered* from the power of darkness.
- that we *turn* to God for salvation and the forgiveness of our sins.

"As far as the east is removed from the west,
My sins are remembered no more;
Forever my soul is at perfect rest,
My sins are remembered no more.

"Forgiven, forgotten, all cleansed in the Blood,
My sins are remembered no more;
Atoned for by Jesus in Calv'ry's flood,
My sins are remembered no more. "[3]

PERSONAL JOURNAL NOTES
(Reflection & Response)

1. The most important thing that I learned from this lesson was:

2. The area that I need to work on the most is:

3. I can apply this lesson to my life by:

4. Closing Statement of Commitment:

---

[1] Walter B. Knight. *3,000 Illustrations for Christian Service* (Grand Rapids, MI: Eerdman's Publishing Company, 1947), p.288.

[2] Craig B. Larson, Editor. *Illustrations for Preaching & Teaching*, p.133.

[3] *Anonymous.* Walter B. Knight. *3,000 Illustrations for Christian Service*, p.290.

	B. God & Christ (Part I): The Person of Christ, 1:15
1. Jesus Christ is the image of the invisible God 2. Jesus Christ is above all things	15 Who is the image of the invisible God, the firstborn of every creature:

SECTION II
THE PREEMINENT CHRIST: GOD'S DEAR SON
Colossians 1:12-23

Study 2:   GOD AND CHRIST (PART I): THE PERSON OF CHRIST

Text: Colossians 1:15

Aim: To focus on the uniqueness of Jesus Christ as a person.

Memory Verse:
"Who being the brightness of His glory, and the express image of His person, and upholding all things by the word of His power, when He had by Himself purged our sins, sat down on the right hand of the Majesty on high" (Heb.1:3).

INTRODUCTION:

A married couple can live together for years but fail to really know each other. An example: for many years a wife made her husband beets for supper because she thought he liked them. One day, the husband let the cat out of the bag and told her: "I do not like beets; I never have liked beets; I never will like beets! Why are you fixing me beets?" Her reply, "You never told me!" Obviously, they had failed to communicate. An assumption here, a guess there—and the truth was never known!

There are many Christians whose experience with Jesus Christ is based on the "best guess" method. Assumptions of who He is have been programmed into their minds. How are we to know the "real Jesus"?

This Scripture tells us. It is one of the most important passages ever written. It does two very significant things.
⇒ It destroys false teaching and false thoughts about God and Jesus Christ.
⇒ It reveals exactly who God and Jesus Christ are.

This was the very purpose of Paul in writing Colossians. False teaching had seeped into the church, false teaching that attacked Jesus Christ. It was called Gnosticism. This was one of the major reasons the pastor of the Colossian church (Epaphras) had visited Paul: to get Paul's advice in dealing with the heresy. The unfortunate thing is this: the teachings of Gnosticism have continued to plague the church down through the centuries, even today. In one form or another, similar teachings are always being used to attack the church. Because of this, the teachings of Gnosticism and its *modern counterpart* will be dealt with in the points where they apply. The point to remember is this: throughout this passage Paul is answering the false teaching that had seeped into the church. And there is no better way to counteract false teaching than to present the truth. The false teaching was an attack against Jesus Christ, against both His work and Person. Therefore, Paul takes up the pen and proclaims God and Christ (Part I): the Person of Jesus Christ.

OUTLINE:
1. Jesus Christ is the image of the invisible God (v.15).
2. Jesus Christ is above all things (v.15).

1. JESUS CHRIST IS THE IMAGE OF THE INVISIBLE GOD (v.15).

The word "image" means an exact likeness, the tangible or visible representation of something or someone.

⇒ It means that Jesus Christ was *God in every respect*. He was the physical image and representation of God.

⇒ It means that Jesus Christ was the perfect manifestation or revelation of God. God is invisible or unseen, but Jesus Christ reveals God to the world.

The impact of this truth about Jesus Christ has explosive repercussions for man. It destroys all false teaching about God and Christ, and it reveals God to man. It shows man who God is and what He is like. As stated in the introduction, this was the very purpose of Paul. False teaching had seeped into the Colossian church, false teaching that had attacked who Jesus Christ was. Note how forcefully the truth destroys the error.

1. Gnosticism said there were many mediators between God and man, that Jesus Christ was not the only mediator.

    a. The parallel with false teaching down through the centuries is clearly seen. There have been and always will be those who proclaim that...

      • Jesus Christ is not the only person who can bring us near God; that He is not the only mediator between God and man; that there are other mediators and intermediaries of God—other great teachers who are just as important as Jesus Christ—who can bring us in touch with God. (Cp. Buddha, Mohammed, other leaders of various cults, and self-proclaimed messiahs.)

APPLICATION:

There are movements within every age that tell us that we are _all_ gods—that every person has the power within himself to attain whatever he wishes. Compare the "new age" movement of the late 20th century. Sadly, millions who are searching for some deep experience to give meaning to their lives fall for such movements, looking for fulfillment, peace, and even salvation within themselves instead of through God.

> **"As I passed by, and beheld your devotions, I found an altar with this inscription, TO THE UNKNOWN GOD. Whom therefore ye ignorantly worship" (Acts 17:23).**

QUESTIONS:
1. Have you ever known someone who believed or followed some false movement or teaching? What was his reason? What was the attraction? Did you share Christ with him?
2. Have you ever believed or followed some false movement or teaching? What was your reason? What was the attraction? Who witnessed to you about the true and living God?

    b. However, note how the truth destroys this false teaching. Jesus Christ, who lived and walked among men, is the express image of God, the very Lord of the universe. This means a most significant thing: God is not what most men think. He is not an unconcerned and distant God who is off in outer space someplace. He is not separated from man by a host of intermediaries, by many different ways to reach Him. God is not out of touch with the world; He has not made it difficult to reach Him. He is close at hand, so close that He has come to earth and lived as a Man among us. And in doing so, He has done two great things for us through the Lord Jesus Christ. First, He has shown us exactly who He is and what He is like; and second, He has shown us the way to reach Him.

Think for a moment about all that Jesus Christ shows us about God.

⇒ The fact that He came to earth from heaven shows us that He and He alone is the Supreme Person who can take us to God.

⇒ The fact that He (as God the Son) came to earth shows us that God is near.

⇒ The fact that Jesus Christ lived as a Man, ministering and helping, shows us that God cares.

⇒ The fact that Jesus Christ died at the hands of men shows that God is love—He willingly sacrificed Himself. Being God He did not have to die. As Scripture says, He could have called down a host of angels to deliver Him.

⇒ The fact that Jesus Christ proclaimed salvation to man shows that God is a Savior.

⇒ The fact that Jesus Christ proclaimed judgment upon evil and warned men of destruction shows that God is a just Lord.

The list could go on and on, but the point is clearly seen. God is not so unconcerned and far away from man that He has left man to grope and stumble through life on his own seeking after God. God loves and cares so much for man that He has shown man exactly who He is and what He is like and the way to reach Him. Jesus Christ alone is the image of God, the Supreme Person of the universe. He alone is the Mediator between God and Man. God is as close as Jesus Christ is.

APPLICATION:

What other god, cult leader, or man-made idol (such as a football or fame), knows us by name, ministers to and cares for us, hears and answers our prayers, and has sacrificially given of himself to save us from our sins? None but Jesus. No other gods can claim to have done anything for us—they are powerless. There is only one living and true God.

> **"For there is one God, and one mediator between God and men, the man Christ Jesus" (1 Tim.2:5).**

QUESTIONS:

1. What are some of the false gods or idols that men make in society?
2. What good thing can a false god do?
3. What harm can a false god do?

2. Gnosticism said the human body was evil. This teaching resulted in two different attitudes toward the body and life.

⇒ Some said the body needed to be disciplined, controlled, and taken care of as much as possible. By controlling its urges and appetites and keeping it fit, the corruption and evil of the body could be mastered more easily.

⇒ Others said the very opposite: what was done with the body mattered little, for it was evil and doomed to death. Therefore, once a person took care of his spirit, he could then eat, drink, and be merry.

a. The parallel with the false teaching of today is clearly seen.

⇒ Some concentrate upon the body and its health through recreation, discipline, and strict living, seeking to overcome the evil, that is, the corruption, disease, aging, and dying of the body, as much as possible.

⇒ Others live as they please, eating and drinking and partying as they wish, thinking that it matters little how they live. Just think how many people feel they can do their own thing—what they want, when they want—just so they believe in and worship God and do a good deed here and there.

The point to see is this: each gives attention to the spiritual only as he wishes, only as much as he feels is necessary to keep his spirit in touch with God. But his concentration is the body and its pleasure, whether the pleasure is the exhibition of discipline and control or the stimulating of the flesh.

APPLICATION:

Some have made their bodies their gods. With the focus on the physical and sensual, doing whatever it takes to get the "perfect body" and please our physical appetites is in vogue. Exercising and working out are good for our health, but what is the real motive behind it?

⇒ To please our Lord by keeping His temple fit and thus being able to serve Him better?

⇒ To please ourselves and our fellow man by *looking good* and attracting men and women?

b. Note how the truth destroys this life-style and teaching. The human body is not evil; Jesus Christ shows us this. He is the image of God—the very Son of God Himself—who came to earth in a human body. Therefore, the human body could not be evil, for God cannot be touched with evil.

The human body has to be honorable or else Jesus Christ would not have wrapped Himself in a human body and come to earth. The conclusion is shocking and convulsive for the life of man. Since the body is honorable, it means that everything a man does with his body is important to his spiritual welfare. What he does with his body determines his relationship and destiny with God. It is totally impossible to keep one's spirit right with God and let one's body go its own way. A person is both spirit and body. Therefore, he is to honor God with *both his spirit and body*, just as Jesus Christ did *in the body* given him by God.

APPLICATION:

How many Christians condemn others for drinking, smoking, doing drugs, and other sins of the body, and yet they do not control their eating nor take care of their bodies by exercising enough? When Christ said, "Let your moderation be known unto all men" (Ph.4:5), did He mean that we could pick and choose which things we want to be moderate in? We must be careful not to judge others for what we are guilty of!

"What? know ye not that your body is the temple of the Holy Ghost which is in you, which ye have of God, and ye are not your own? For ye are bought with a price: therefore glorify God in your body, and in your spirit, which are God's" (1 Cor.6:19-20).

QUESTIONS:
1. Do you ever justify something you've done (overeating, drinking, smoking, etc.) by claiming that it is not hurting anyone?
2. Do you think the Holy Spirit cares what you do to your own body? Why?
3. What should be your attitude toward caring for your body?
4. How can you keep from adopting a worldly attitude toward your body?

3. Gnosticism said the way to God was through learning a certain amount of knowledge and certain key words that would assure the opening up of spiritual insight. The emphasis was upon the intellect and learning, knowledge and insight, personal improvement and self-effort in achieving acceptance with God.

a. The parallel with so much of man's natural thinking is evident. So many feel safe and secure if they...
- know about God and religion.
- know religious phrases and words and can talk in pious and religious language.
- are religious enough to learn about God and religion.

APPLICATION:
Note: knowing about someone is not knowing the person; it is not personal knowledge. People all over the world can identify with some famous historical figure such as George Washington or Hitler. We know *about* them. But we do not know them personally. Likewise we can know *about* God without knowing God personally. How many professing Christians know God *personally*? Do you? How *can* we know Him personally?

b. The truth revealed by Jesus Christ strikes at the very foundation of such thoughts and teachings. God does not save a person because he thinks about God and knows some things about religion and God. God saves the uneducated as well as the educated, the simple as well as the intellectual, the ignorant as well as the knowledgeable, the poor as well as the rich, the young as well as the adult. This is seen in that Jesus Christ, who is the image of God...
- came to earth as a baby.
- was reared by simple, poor parents.
- was not educated at a university or any other school beyond the local community synagogue.
- always ministered and reached out to the needy of the world—those who had need, regardless of age, simplicity, suffering, ignorance, or any other unfortunate circumstance.

Jesus Christ reveals that God saves all who come to the Father through Him—through Him who redeems us and forgives our sins (Col.1:14).

"For there is no difference between the Jew and the Greek: for the same Lord over all is rich unto all that call upon him. For whosoever shall call upon the name of the Lord shall be saved" (Ro.10:12-13).

The conclusion is forceful: Jesus Christ is the express image, the exact representation, the perfect manifestation, the very Person of God Himself. There is no other person who can bring us near God and no other life-style to follow in reaching God. Jesus Christ is the Sovereign Majesty of the universe who came to earth as God to save men.

"And without controversy great is the mystery of godliness: God was manifest in the flesh, justified in the Spirit, seen of angels, preached unto the Gentiles, believed on in the world, received up into glory" (1 Tim.3:16).

ILLUSTRATION:
Jesus Christ is the express image of God. Imagine if you will the excitement of a news editor who might have been living at the time of Christ.

Bernie Newsome, the religion editor, glanced at a memo on his desk from one of his investigative reporters. It read "Bernie...Rumor has it that God's Son has come in the flesh...Looks like a breaking story...Send me an artist...I think a Pulitzer Prize is ours...Please advise soon. An in-

former told me that God's Son would be betrayed and would not be available for any interviews." Signed, I.B. Wright.

Bernie took out his pen and wrote these instructions:

"Good work I.B. Forget the interview...Just get me his picture!" As Bernie thought about what his reporter was working on, he wondered outloud, "I wonder what God's Son is going to look like? Will He resemble His Father?" Then a thought shot through Bernie's mind—"What does His Father look like?"

Remember: Jesus Christ is the exact image of God. He shows us exactly what God looks like. If you have seen the Son, you have seen the Father. If you know the Father, then you know the Son. You cannot know one without knowing the other.

QUESTIONS:
1. What one thing stands out in your mind as you think about the person of Christ? Why? How meaningful is it to you that Christ and the Father are equal?
2. What are the flaws of gnosticism? Share some examples of Gnostic thought in the Christian church today. What is the end result of this false teaching?
3. How does this verse help you to better understand the relationship between Jesus Christ and the Father?

2. JESUS CHRIST IS ABOVE ALL THINGS (v.15).

The word "firstborn" does not mean that Jesus Christ was the first created being of the universe. It means *priority, superiority, preeminence, supremacy*. It means that He existed before all creation as the Supreme Being of the universe. All creation is His heritage. Nothing is superior to Him. Therefore, everything is under Him and owes its existence, worship, and service to Him.

"I and my Father are one" (Jn.10:30).
"In whom the god of this world hath blinded the minds of them which believe not, lest the light of the glorious gospel of <u>Christ, who is the image of God</u>, should shine unto them" (2 Cor.4:4).

ILLUSTRATION:
If we do not take great care, our focus will subtly shift away from the Lord Jesus.

"Leonardo da Vinci took a friend to criticize his masterpiece of the 'Last Supper,' and the remark of the friend was, 'The most striking thing in the picture is the cup!' The artist took his brush and wiped out the cup as he said, 'Nothing in my painting shall attract more attention than the face of my Master!'"[1]

How we all need to be careful of distractions! Our focus should be upon Jesus Christ, first and foremost.

QUESTIONS:
1. What are the most common distractions that keep you from focusing upon Jesus Christ? Do you sometimes fail to wipe out the distractions?
2. What are some of the natural results of too many distractions as you follow Jesus?
3. Jesus Christ is superior. What difference should this make when you share the gospel with someone from another religion? What kinds of things would you share?

SUMMARY:

In a day when there are so many self-proclaimed messiahs, cults, and worldly religions, we must stand strong for the truth: Jesus is God, the Supreme Creator of the universe. He alone is the Truth; He alone is the Way to eternal life. Nothing less and nothing else is acceptable to God the Father. Remember:

1. Jesus Christ is the image of the invisible God.
2. Jesus Christ is above all things.

PERSONAL JOURNAL NOTES:
(Reflection & Response)

1. The most important thing that I learned from this lesson was:

2. The area that I need to work on the most is:

3. I can apply this lesson to my life by:

4. Closing Statement of Commitment:

---

[1] Walter B. Knight. *3,000 Illustrations for Christian Service*, p.379.

	C. God & Christ (Part II): Christ the Creator, 1:16-17

1. Christ created all things
  a. In heaven & in earth
  b. Visible & invisible
	16 For by him were all things created, that are in heaven, and that are in earth, visible and invisible, whether they be thrones, or dominions, or principalities, or powers: all things were created by him, and for him:

2. Christ created all things for Himself 3. Christ is before all things, v.17 4. Christ holds all things together	17 And he is before all things, and by him all things consist.

SECTION II
THE PREEMINENT CHRIST: GOD'S DEAR SON
Colossians 1:16-17

Study 3:   **GOD AND CHRIST (PART II): CHRIST THE CREATOR**

Text: **Colossians 1:16-17**

Aim: To recognize and honor Christ as the Creator of the world.

Memory Verse:
     "And He is before all things, and by Him all things consist" (Colossians 1:17).

INTRODUCTION:
     This passage concerns the creation of the universe. It deals with such questions as...
- What is the origin of the universe?
- What was the force that brought forth the universe?
- Is there more than one world or universe? More than the physical dimension of being?
- What is the purpose of creation?
- What holds things together? What is the power behind the laws of nature such as gravity?

     There are basically three views of creation.
     1. *There is the secularist or humanist view, the idea that the world just happened by chance.* No force or power created the world. There was *nothing*, and then by some means some gas or some element just appeared...
- out of nothing.
- out of nowhere.

     Then through the ages, the single gas or element became two elements, and the evolutionary process began until eventually the world was created. Of course, there have been and always will be various ideas as to how the evolutionary process happened (cp. the present idea of the Big Bang theory that is somewhat popularized). However, the essence of the secularist or humanist is that the world or universe began out of nothing and out of nowhere.

52

<u>ILLUSTRATION:</u>
"The probability of life originating [by] accident is comparable to the probability of the...dictionary resulting from an explosion in a printing shop."[1]

2. *There is the view that some god did create the world, but he is far off and removed from the world.* The far off god is thought of in various ways:
⇒ Some see him as good; others as evil.
⇒ Some think he created the world himself; others think that he used other forces.
This was the view of Gnosticism, the false teaching that had seeped into the church at Colosse. It is also the view held by men in today's society. They just *feel* that God is far away, completely removed from the world. If they think about creation at all, they cannot see God as having created the world, for He is too far removed from it. He must have used other forces or beings to make the world.

3. *There is the pure Christian view, the truth that God Himself, the Sovereign Majesty of the universe, created the world in the person of Jesus Christ.* This is the discussion of this passage. As it is studied, note the force of the statement in Scripture: it declares in no uncertain terms how the universe began. Note also how the statement destroys all false teaching, and note how much more logical and understandable the truth is in comparison to the false beliefs. Christ is the Creator of the universe.

OUTLINE:
1. Christ created all things (v.16).
2. Christ created all things for Himself (v.16).
3. Christ is before all things (v.17).
4. Christ holds all things together (v.17).

1. JESUS CHRIST CREATED ALL THINGS (v.16).

This is a matter of fact statement, yet note how profound the truth is and how much is covered in the verse.
1. The words "by Him" mean *in Him*; that is, creation took place *in* Christ, *within* His very being.
⇒ The heart of Christ desired the world.
⇒ The mind of Christ planned the world.
⇒ The will of Christ destined the world.
⇒ The Word of Christ created the world.

The creation of the world took place within Christ, within His very being.
⇒ It was the *love of Christ* that moved His heart to create the world.
⇒ It was the *knowledge of Christ* that aroused His mind to plan the world.
⇒ It was the *riches of His grace* that stirred Him to will the world.
⇒ It was the *power of His Word* that energized or brought the world into existence.

2. The words "all things" are very significant. They mean...
• "all things" collectively, that is, all the things within the universe were created by Christ.
• "all things" individually, that is, every single detail of creation was created by Christ.
The point is that nothing exists that was not created by Christ. All things were made by Him, even the very details of every single thing. *"God is as great in minuteness as He is in magnitude."*[2]

APPLICATION:

Just imagine all the details involved in the process of insemination, birth, and growth—whether it be a flower or a person. Imagine the knowledge that God must have to create and plan every step of the process. What human being could conceivably think up, design, or plan the process with all its intricate details? Man does not even know or understand all that is involved today in the process of birth or growth—new discoveries are being made about it every day by the most knowledgeable men. Who but God could have started it all in motion?

3.   The words "were created" simply mean that creation was an historical event. There was a time, a day, an hour, a moment when Jesus Christ spoke the Word and all things in their intricate detail came into being.

4.   The creation of Christ includes all the worlds of all the dimensions of being. This is what is meant by the statement "that are in heaven, and in earth, visible and invisible, whether they be thrones, or dominions, or principalities, or powers." Note how all inclusive the statement is:

⇒   If there are other visible and living planets and beings in outer space, Christ created them.

⇒   If there are invisible worlds and beings in other dimensions, Christ created them.

"All things were made by him; and without him was not any thing made that was made" (Jn.1:3).

ILLUSTRATION:

Just think for a moment: man's best attempts at perfection *always* sinks into a dismal failure. Christ provides all of the perfection that we need.

"In the town hall in Copenhagen stands the world's most complicated clock. It took forty years to build at a cost of more than a million dollars. That clock has ten faces, fifteen thousand parts, and is accurate to two-fifths of a second every three hundred years. The clock computes the time of the day, the days of the week, the months and years, and the movements of the planets for twenty-five hundred years. Some parts of that clock will not move until twenty-five centuries have passed.

What is intriguing about that clock is that it is not accurate. It loses two-fifths of a second every three hundred years. Like all clocks, that timepiece in Copenhagen must be regulated by a more precise clock, the universe itself. That mighty astronomical clock with its billions of moving parts, from atoms to stars, rolls on century after century with movements so reliable that all time on earth can be measured against it."[3]

QUESTIONS:
1.   What kinds of claims does this verse make about Christ? Why is it important to know that Christ is the creator of the universe?
2.   How would you handle objections to your faith in God by an unbeliever?
3.   Have you ever thought about *why* Christ brought you into the world? Are you satisfied with yourself? How does trusting God help you to accept yourself?

2. CHRIST CREATED ALL THINGS FOR HIMSELF (v.16).

Think for a moment: if Christ really created all things, who should creation praise and honor, worship and serve? The answer is obvious: creation owes its existence to Christ. Jesus Christ created the universe...

- to love
- to bless
- to redeem.

- to receive
- to save
- to exalt.

...that in the ages to come He might show the riches of His grace and kindness (Eph.2:7).

...that He might reveal His glory (Ro.8:18).

> "For of him, and through him, and <u>to him</u>, are all things: to whom be glory for ever" (Ro.11:36, cp. 1 Cor.15:28; Eph.1:10; Col.1:19-20; Heb.1:2; 2:10).

QUESTIONS:
1. Does God have the right to impose His rules on people? On you?
2. What should your response be to Christ when He requires something from you?
3. Are there any circumstances when you should not obey Christ? What steps are you willing to take in order to have a willing heart?
4. Why do some people tend to think that "God owes them something"? Does He?

3. JESUS CHRIST IS BEFORE ALL THINGS (v.17).

This is a critical point; it means two things.

1. Jesus Christ was before all things *in time*. Before the first thing was ever created, Jesus Christ was already there. He is not a created being; He is the Creator. There was nothing existing in the universe when He created. Before the beginning of time, before the universe ever existed, He was there. God alone is eternal.

APPLICATION:
A person might ask, when did God begin? Who created Him? How can something or someone have no beginning? Consider a ring worn on someone's finger: turn it all around and try to find where it begins and where it ends. It can't be done—for there is no beginning or ending to the ring; it is continuous. So it is with God; He has no beginning and no ending. We may not understand it, but we must accept it. He *always has been* and *always will be*. We must believe and accept it by faith.

> "Before the mountains were brought forth, or ever thou hadst formed the earth and the world, even from everlasting to everlasting, thou art God" (Ps.90:2).

2. Jesus Christ is before all things *in importance and supremacy*. Nothing is superior to Him. He alone is the Sovereign Majesty of the universe. All else—every single thing—stands under Him owing their existence, worship, and service to Him.

> "Christ came, who is over all" (Ro.9:5).

APPLICATION:
This point destroys all ideas that Jesus Christ is only a great teacher, only one among many great men who can lead us to God. God tells us clearly in His Word that Christ is *over all*—without exception.

QUESTIONS:
1. What kinds of claims does this verse make about Jesus Christ? How meaningful is Christ's eternity to you when compared to other religious leaders?
2. How does trusting God help you deal with this Scripture? Do you need to make any adjustments in your relationship with Him?

4. JESUS CHRIST HOLDS ALL THINGS TOGETHER (v.17).

William Barclay is descriptive in his commentary:

> "...it is the Son who...holds the world together. That is to say, all the laws by which this world is an order and not a chaos are an expression of the mind of the Son. The law of gravity and all the so-called scientific laws are not only scientific laws; they are divine laws. They are the laws which make sense of the universe. They are the laws which make this a reliable and a dependable world. Every law of science and of nature is, in fact, an expression of the thought of God. It is by these laws, and therefore by the mind of God, that the universe hangs together, and does not disintegrate in chaos."[4]

The point is clear: Jesus Christ is what holds the world together. It is His love and power and energy...
- that keeps the universe from flying apart and disintegrating.
- that keeps all creatures from utterly destroying themselves through savagery.

> **"Who being the brightness of his glory, and the express image of his person, and <u>upholding all things by the word of his power</u>, when he had by himself purged our sins, sat down on the right hand of the Majesty on high" (Heb.1:3).**

APPLICATION 1:
The very nature of Christ is...
- to exist *eternally*.
- to exist *in a perfect state of being*.
- to exist *in perfect communion* and fellowship eternally with God (cp. 1 Jn.1:3).

And note: it is the very nature of Christ that will be given to us as believers; therefore, all three things will become our nature: eternal existence, perfected state of being, and perfect communion and fellowship with God.

> **"But we all, with open face beholding as in a glass the glory of the Lord, are changed into the same image from glory to glory, even as by the Spirit of the Lord" (2 Cor.3:18).**

APPLICATION 2:
Not only is Jesus Christ perfect and eternal, but He created the universe to be perfect and eternal. Man has corrupted the world and himself, but Christ reveals that God is wonderful, far beyond anyone we could have ever dreamed. He is loving and caring, full of goodness and truth. He will not tolerate injustices: murder and stealing, lying and cheating, abuse and mistreatment, ignoring and neglect of husband, wife, child, neighbor, brother, sister or stranger. God loves, and He is working and moving toward a perfect universe that will be filled with people who choose to love, worship, live, and work for Him. This should give us all great hope for the future. We can look forward to the day when not only our bodies will be perfected but also the whole world—all of creation!

ILLUSTRATION:
Do you realize the power that Christ has at His disposal? He holds *everything* together. For example,

> "A guide took a group of people through an atomic laboratory and explained how all matter was composed of rapidly moving electric particles. The tourists studied models of molecules and were amazed to learn that matter is made up primarily of space. During the question period, one visitor asked, 'If this is the way matter works, what holds it all together?' For that, the guide had no answer.
> "But the Christian has an answer: Jesus Christ!"[5]

QUESTIONS:

1. What kinds of burdens do you carry that seem to make your life fall apart? What kinds of promises does this Scripture give to you?
2. Recall a previous experience where you sensed Christ's "keeping power." Looking back, what kinds of lessons did you learn?
3. What kind of counsel would you give to a person who is spending all his energy trying to hold his life (i.e. marriage, finances, families, etc.) together by using his own strength?

SUMMARY:

We must recognize that Christ is not only the Creator of all things but that all things were created *for* Him—all things *belong to* Him, all things are held together *by* Him. He alone is supreme. As Christian believers, we should be challenged to live every day keeping these things in mind, honoring God with every action and doing all for the glory of God, for His pleasure.

1. Christ created all things.
2. Christ created all things for Himself.
3. Christ is before all.
4. Christ holds all things together.

PERSONAL JOURNAL NOTES
(Reflection & Response)

1. The most important thing that I learned from this lesson was:

2. The area that I need to work on the most is:

3. I can apply this lesson to my life by:

4. Closing Statement of Commitment:

---

[1] Eleanor Doan. *The New Speakers Source Book* (Grand Rapids, MI: Zondervan Publishing House, 1968), p.108. As quoted by Edwin Conklin.
[2] Eleanor Doan. *The New Speakers Source Book*, p.108.
[3] Craig B. Larson, Editor. *Illustrations for Preaching & Teaching*, p.45.
[4] William Barclay. *The Letters to the Philippians, Colossians, and Thessalonians*, p.144.
[5] Warren W. Wiersbe. *The Bible Exposition Commentary, Vol.2*, p.116.

	D. God & Christ (Part III): Christ is the Head of the Church, 1:18-19
1. Christ is the head of the church	18 And he is the head of the body, the church: who is the beginning, the first-born from the dead; that in all things he might have the preeminence.
2. Christ is the beginning of the church	
3. Christ was the first to arise from the dead	
4. Christ is supreme in all things	
5. Christ is filled with all the fulness of God Himself	19 For it pleased the Father that in him should all fulness dwell;

SECTION II
THE PREEMINENT CHRIST:
GOD'S DEAR SON Colossians 1:12-23

Study 4:   GOD AND CHRIST (PART III): CHRIST IS THE HEAD OF THE CHURCH

Text: Colossians 1:18-19

Aim: To recognize Jesus Christ as the true Head of the church.

Memory Verse:
  "And hath put all things under his feet, and gave him to be the head over all things to the church" (Eph.1:22).

INTRODUCTION:
    When the head of a human body is removed, the conclusion is obvious: the body dies. The same is true of the church. When the true Head, Jesus Christ, is removed, the church body dies. And when a foreign head is placed on the body of Christ, a monster is created. And in far too many cases, Jesus Christ has been pushed aside and removed as the Head of the church. Who has replaced Him—the pastor, the board of directors, the richest families, the denomination itself? All of these have become the head in far too many churches.
    This is the agenda in the study today: to give Jesus Christ His proper place at the head of the church, lest we forget and create a monster.
    This part of the Bible is one of the great pictures of Christ and of the church. It pictures in clear terms what the relationship is between Christ and the church. It is a passage that should be studied by every local church and church member time and again.

OUTLINE:
    1.   Christ is the head of the church (v.18).
    2.   Christ is the beginning of the church (v.18).
    3.   Christ was the first to arise from the dead (v.18).
    4.   Christ is supreme in all things (v.18).
    5.   Christ is filled with all the fulness of God Himself (v.19).

1. JESUS CHRIST IS THE HEAD OF THE CHURCH (v.18).

    Before discussing Christ's place as the head of the church, what does the word church mean? It means to call out a gathering, an assembly. In the Greek there is no spiritual significance ascribed to the word church. An example is the town meeting in Ephesus which was "called out." It was only an official city-wide meeting.

What is the difference then between such a secular meeting and the church of God?

⇒ It is God who calls together and gathers His church. His church is the body of people "called out" from the world by Him.

⇒ God dwells within the very presence of those He calls together.

⇒ The gathering of God meets together for two purposes—worship and mission. God is the object of worship, and His mission becomes the objective of the church.

With that significant difference in mind, the importance of verse 18 becomes clear. This passage (v.18) is the most common description of Christ and the church: the picture of the human body with Christ as the Head and the church as His body. When the church is called the body of Christ, at least three ideas are pictured.

1.   There is the idea of *life*, of the most vital connection and relationship. A body cannot live apart from the head, and a head cannot live apart from the body. Both the head and body are absolutely necessary for there to be life. Without Jesus Christ, the church does not exist; and without the church, the life of Christ on earth could not be known or exist. Christ is made known only through the lives of His people, the church. That is His chosen method to make Himself known.

APPLICATION:
This means something critically important.
1)   If any part of the world is without the church (His body), that part of the world cannot know Christ the Head.
2)   If the world sees a body of people with some head other than Christ, then that body of people is not the true church, not the body of Christ.

2.   There is the idea of *activity* and its *source*. It is the body that acts, but it is the head that tells the body to act. It is the head that...

- plans for the body
- directs the body
- guides the body
- inspires the body

- arouses the body
- activates the body
- drives the body

The body does nothing without the head.

APPLICATION:
All that the body does begins in the head. This is significant. It means that the church is totally dependent upon the Head, Jesus Christ. The body finds its purpose, meaning, and significance in the Head who is Jesus Christ. Therefore, the body or church must learn more and more to acknowledge and honor the Head. The body must learn to look to the Head for its plans, guidance, and motivation.

3.   There is the idea of *control*. The head is to rule and reign over the body. The body is to be controlled by the head. The body is not to act apart from the head. But note: sometimes a body does act apart from the head. But when it does, it is because of disease, handicap, or injury. There is some malfunction—some physical, emotional or mental problem. So it is with the church. When Christ does not control the church body, it is because there is some malfunction, some problem within the body.

APPLICATION:
The church body is to let Christ control it. The church is to walk a disciplined, controlled life just like Christ says. When the church lives like Christ dictates, then the church body lives a life free of disease and injury.

"And hath put all things under his feet, and gave him to be the head over all things to the church" (Eph.1:22).

ILLUSTRATION:

When Jesus Christ is removed as the Head of the local church, that body will eventually die.

> *"I heard of a poor half-witted fellow whose companion, working beside him, dropped dead. He was found trying to hold up the dead man, trying to make him stand and sit upright. Finding his effort without avail, he was saying to himself, 'He needs something inside him.' I suspect that is the reason we live at a poor dying rate. We need a living Spirit within to control and uphold us"[1]*

How are your vital signs? Only the Head can give you a pulse. Only His Spirit will hold you up.

QUESTIONS:
1. If you were a doctor, what kinds of things would alarm you as you gave your church a physical check-up? What kind of treatment would you recommend?
2. What sort of relationship should be between the head and the body? What is the implication if the body does not respond to commands from the head?
3. When you need to eat, rest, sit, work, etc., your head is what tells you to do these things. They are automatic to you. When the head of the church, Jesus Christ, tells you to do something (witness, worship, pray, or serve someplace), do you do it automatically? Do you hesitate? Do you waiver in your obedience?
4. How does this verse help you to understand God's plan for the Church?

2. JESUS CHRIST IS THE BEGINNING OF THE CHURCH (v.18).

The word "beginning" has a twofold idea.

1. "Beginning" means *creative power*. When something first begins, it is created or brought into being by some person or thing greater than itself. Jesus Christ was the Person who gave birth to the church. He is greater than the church; therefore, He had the power to create the church and bring it into existence.
   ⇒ The church is the idea of His mind: He was the One who dreamed of the church, thought it up, and saw the great purpose it could accomplish upon earth.
   ⇒ The church is the plan of His heart: He saw how the church could be founded and built upon the earth and His heart wanted it.
   ⇒ The church is the desire of His will: He desired and longed for the church; therefore, He willed to create it.
   ⇒ The church is the activity of His hands and life: Jesus Christ came to earth and gave birth to the church.
   ⇒ The church is the result of His love: He loved the world; therefore, He founded His church and He reaches out to the world through His church.
   ⇒ The church is the subject of His care: He looks after and oversees the welfare of His church, making sure that it fulfils its purpose on earth. Even the very gates of hell cannot prevail against the church because of His love and care (Mt.16:18).

The point is this: Jesus Christ began the church. He is the beginning, the creative power who founded and gave birth to the church.

APPLICATION:

Jesus Christ is the only Person who is to be honored and acknowledged as the beginning of God's church on earth. No other person is to ever usurp the place of Christ in the church. He and He alone is to be praised as the Source of the church's life and being. He and He alone can bring men to God. Think how many men in the world today are honored as "founders" of a church, a religion, or a cult. Instead of honoring God, their members honor just a man—a sinful man who is trying to usurp God's rightful place. We, too, must be careful when we honor and praise men, careful that we are not giving glory to men that belongs to God.

2. "Beginning" means *first in time*. Jesus Christ was the first Person of the church. He began the church; therefore, He was the first member, the great and glorious Founder of the church. All others who come into the church follow Him.

APPLICATION:

This means something of extreme significance. A person who does not follow Christ the Founder fails to really enter the church which He founded. A person may sit in the pews of a building and hear the voice of the preacher, but unless he follows Christ, he is not in the body and movement of the church. He follows some other body and movement. And one thing must be noted: Christ was very clear about His body and movement—about how His church and followers are to live. Therefore, to be a part of His church, a person has to live in the will and movement which Christ established.

> "That we henceforth be no more children, tossed to and fro, and carried about with every wind of doctrine, by the sleight of men, and cunning craftiness, whereby they lie in wait to deceive; but speaking the truth in love, may grow up into him in all things, which is the head, even Christ" (Eph.4:14-15, cp. Col.2:18-19; 1 Jn.2:23-24).

QUESTIONS:
1. Why did Jesus Christ create the Church?
2. How do you think God feels about those who claim to be founders of a church or denomination? Why do you suppose some Christians want the title of founder? What would be some of the characteristics that would come out of these churches or denominations?
3. What are the true qualifications of becoming a member of the Church? Do you think it is possible to be a true member of the Church without following Christ?

3. JESUS CHRIST WAS THE FIRST TO ARISE FROM THE DEAD (v.18).

There are three ways that the resurrection of Christ and the church are closely related.

1. The resurrection of Christ is the very *reason the church exists*. If Jesus Christ had not risen from the dead, there would be no church. Why? Because God loves man and longs for man to live forever in His presence. He made this possible through the resurrection of Jesus Christ and by establishing the church. What happened was this: Jesus Christ became the first person who ever arose from the dead and who never had to die again. He conquered death. Therefore, when a person truly believes in the resurrection of Christ, God takes that belief and counts the person as being *in Christ*. So, when the man is ready to leave this world, the Lord's energy and power transfers the person right into the presence of God.

Now note: this is the message and hope of the gospel. It is the people who believe in the resurrection of Christ who make up the church. This is what the church is: a body of people who have trusted the power of Christ's resurrection to conquer death for them and to transfer them into the eternal presence of God. *Apart from the resurrection of Christ, there would be no hope and no message of conquering power; therefore, there would be no church.*

APPLICATION 1:

The resurrection of Christ and the church are tied together.

⇒ Every person who truly believes in the resurrection of Christ is a true member of the Lord's church.

⇒ Every true member of the church is a person who has truly believed in the resurrection of Christ.

APPLICATION 2:

The church is a body of people who truly believe in the resurrection of Christ. The conquest of death is the church's great message of hope. It is this very belief that distinguishes it from all other organizations of men such as social and civic clubs.

2. The resurrection of Christ and the life of the church means *there is a new life available* for people. When Christ was raised from the dead, His body and life were entirely different from His former body and life. He had a changed body and life; He was raised to live a new life, to live face to face with God forever. So it is with the church. The church is to be a picture of the resurrected and changed life of Christ. The church is...

• to be entirely different from the world.

• to be separated from the world and given over completely to God.

• to live its life as though it is face to face with God.

APPLICATION:

How many churches today are entirely different and separated from the world? How many could look at God face to face without shame? Think of the churches that are endorsing immoral relationships and marriages, even ordaining gay and lesbian ministers! Such churches have not separated from the world, but rather have joined forces with the world—accepting worldly and immoral practices among its members without raising a voice against such ungodliness. We must all, as individuals and as church bodies, be sure that in no way are we guilty of joining forces with the world.

3. The resurrection of Christ is the *power by which the church is to live*. The resurrection of Christ proves there is unlimited, enormous power available for living and conquering all the foes of life, even the foes of death and judgment. The church is to live as resurrected beings— beings with a new life, a life of power and energy that conquers all the trials of life. Just imagine! Such power is available, and it is to be *alive and active* in the church. In fact, the resurrected power of the Lord Jesus Christ is to be the very life blood of the church.

APPLICATION:

What trial or temptation is too great to handle for a God who has the power to raise His Son from the dead? None! God has made this power available to us through our faith in Jesus Christ—but His power is only as strong as our faith!

> **"And what is the exceeding greatness of his power to us-ward who believe, according to the working of his mighty power, which he wrought in Christ, when he raised him from the dead, and set him at his own right hand in the heavenly places" (Eph.1:19-20).**

QUESTIONS:

1. The resurrection of Christ and the Church are vitally linked together. What difference should this make in a church's life?

2. Why do you think some churches blend together with the world? What types of boundaries or principles must be established in a local church to keep it from looking like the world?

3. Remember: *the resurrection of Christ is the power by which the church is to live*. What are some areas in your church where Christ's power is being displayed? What are some examples of some person exerting his own power in a church?

4. JESUS CHRIST IS SUPREME IN ALL THINGS (v.18).

God the Father has only one child, the Lord Jesus Christ who is God the Son. Note two points.

1.   God the Son willingly came to earth to die and to arise again for man's salvation. Therefore, God the Father is bound to love God the Son with a supreme love. He is bound to do the ultimate for Christ, to give Christ the preeminence in all things. He is bound to do everything and to arrange everything to focus around His only Son.

The point is this: God's great love for His Son explains why the church exists. God had created the world and man to worship and serve Him, but when man rebelled and refused to honor Him, God had to accomplish His purpose some other way. All men were not going to worship and serve Him, but He knew that some would if He provided a way. This God did. He provided the way through His Son Jesus Christ and the church. The person who believes in His Son Jesus Christ is forgiven for his rebellion and accepted into the new body of people God created, the body called "the church."

⇒   This is what the church is: a body of people who have approached God through the Lord Jesus Christ to worship and serve God.

2.   Jesus Christ is to have the preeminence in all things: He is the Person who came to earth to suffer and die. He is the One who has loved and given Himself for the church. He is the One who died to establish the church (Eph.5:25). Therefore, God has made Christ the preeminent and supreme Majesty of the universe.

⇒   Jesus Christ has been exalted to the right hand of God the Father.

> **"So then after the Lord had spoken unto them, he was received up into heaven, and sat on the right hand of God" (Mk.16:19).**

⇒   Jesus Christ has been given a name above every name.

> **"Wherefore God also hath highly exalted him, and given him a name which is above every name" (Ph.2:9).**

⇒   Jesus Christ has been given all things.

> **"Saying with a loud voice, Worthy is the Lamb that was slain to receive power, and riches, and wisdom, and strength, and honour, and glory, and blessing" (Rev.5:12).**

⇒   Jesus Christ has been made both Lord and Christ (Messiah, Savior).

> **"Therefore let all the house of Israel know assuredly, that God hath made that same Jesus, whom ye have crucified, both Lord and Christ" (Acts 2:36).**

⇒   Jesus Christ has been exalted above all.

> **"He that cometh from above is above all: he that is of the earth is earthly, and speaketh of the earth: he that cometh from heaven is above all" (Jn.3:31).**

⇒ Jesus Christ is Lord of both the living and the dead.

> **"For to this end Christ both died, and rose, and revived, that he might be Lord both of the dead and living" (Ro.14:9).**

⇒ Jesus Christ has a more excellent name than the angels.

> **"Being made so much better than the angels, as he hath by inheritance obtained a more excellent name than they" (Heb.1:4).**

⇒ Jesus Christ has more glory than even the greatest of men.

> **"For this man was counted worthy of more glory than Moses inasmuch as he who hath builded the house hath more honour than the house" (Heb.3:3).**

⇒ Jesus Christ is the Alpha and Omega, the first and the last.

> **"Saying, I am Alpha and Omega, the first and the last" (Rev.1:11).**

⇒ Jesus Christ has all things put under His feet.

> **"And hath put all things under his feet, and gave him to be the head over all things to the church" (Eph.1:22).**

⇒ Jesus Christ has all things subject to Him.

> **"Who is gone into heaven, and is on the right hand of God; angels and authorities and powers being made subject unto him" (1 Pt.3:22).**

ILLUSTRATION:
There is no need for the Christian believer to get into an argument with a lost person. What good will it do if we win the argument but lose the soul?

> *"In 1893, the World's Columbian Exposition was held in Chicago, and more than 21 million people visited the exhibits. Among the features was a 'World Parliament of Religions,' with representatives of the world's religions, meeting to share their 'best points' and perhaps come up with a new religion for the world.*
> *"Evangelist D.L. Moody saw this as a great opportunity for evangelism. He used churches, rented theaters, and even rented a circus tent (when the show was not on) to present the Gospel of Jesus Christ. His friends wanted Moody to attack the 'Parliament of Religions,' but he refused. 'I am going to make Jesus Christ so attractive,' he said, 'that men will turn to Him.' Moody knew that Jesus Christ was the preeminent Saviour, not just one of many 'religious leaders' of history.*
> *"The 'Chicago Campaign' of 1893 was probably the greatest evangelistic endeavor in D.L. Moody's life, and thousands came to Christ"[2]*

What a lesson for all generations of the world—to acknowledge and proclaim that Jesus Christ is the only Savior, the only true and living God!

QUESTIONS :
1. According to this verse, on what basis does the Church exist?
2. How does understanding the relationships between God the Father, Jesus Christ, and the Church help you better relate to other Christian believers?
3. As a Church member, what sort of attitude are you to have about Christ?

5. JESUS CHRIST IS FILLED WITH ALL THE FULNESS OF GOD HIMSELF (v.19).

All that God is dwells in Jesus Christ. This is what this verse means. *Jesus Christ is fully God in all God's divine nature.* The word "dwell" means to make *permanent* abode or to be at home *permanently*. All the fulness of God was *at home* in Christ before He came to earth, *at home* in Him while He was on earth, and will continue to be *at home* within Him throughout all eternity. Jesus Christ is God, the Son of God who possesses the perfect nature of God the Father in all His Being and characteristics.

This is significant for the church because it means...
- that God is the Head of the church.
- that God is the beginning of the church.
- that God is the One who came to earth, died, and arose from the dead.
- that God is the preeminent Person of the universe.
- that God in all His fulness dwells in Jesus Christ, the Son of God.

It means that the church worships God when it worships the Son of God. It means that God the Father is honored when God the Son is honored. Both the Father and the Son have the same perfect nature; therefore, what is done for the Son is done for the Father. The Son is to be worshipped and served even as the Father is. In fact, because of what God the Son has done in coming to earth—dying and arising from the dead—God the Father wants His Son to have the preeminence. Note the word "pleased": it pleases the Father that His Son has His nature and is the preeminent majesty of the universe.

APPLICATION:
The church can please the Father only by praising and serving the Son, the Lord Jesus Christ, the One in whom all the fulness of God dwells. It is nice and sometimes appropriate when we give honor and praise to men, but our focus must always be on the Lord Jesus Christ—on what has been done through Him, by Him, and for Him.

"In the beginning was the Word, and the Word was with God, and the Word was God. The same was in the beginning with God" (Jn.1:1-2).

QUESTIONS:
1. What does this verse teach about the deity of Christ? What does it mean "to dwell"? Why is it important that Christ is filled with all the fulness of God Himself?
2. Do you think you can please the Father if the Son does not have His proper place in your heart? What kinds of adjustments do you need to make to give Christ His proper place in your life?

SUMMARY :

Christ is the founder of the church as well as the head of it. The church exists only *because* of Christ and only *for* Him. We owe our allegiance to Him and Him alone—He paid the supreme sacrifice so that we might have the hope of resurrection and eternal life with Him.

1. Christ is the head of the church.
2. Christ is the beginning of the church.
3. Christ was the first from the dead.
4. Christ is supreme in all things.
5. Christ is filled with all the fulness of God Himself.

PERSONAL JOURNAL NOTES
(Reflection & Response)

1. The most important thing that I learned from this lesson was:

2. The area that I need to work on the most is:

3. I can apply this lesson to my life by:

4. Closing Statement of Commitment:

---

[1] Walter B. Knight, *Knight's Master Book of 4,000 Illustrations.* (Grand Rapids, MI: William B. Eerdmans Publishing Company, 1956), p.289.

[2] Warren W. Wiersbe, *The Bible Exposition Commentary, Vol.2*, p.117.

	E. God & Christ (Part IV): Christ the Reconciler of All Things, 1:20-23	works, yet now hath he reconciled	God—through Christ
1. God has reconciled all things to Himself—through Christ	20 And, having made peace through the blood of his cross, by him to reconcile all things unto himself; by him, I say, whether they be things in earth or things in heaven.	22 In the body of his flesh through death, to present you holy and unblameable and unreproveable in his sight:	**3. God had one great purpose in reconciliation: To present the believer perfect before Him**
a. The need: To make peace		23 If ye continue in the faith grounded and settled, and be not moved away from the hope of the gospel, which ye have heard, and which was preached to every creature which is under heaven; whereof I Paul am made a minister;	**4. God has made reconciliation conditional**
b. The means: The cross			a. Must continue in the faith
c. The result: All things in heaven & earth reconciled			b. Must not be moved away from the gospel
2. God has reconciled those who were alienated & enemies of	21 And you, that were sometime alienated and enemies in your mind by wicked		

SECTION II
THE PREEMINENT CHRIST: GOD'S DEAR SON
Colossians 1:12-23

Study 5: GOD AND CHRIST (PART IV): CHRIST THE RECONCILER OF ALL THINGS

Text: Colossians 1:20-23

Aim: To clearly see Christ as the way to reconciliation with God.

Memory Verse:
> "And having made peace through the blood of His cross, by Him to reconcile all things unto Himself; by Him, I say, whether they be things in earth, or things in heaven" (Colossians 1:20).

INTRODUCTION:

All over the world men are seeking peace. They are seeking peace with family members, neighbors, co-workers, employers, governments, and races of people. Solution after solution will be tried over and over again, but man-made solutions to peace only serve as temporary Band-Aids to terminal problems. The only lasting solution to peace is for man to find peace with God. This will be seen in the points that follow.

But for now, what is the secret to peace with God? The secret to peace and reconciliation with God is the cross. But not an ordinary cross. Many men have died through the ages on crosses for many causes. True and lasting peace comes to men because of *the blood of the cross, because of Jesus Christ*. The blood which Jesus Christ shed upon the cross is the only thing that can bring permanent peace to the heart of man.

This passage is one of the great studies of Scripture, the message of *reconciliation*. What does *reconciliation* mean? It means to restore friendship, harmony, or communion; to cause to accept. Man can now be reconciled to God, that is, restored to God and accepted by God, because of Christ. It is an astounding passage, for it reveals that God has not only reconciled man to Himself, but He has reconciled the whole universe—all of creation—to Himself.

OUTLINE:
1. God has reconciled all things to Himself—through Christ (v.20).
2. God has reconciled those who were alienated and were enemies of God—through Christ (v.21-22).
3. God had one great purpose in reconciliation: to present the believer perfect before Him (v.22).
4. God has made reconciliation conditional (v.23).

1. GOD HAS RECONCILED ALL THINGS TO HIMSELF—THROUGH CHRIST (v.20).

This is one of the great verses of Scripture, but it is a shocker, an eye-opener. It seems to be teaching universal salvation, that is, that everything in heaven and earth has been saved through the blood of Christ. This, of course, could not be what Paul meant, for it is not what the rest of Scripture teaches. Note three significant facts.

1. There is a great need for peace between God and man. Man is not at peace with God. His soul is restless and disturbed, lonely and empty, without direction and purpose. His soul is as separated from God as it can be. Man's relationship with God can be described in three ways.

    a.   Man is not at *peace with God*. Note the word *"with."* Peace *with* God refers to man's relationship with God. Man does not know God personally; he is not near God nor close to God. He often questions the very existence of God, and even if he believes that God exists, he knows little if anything about talking and sharing with God. Instead of sensing *peace with God*, he senses separation from God, as though God is out in space someplace, far away from the earth.

> **"Therefore being justified by faith, we have peace with God through our Lord Jesus Christ" (Ro.5:1).**

    b.   Man does not experience the *peace of God*. Note the word *"of."* The peace *of* God refers to possessing the peace of God within one's heart and life. As man walks throughout the day taking care of his affairs, his heart is not settled; he lacks peace; he knows little if anything of the peace of God. He lacks complete assurance as he faces the circumstances, problems, difficulties, trials, and temptations of life.

> **"Be careful for nothing; but in every thing by prayer and supplication with thanksgiving let your requests be made known unto God. And the peace of God, which passeth all understanding, shall keep your hearts and minds through Christ Jesus" (Ph.4:6-7).**

    c.   Man does not experience the *God of peace* dwelling within his heart and flooding his soul. As he walks through life, he does not know what it is to have the presence of God with him; he does not know what it means to have the God of peace helping him face the affairs and trials of daily life.

> **"Finally, brethren, whatsoever things are true, whatsoever things are honest, whatsoever things are just, whatsoever things are pure, whatsoever things are lovely, whatsoever things are of good report; if there be any virtue, and if there be any praise, think on these things. Those things, which ye have both learned, and received, and heard, and seen in me, do: and the God of peace shall be with you" (Ph.4:8-9).**

APPLICATION:
    The point is this: man has a great need for peace with God. God has met that need by reconciling all men to Himself through His Son, Jesus Christ.

QUESTIONS:
1. What are some signs that men are not at peace *with* God?
2. What is the peace *of* God? Do you have this?
3. If a person did not have the *God of peace* dwelling within him, what would be some indications of this in his life?

2. There is the means of reconciliation: the blood of the cross. How does the *blood of the cross* reconcile us to God? There are three pictures that show us.

    a. *There is the picture of unjust punishment and death.* The cross was the place where criminals were executed. This means that Jesus Christ died as an unjust criminal, yet He was not a criminal. He did not deserve to die, for He had broken no law. He was not upon the cross because He deserved to die; He was not there because of His own sins. Therefore, He was bound to be dying for someone else, as a substitute. He was the Righteous dying for the unrighteous, the Just dying for the unjust.

    This is very significant. If the sinless Son of God died for sinners, then the penalty for our sins has already been paid. We are freed from the charge of being sinners: we are no longer considered unjust. How? By faith. When we truly believe that the Christ died for our sins, God counts it so. God takes our faith and *accepts it as our identification with Christ*. Being freed from the charge of sin, we become acceptable to God. We are reconciled and brought near God by Christ's dying for our sins.

> **"For Christ also hath once suffered for sins, the just for the unjust, that he might bring us to God, being put to death in the flesh, but quickened by the Spirit" (1 Pt.3:18).**

    b. *There is the picture of blood or of sacrifice.* When the blood of Christ is mentioned, the idea of sacrifice is meant. The blood of Christ is tied to the blood of animal sacrifices in the Old Testament. Down through the centuries God had told man that sin was very serious—a matter worthy of death. It was sin that separated man from God. Therefore, man either had to die for his sins or else someone else who was innocent and without transgression had to be sacrificed for him. That Someone, of course, had to be God Himself, for no one else is innocent and perfect. But it was not yet time for God to come to earth in the person of His Son, the Lord Jesus Christ; the fulness of time had not yet come. Man had not yet learned the awfulness of sin and the great price that God would be paying in sacrificing His Son for man.

    Animal sacrifice was one of the ways God was going to teach these truths to man. A man was to believe that the animal was sacrificed for him. If he truly believed, then God accepted the animal sacrifice as bearing his sins. This, of course, meant the man was freed from the charge of sin. He was thereby reconciled and made acceptable to God by the blood that was shed.

    The point is this: the shed blood of Christ is the supreme sacrifice. The perfect blood of God's own Son has now been sacrificed for man's sins. If a man believes that the blood of Christ (His life) was sacrificed for his sins, then God accepts his faith as the fact. The believer is identified with the death of Christ, as having already died. Therefore, he never again has to die. He is reconciled and brought near God by the blood or sacrifice of Christ.

> **"Who his own self bare our sins in his own body on the tree, that we, being dead to sins, should live unto righteousness: by whose stripes ye were healed" (1 Pt.2:24).**

APPLICATION:

The blood of Christ is one of the most profound statements that Christianity makes to the world—His shed blood has been sacrificed so that we may live.

QUESTIONS:

1. Do you believe that the sacrifice of Jesus Christ has been made for you and is a once-for-all action? Why do some people struggle with this reality?
2. Do you ever feel compelled to try to win God's favor with some action? Does it improve your standing with God?
3. Once you accept Christ as your Savior, God does not see your past sins anymore because you are in Christ. Do you find yourself doubting that the sacrifice of Christ could possibly cover all your sins? (Remember: there could be no greater sacrifice than that of Jesus Christ, the sinless, perfect Son of God.)

c. *There is the picture of the cross or of being cursed.* The death of Christ on the cross is always the picture of a curse:

"Cursed is everyone that hangeth on a tree" (Gal.3:13).

The curse, of course, is death. Everyone who ever hung on the cross was doomed to die as a criminal. However, the picture goes much deeper than physical death. Spiritual and eternal death are also meant. Man is doomed to spiritual and eternal death, and there is no escape other than Christ. When Christ hung on the cross, He bore the curse of condemnation, punishment, and death for man. The man who truly believes that Christ bore his curse and condemnation becomes acceptable to God. Very simply, God loves His Son so much that He will accept any person who honors His Son through genuine trust and belief. If a person believes that his sins are forgiven through the cross of Christ, then God will forgive his sins. God loves His Son that much. Therefore, if a person believes that the blood of Christ reconciles him to God, God will reconcile him. God will honor His Son by doing it; God will allow the person of true faith to draw near Him.

"But God commendeth his love toward us, in that, while we were yet sinners, Christ died for us. Much more then, being now justified by his blood, we shall be saved from wrath through him" (Ro.5:8-9).

3. There is the result of the death of Christ. All things are reconciled to God, whether they be things in earth or things in heaven. As stated earlier, *this does not mean universal salvation.* Scripture does not teach that every person will be reconciled to God. Common sense and looking around with a dose of honesty tell us this. The next verse and point make it clear that only true believers are reconciled to God. The height of injustice would be for the unjust to be accepted by God. If the unjust continues to deny and curse God and to act selfishly toward his neighbor, God would not be God if He accepted the unjust. What this verse means is this:

a. God has reconciled all things in earth: both man and his world have been reconciled to God. The door of reconciliation with God is now open, and man is to enter and live with God forever. God has done all He can: He has made it possible for man to draw near Him through reconciliation. It is up to man to draw near. God has done His part; man must now do his part. Man must now turn to God through faith in the blood of Christ.

Note another point as well. The reconciliation of "all things" includes all of creation, the world itself. The earth was created for man, to be his place of residence; therefore, creation shall be redeemed even as man shall be redeemed. There shall be a new heaven and a new earth even as there shall be a new man that lives eternally.

"But the day of the Lord will come as a thief in the night; in the which the heavens shall pass away with a great noise, and the elements shall melt with fervent heat, the earth also and the works that are therein shall be burned up. Seeing then that all these things shall be dissolved, what manner of persons ought ye to be in all holy conversation and godliness, looking for and hasting unto the coming of the day of God, wherein the heavens being on fire shall be dissolved, and the elements shall melt with fervent heat? Nevertheless we, according to his promise, look for new heavens and a new earth, wherein dwelleth righteousness" (2 Pt.3:10-13).

b. God has reconciled all things in heaven: by heaven God probably meant all the worlds of all dimensions. No matter what dimensions there are—even if there is only one other dimension, the spiritual dimension—every being in it has been reconciled to God through the death of Christ.

Note: the idea of the verse is looking ahead to the life that will exist in the new heavens and earth. The life of the future will be a life of reconciliation with God, a life that will see everything in the new heavens and earth reconciled to God. This does not mean that murderers, adulterers, idolaters, and the host of other unbelievers will be there. It means that everyone who is there will be reconciled to God.

"And all things are of God, who hath reconciled us to himself by Jesus Christ, and hath given to us the ministry of reconciliation; to wit, that God was in Christ, reconciling the world unto himself, not imputing their trespasses unto them; and hath committed unto us the word of reconciliation" (2 Cor.5:18-19).

QUESTIONS :
1. What does this verse tell you about God's promise for you? How do you think God wants you to respond to Him?
2. What did God use as the means of reconciliation? How does this knowledge help you to live a full life?
3. Why do you think Christ, a perfect and sinless man, had to die? Couldn't God have done it differently?

2. GOD HAS RECONCILED THOSE WHO WERE ALIENATED AND WERE ENEMIES OF GOD—THROUGH CHRIST (v.21-22).

God has reconciled those who were alienated and were enemies of God. This verse shows that Paul was not thinking about universal salvation. He is addressing believers, those who truly believe that the blood of Jesus Christ has reconciled them to God. He wants them to remember how wonderful reconciliation is. God had done a marvelous thing for them.

APPLICATION:
Just as a manual on how to fly an airplane is not written for someone who drives a truck, the Bible is not written for unbelievers. It is written for believers. Just as the truck driver can begin to learn about flying a plane by reading the airplane manual, an unbeliever can begin to learn about how to be saved by reading the Bible. But the Bible was written *for* believers! Therefore, when Paul here speaks to those who were alienated and sometimes enemies, he is speaking to believers who have drifted or fallen away from the faith. This should alert us to realize that we, too, as believers, are subject to drifting or falling away!

1.   Believers had been *alienated* from God. The word means estranged and separated because of dislike; it means to be unattached because of indifferent and unfriendly feelings. Man is alienated from God...

- because he dislikes who God is. Man is unwilling to submit to the sovereignty of God and to the Lordship of Christ.
- because he dislikes what God says. He refuses to give up all he is and has to obey God fully.
- because he feels God will overlook his sin. Man just feels that God would never condemn him, not in the final analysis.
- because he thinks God is far away, mostly removed from the world and the affairs of daily life. Man thinks God is unconcerned and has little interest in our day-to-day living.

2.   Believers had been *enemies* of God. The word means hostile, hateful, and rebellious. Just think for a moment: think about how men act toward God. They...

- ignore Him
- curse Him
- blaspheme Him
- mock Him
- neglect Him

- deny Him and His very existence
- disobey Him
- falsely profess Him
- half-heartedly serve Him

Note where rebellion takes place: in the mind and in the thoughts. A man thinks about doing something that he knows is against God's will and Word. But the thought is planted in his mind, and he harbors the thought. Any behavior or act that is not in accordance with God's will is rebellion and insurrection. It is going contrary to the *explicit orders* of the King of kings. The terrible tragedy is that every person has rebelled against God. Every human being has stood upon the earth as an enemy of God, an enemy who is in open defiance against God. Every human being has refused to obey the commandments of the King, and every human being who is open and honest knows it. The great task of man...

- is not to disprove the charge that he is an enemy of God.
- is not to prove that he is good enough to be acceptable to God.
- is not to deny and disprove God (denial and disproof can never eliminate truth and fact).

The fact of man's alienation—that he is an enemy of God—is clearly seen. The great task of man is to seek how to be reconciled to God.

ILLUSTRATION:
Just how intense is an unsaved man's hatred for God? J. Vernon McGee illustrates this point with a personal example:

> "A great many people think that men are lost because they have committed some terrible sin. The reason people are lost is that their minds are alienated from God. I think this explains the fierce antagonism toward God on the part of the so-called intellectuals of our day. There is an open hatred and hostility toward God.
> "Some time ago I had the funeral of a certain movie star out here in California. The Hollywood crowd came to the funeral. One of the television newscasters commented on the funeral, and I appreciated what he had to say about it. He said, 'Today Hollywood heard something that it had never heard before.' But I also saw something there at that funeral that I had never seen before. I had never seen so much hatred in the eyes of men and women as I saw when I attempted to present Jesus Christ and to explain how wonderful He is and how He wants to save people. There is an alienation in the mind and heart of man."[1]

3.   Believers have been reconciled to God by the body of Jesus Christ *through death*. Note the unique wording of this statement (v.22ª). The body of Jesus Christ is being stressed. He came to earth in the body of a human being.

    a.   Jesus Christ had to have a real body so that He could secure perfection for the human body. He had to live a perfect and righteous life; He had to live a sinless life as a Man. By living a perfect and sinless life, He became the Ideal and Perfect Pattern of righteousness for all men. All men who really trust Him are covered by His perfection and righteousness. Thereby they become acceptable to God.

    b.   Jesus Christ had to have a real body so that He could bear the sins and condemnation of men and die for man. Jesus Christ was willing to bear the condemnation of sin for men. When a man really believes that Christ died for him, God takes the *man's faith* and counts it as his death. Therefore, the man never has to die spiritually or eternally. When he passes from this life into the next, he will never taste or experience spiritual or eternal death. Quicker than the blink of an eye, God will transfer the believer into His presence. Why? Because the death of Jesus Christ covers him. Jesus Christ has already paid the penalty and suffered the condemnation of the believer's sin. The believer is freed from sin; he is reconciled to God by the death of the body of Christ.

> **"But God commendeth his love toward us, in that, while we were yet sinners, Christ died for us" (Ro.5:8).**

QUESTIONS:
1. Do you ever have feelings of alienation from God? What causes these feelings? What kinds of things can you do in order to have an intimate relationship with God?
2. Before you invited Christ into your life, you were an enemy of God. What kinds of things are hostile to God? What kinds of hostile things do you still do to God? Why do you think this still happens? What can you do in order to change the way you treat God?
3. What is the secret to being reconciled with God?

3. GOD HAD ONE GREAT PURPOSE IN RECONCILIATION—TO PRESENT THE BELIEVER PERFECT BEFORE HIM (v.22).

A great day of coronation is coming, a day when every believer will be presented to God face to face. What a moment! Being ushered into the presence of God to be presented to Him. The excitement, awe, reverence, and ecstasy of the moment will be beyond imagination. This is the reason for the death of Christ. Three things are essential for us to be allowed to stand before God.

1. We must be holy: separated, set apart, and consecrated to God.
    ⇒   We must live lives that are set apart to Christ and to the belief that He died for our reconciliation and that His death covers us.
    ⇒   We must live lives that are separated from worldliness and selfishness and from the flesh and its sins.
    ⇒   We must live lives that are set apart and consecrated to God and His service, lives that live for His cause.

2.   We must also be "unblameable": without blemish, without spot, faultless, without any defect whatsoever.

3.   We must also be "unreproveable": beyond reproach, blameless, unchargeable. Imagine standing before God holy, unblameable, and beyond reproach. Imagine how pleased God would be that we had honored Christ, His only Son, by trusting Him so much! As we are presented to God, what would He say? What would His first words be to us? We would be speechless, no doubt. But what a day of coronation, of glory, of greatness—standing face to face with our Fa-

ther, the God of all glory, the Sovereign Majesty of the whole universe. This is God's one great purpose in reconciliation: to present us perfect before Him.

> **"I beseech you therefore, brethren, by the mercies of God, that ye present your bodies a living sacrifice, holy, acceptable unto God, which is your reasonable service. And be not conformed to this world: but be ye transformed by the renewing of your mind, that ye may prove what is that good, and acceptable, and perfect, will of God" (Ro.12:1-2).**

QUESTIONS:
1. What is the end result of reconciliation? Who has taken the initiative in this: you or God? What kind of role do you play in reconciliation?
2. What kinds of things allow us to stand before God? In which of these areas do you need to take some action?
3. If you were to die today, would you be satisfied with your current spiritual condition? Why or why not?

4. GOD HAS MADE RECONCILIATION CONDITIONAL (v.23).

There are two conditions.

1. A person must *continue* to believe in Jesus Christ and to grow in his belief. He must become more and more grounded and settled in his belief in Christ.
   - ⇒ The word "continue" means to persist, ever moving on; to carry on or keep up; to maintain a certain course or action without interruption.
   - ⇒ The word "grounded" means to be grounded in Christ like the firm, solid foundation of a building. The believer must be so grounded in Christ that he can withstand the severest storms of life.
   - ⇒ The word "settled" means stedfast. The believer must actually stand firm and continue on in being stedfast if he wishes to be presented perfect before God.

ILLUSTRATION:
It has been said that if you are not growing then you are dying. This is particularly true with the believer. Here is a practical illustration which shows us that growth is not always easy. Here's why.

> *"Every member of a family was puzzled over the mystery of a fern that would not grow. Sulking, seemingly, the plant refused to put out new stems. That there might be no injury from transplanting, it had been taken up carefully, and sheltered until it should have been well rooted. Everything in the way of plant food had been provided, but there it stood, no larger than when brought to the house, an awkward, ugly thing, in a mockingly large flower pot.*
> *"Then arrived a guest who was a horticulturist. He forced a wire down into the earth about the fern's roots, and diagnosed the trouble at once. The plant had been set in stiff clay, and this had become packed hard. Reset in loose soil, the fern grew luxuriously. Even the flower of God's planting cannot find root in a heart choked by the cares and riches and pleasures of this life "[2]*

Where are your roots? In a hard heart of clay? Or in a heart filled with fertile soil?

2.   A person must not be moved away from the hope of the gospel. What is it that would move a person away from the gospel?

⇒ worldliness	⇒ pride	⇒ friends
⇒ lust	⇒ fame	⇒ persecution
⇒ greed	⇒ power	⇒ job
⇒ comfort	⇒ family	⇒ false teaching

What is the hope of the gospel? That we might be reconciled to God and presented perfect before Him, holy and blameless—that we might be given the wonderful privilege of living forever with Him, worshipping and serving Him throughout the universe—all to the glory of Christ Jesus our Lord.

APPLICATION:

It is not enough to profess Christ. A person must live for Christ. A person who professes Christ and does not live for Christ is living a lie. A person has to continue in the faith and grow to such a degree that he will never be moved away. If he moves away from Christ and stays moved away, he will never be presented to God as perfect. He will have denied the faith. Continuing on with Christ is an absolute essential. It is the one condition for reconciliation with God.

> **"Therefore, my beloved brethren, be ye stedfast, unmoveable, always abounding in the work of the Lord, forasmuch as ye know that your labour is not in vain in the Lord" (1 Cor.15:58).**

QUESTIONS:
1.   What does this verse teach about spiritual growth? Do you believe that you are growing or backsliding? What examples support your answer?
2.   What do you think your role is in spiritual growth? What is God's role?
3.   What kinds of barriers hinder your spiritual growth? What sorts of things can you do to break free from those things?

SUMMARY:

Christ has made it possible for us to be restored to God—all through His death on the cross. We can be presented to God holy, blameless, and perfect because of the sacrifice of Christ. We must accept what Christ has done for us by faith, and then we must continue on in our faithfulness until the glorious day when we meet the heavenly Father face to face.

1.   God has reconciled all things to Himself—through Christ.
2.   God has reconciled those who were alienated and were enemies of God—through Christ.
3.   God had one great purpose in reconciliation: to present the believer perfect before Him.
4.   God has made reconciliation conditional.

PERSONAL JOURNAL NOTES:
(Reflection & Response)

1. The most important thing that I learned from this lesson was:

2. The area that I need to work on the most is:

3. I can apply this lesson to my life by:

4. Closing Statement of Commitment:

---

[1] J. Vernon McGee, *Thru The Bible, Vol.5* (Nashville, TN: Thomas Nelson Publishers, 1983), p.342

[2] *Methodist Times.* Walter B. Knight, *3,000 Illustrations for Christian Service*, p.328.

	III. THE NEEDS OF THE CHURCH, 1:24-2:7 **A. A Minister Who Tirelessly Labors For the Church, 1:24-29**	which hath been hid from ages and from generations, but now is made manifest to his saints:	share the great mystery of God— "Christ in you, the hope of glory"
1. A minister who will willingly suffer for the church	24 Who now rejoice in my sufferings for you, and fill up that which is behind of the afflictions of Christ in my flesh for his body's sake, which is the church:	27 To whom God would make known what is the riches of the glory of this mystery among the Gentiles; which is Christ in you, the hope of glory:	
		28 Whom we preach, warning every man, and teaching every man in all wisdom; that we may present every man perfect in Christ Jesus:	**4. A minister who will preach Christ, warning & teaching every man**
2. A minister who has been chosen by God to proclaim the Word of God	25 Whereof I am made a minister, according to the dispensation of God which is given to me for you, to fulfil the word of God;		
		29 Whereunto I also labour, striving according to his working, which worketh in me mightily.	**5. A minister who will labor & work: Strive laboriously, depending upon Christ for energy**
3. A minister who will	26 Even the mystery		

SECTION III
THE NEEDS OF THE CHURCH
Colossians 1:24-2:7

Study 1: **THE CHURCH NEEDS A MINISTER WHO WILL TIRELESSLY LABOR FOR THE CHURCH**

Text: **Colossians 1:24-29**

Aim To stir you to work tirelessly for the church.

Memory Verse:
> "And I thank Christ Jesus our Lord, who hath enabled me, for that he counted me faithful, putting me into the ministry" (1 Tim.1:12).

SECTION OVERVIEW:
This study and the next study (13 verses all together, Col.1:24-2:7) deal with a most important subject: the needs of the church. Two basic needs are discussed.
1. The need for a minister who will tirelessly labor for the church.
2. The need for believers who will tirelessly labor for the church.

INTRODUCTION:
Today's study is Col.1:24-29. One of the most basic needs of the church is to have a minister who arduously labors for the church. This is not just a word for the professional clergy. God has called every believer--each one of us--to be a minister. But for now, concentrate on the role of your 'Senior Pastor, Minister, or Preacher.' What does this role involve? Is your minister supposed to be responsible for everything—the administration, choir, visitation, new members, every committee meeting at every level, and on and on?

For a moment, leave behind any preconceived concept of a minister's role and investigate what God says in these Scriptures. For a lot of us, ministry will never be the same again.

OUTLINE:
1. A minister who will willingly suffer for the church (v.24).
2. A minister who has been chosen by God to proclaim the Word of God (v.25).
3. A minister who will share the great mystery of God: "Christ in you, the hope of glory" (v.26-27).
4. A minister who will preach Christ, warning and teaching every man (v.28).
5. A minister who will labor and work: strive laboriously, depending upon Christ for energy (v.29).

1. THE CHURCH NEEDS A MINISTER (SERVANT) WHO WILL WILLINGLY SUFFER FOR OTHERS, THAT IS, FOR THE CHURCH, THE BODY OF CHRIST (v.24).

Paul was such a minister. He paid any price and went to any length of suffering in order to reach and grow people for Christ. He literally poured out his life: he suffered much, and the suffering he bore, he bore willingly for the cause of Christ and His church. This is the message of this verse. It teaches a most wonderful thing: the minister of God actually *completes the sufferings of Christ*. When Christ was upon the earth, He loved the church and gave Himself for it; therefore, He poured out His heart and life for the church, that is, for believers. Christ ministered, served, worked, labored—and He did it all consistently and faithfully. Every day of His life He suffered to the point of exhaustion and fatigue, striving to reach and minister to people. Christ bore whatever was necessary in order to build up the church. And in so doing, He left the *pattern* for all those who would follow after Him. When He left the earth, He expected all believers to *follow in His steps*, to give their lives to suffer whatever is necessary to reach and minister to people. Christ expects every minister and believer to suffer for the church: to pay whatever price is necessary to build the church.

APPLICATION:
Working and laboring for Christ on this earth is not easy. Serving the church in this world is not easy. The reason is due to the ideas and behavior of men toward Christ and His church. Men's ideas and behavior are corrupt. When they look at Christ and His church, they feel that the church is...
- meaningless for modern man.
- acceptable just so it stays in its place.
- all right as a social service to the community.
- needed to lift high the volumes of morality and justice.
- good in that it meets the religious needs of man.

The list could go on and on, for the feelings of people about Christ and the church are almost endless. Some persons look at Christ and deny His relevance and curse His name. They could care less about His church. When it comes to the church, they...
- ignore It
- neglect it
- abuse it
- ridicule it
- persecute it
- attempt to destroy it

Other persons profess Christ and join His church, but their commitments are almost meaningless. They are...
- inactive
- sleepy-eyed
- complacent
- unconcerned
- non-supportive
- lacking vision

On top of all this, there are always those within the church who are...
- worldly
- carnal
- divisive
- critical
- gossiping
- whispering
- murmuring
- making trouble

It is such ideas and behavior that put so much pressure and weight upon the leaders of the church. This is what causes so much suffering for the genuine servant of Christ. The genuine servant longs for people to know Christ and the abundance of life which Christ brings. He wants people to grow into the image of Christ and to keep their eyes fixed upon the hope of glory which is to be given to every true believer. He knows that without Christ men are lost and doomed to judgment. Therefore, he suffers whatever burden and pain is necessary to reach and grow people.

> "Remember the word that I said unto you, The servant is not greater than his lord. If they have persecuted me, they will also persecute you; if they have kept my saying, they will keep yours also" (Jn.15:20).
> "For unto you it is given in the behalf of Christ, not only to believe on him, but also to suffer for his sake" (Ph.1:29).

QUESTIONS:
1. What are some of the ways you suffer or labor to the point of exhaustion for others? What is your greatest challenge in being willing to suffer and to labor tirelessly for others?
2. Are you willing to suffer for the sake of the church? What kinds of things would cause you to avoid suffering?
3. What are some of the reasons this Scripture gives for suffering? How does trusting God help you to live out the truths of this Scripture?

2. THE CHURCH NEEDS A MINISTER WHO HAS BEEN CHOSEN BY GOD TO PROCLAIM THE WORD OF GOD (v.25).

Note two significant points.

1. Paul was made a minister by God. Paul was a minister because God had called him to be a minister. He was not in the ministry...
- because he thought the ministry was a good profession to enter.
- because some friends thought he would make a good minister.
- because he had the natural talents for the ministry.
- because he wanted to commit his life to teach the highest principles of morality and justice.

APPLICATION:
Note a most significant fact. The word "dispensation" in v.25 refers to the steward who oversees the household and property of the owner. The minister is the steward of God, the person chosen to oversee the house or church of God. This fact is almost unbelievable, but it is true: God has actually chosen some persons to oversee His affairs for Him. The minister has been chosen by God to be the steward of His (God's) church and His (God's) people. God has literally taken His church and people and placed them into the hands of His ministers, into...
- their stewardship
- their supervision
- their administration
- their ministry
- their responsibility
- their management
- their care
- their lives
- their love

What an enormous call and responsibility! Yet it comes from God; therefore, it must be fulfilled.

> "For though I preach the gospel, I have nothing to glory of: for necessity is laid upon me; yea, woe is unto me, if I preach not the gospel! For if I do this thing willingly, I have a reward: but if against my

will, a dispensation of the gospel is [still] committed unto me" (1 Cor.9:16-17).

2.   Paul was chosen to fulfil the Word of God, that is, to make the Word of God fully known.

"Preach the word; be instant in season, out of season; reprove, rebuke, exhort with all longsuffering and doctrine" (2 Tim.4:2).

APPLICATION:
    Ministers are to preach the whole Word of God—with its cautions, rebukes, and corrections as well as its promises, mercy, and hope. Too many ministers steer clear of subjects that are controversial—even though the Bible speaks clearly on them. As ministers and believers of God's Word, we are to share the full gospel—as God has chosen us and directed us to do.

ILLUSTRATION:
    The task of the minister is to reach and nourish people, reach and nourish them by using the Word of God in order to affect every area of their lives. Here is an example of how much God's Word meant to a young girl.

"In France, there once lived a poor blind girl who obtained the Gospel of Mark in raised letters and learned to read it by the tips of her fingers. By constant reading,... [her fingers] became callous, and her sense of touch diminished until she could not distinguish the characters. One day, she cut the skin from the ends of her fingers to increase their sensitivity, only to destroy it.
"She felt that she must now give up her beloved Book, and weeping, pressed it to her lips, saying 'Farewell, farewell, sweet word of my Heavenly Father!' To her surprise, her lips, more delicate than her fingers, discerned the form of the letters. All night she perused the form of the letters. All night she perused with her lips the Word of God and overflowed with joy at this new acquisition."

QUESTIONS:
1. The Bible tells us that to whom much is given much will be required. As a minister or servant, what does God require of you?
2. How can you as a servant do a better job of proclaiming God's Word?
3. What do unbelievers do to discourage you from reaching and nourishing people? What can you do to overcome this challenge?

3. THE CHURCH NEEDS A MINISTER WHO WILL SHARE THE GREAT MYSTERY OF GOD—THE GLORIOUS MESSAGE OF "CHRIST IN YOU, THE HOPE OF GLORY" (v.26-27).

What does this mean? Remember that the word "mystery" means secret, some secret that God was not able to reveal to the world until man had been prepared to receive it. What is the mystery that God has kept secret but now has been revealed? It is twofold:

1.   First, the mystery is that Christ actually lives within the believer. It is the *Indwelling Christ* or *Christ dwelling in you* that we read about in Scripture. Christ actually lives within the hearts and lives of believers, and His presence is their guarantee of living forever in glory.
    This is exactly what Christ promised when He was on earth. He was about to face the cross, but right before He died, He said:

"And I will pray the Father, and he shall give you another Comforter, that he may abide with you for ever; even the Spirit of truth; whom the world cannot receive, because it seeth him not, neither knoweth him: but

ye know him; for he dwelleth with you, and shall be in you. **I will not leave you comfortless: I will come to you**" (Jn.14:16-18).

The Holy Spirit is the personal presence of Christ in the believer. Note three facts.

a. Jesus said, "*I will come to you.*" He meant that He would return after He had gone away, that is, died. He would come back to give believers His personal presence. He would not leave them comfortless; the word means to be orphaned, to be without parental help, to be helpless. Jesus would not leave them to struggle through the trials and temptations of life alone.

Jesus' presence with His followers began with His resurrection and with the coming of the Holy Spirit. Jesus was saying that He would come to the believer in the person of the Holy Spirit.

b. The presence of Jesus is a living, eternal presence. He died, but He did not stay dead. He arose and conquered death; He arose to live forever. *Now think: if Jesus Christ is living forever and He dwells within the believer, then that means the believer lives eternally. He never dies.* The believer is made eternal by the eternal presence of Christ *within* him.

c. The presence of Christ is a living union, a *mutual indwelling* between God, Christ, and the believer. "At that day" refers to Jesus' resurrection and the coming of the Holy Spirit.

Now note: when Jesus arose from the dead, believers knew something. His claim was true in an absolute sense. Jesus really was *in* God. God is eternal, so by being *in* God, Jesus was bound to live forever; He was bound to arise from the dead. Something else was known. All that Jesus had said was true. He was placing all believers *in* Himself and Himself *in* them; or to say it another way, when the Holy Spirit came, believers were placed *in* His Spirit and His Spirit *in* them.

This is the glorious truth of "Christ in you"—of Christ's actually living within the believer. It is the first part of the great mystery of God that had been hid but is now revealed to the children of men.

> **"At that day ye shall know that I am in my Father, and ye in me, and I in you" (Jn.14:20).**

2. Second, the mystery of God is that Christ will live within any person, no matter who he or she is—God is no respecter of persons. He shows no partiality and no favoritism. This may be a shock to some people such as Jews and some religionists who feel they are special to God. But this is the proclamation of Holy Scripture. Note the exact words of this passage:

> **"The glory of this mystery among the Gentiles; which is Christ in you."**

It is *in the Gentiles* that Christ dwells; that is, He dwells within anyone who opens his heart and life to Him. When God sent His Son Jesus Christ into the world to die for men, God showed the world that He loves every person equally. He does not favor anyone—not one person—much less a class or nation of people. Every person can now approach God and become acceptable to Him through His Son, Jesus Christ.

APPLICATION:

There is one other thing that needs to be noted: Christ in you is *the hope of glory.* Man's only hope of ever entering and living in glory is Jesus Christ. Jesus Christ must be living in the heart of a person when he dies if the person is to be allowed to enter glory. The guarantee of glory is the presence of Christ and His Spirit within the heart.

> **"Whereby are given unto us exceeding great and precious promises: that by these ye might be partakers of the divine nature, having escaped the corruption that is in the world through lust" (2 Pt.1:4).**

4. THE CHURCH NEEDS A MINISTER WHO WILL PREACH CHRIST AND WILL WARN AND TEACH EVERY MAN (v.28).

This is the great task of the minister.

1. *The minister is to preach Christ.* This point is revolutionary, for it declares the very opposite of what man has always done. Man has always proclaimed principles, ideas, theories, positions, rules, codes, morals, laws, philosophies, institutions, and religions. But this is not to be the theme of the minister's proclamation. As good and as helpful as some of these things are, they are not the task of the minister nor of God's church. The minister is to preach Christ, not things, no matter how good they may be.

> **"For we preach not ourselves, but Christ Jesus the Lord; and ourselves your servants for Jesus' sake" (2 Cor.4:5).**

2. *The minister is to warn every man.* Man must be warned: he cannot enter glory unless Christ is in him. No man is perfect; no man has enough righteousness to make himself acceptable to God. Man cannot earn or do enough to become perfect. Therefore, he shall be cast out of the presence of God, for God is perfect and only perfection can live in God's presence. Man's only hope is Christ, for Christ alone is righteousness. Christ alone is perfect. This is critical for man, for it means that...
   - man's only hope of ever becoming acceptable to God is to have Christ, His righteousness and perfection, living within his body.
   - man's only hope of conquering death when he dies is to have Christ, His righteousness and perfection, living within his body.

Man must be warned: he must repent of his evil and selfishness, turning to God in trust and obedience. He must trust and obey God's only Son, the Lord Jesus Christ. He must surrender his life to Christ and let Christ enter and control his life, or else he will be doomed to separation from God eternally. A person cannot live a life separated and apart from God and then at death expect to enter God's presence. If a person lives a life separated and apart from God, then he will continue on separate and apart from God—continue on eternally. God has done everything He can for man in His Son, Jesus Christ. He can do no greater thing, no more than give the life of His own Son for the salvation of man. There is nothing else to be done. The decision is up to every man. Man must be warned—warned by the person whom God has chosen to warn him, that is, the minister.

> **"Now we exhort you, brethren, warn them that are unruly, comfort the feebleminded, support the weak, be patient toward all men" (1 Th.5:14).**
> **"Cry aloud, spare not, lift up thy voice like a trumpet, and show my people their transgression" (Is.58:1).**

3. *The minister is to teach every man.* It is not enough to warn men. Once they have been warned and have responded to the warning by inviting Christ into their hearts and lives, people need to be taught. They need to learn how to live and walk in Christ. Note the word "wisdom."

This means practical knowledge, knowing how to apply and practice and live out the great teachings of Christ. The minister is to teach "in all wisdom"; that is, he is to be practical in his teaching. Theory and principles, of course, are necessary; but they must be applied to everyday life. Believers must know how to follow Christ day by day as they face the trials and temptations of life.

4. *The minister has one aim: to present every man perfect in Christ* Jesus. The minister is to labor and labor to *present* every person *perfect in Christ Jesus.*

> **"Till we all come in the unity of the faith, and of the knowledge of the Son of God, unto a perfect man, unto the measure of the stature of the fulness of Christ" (Eph.4:13, cp. Mt.5:48; Heb.6:1; Jas.1:4).**

ILLUSTRATION:

The challenge to present every man perfect in Christ is the bottom-line for a minister. Either he does or he doesn't.

> *"A sailor had just returned from a whaling voyage. He heard an eloquent preacher. Asked how he liked the sermon, the sailor replied: 'It was shipshape. The masts just high enough, the sails and the rigging all right, but I did not see any harpoons. When a vessel goes on a whaling voyage, the main thing is to get whales. They do not come because you have a fine ship. You must go after them and harpoon them. The preacher must be a whaler!'"*[2]

The preacher *must go* after men in order to present them to Christ. The preacher must be a worker!

QUESTIONS:
1. Why do some ministers refuse to step on people's toes? What sorts of things lead them to preach and teach this way? What can you do to encourage them to teach the Word of God without ?
2. What is to be the focus of the minister when preaching and teaching?
3. Are there areas of your life that need to be strengthened in this same way? Do you call things as you see them—calling a sin a sin?
4. Have you allowed your minister or pastor to "warn and teach" you? Do you accept his preaching as God's command?

5. THE CHURCH NEEDS A MINISTER WHO WILL LABOR AND STRIVE LABORIOUSLY, DEPENDING UPON CHRIST FOR ENERGY (v.29).

1. The word "labor" means to toil and to struggle in labor and work to the point of exhaustion, fatigue, and pain. It is the picture of an athlete struggling, agonizing, and pushing himself well beyond his capacity in order to achieve his objective. This is the call of God to the minister: to labor and work just as diligently as Paul and as the most dedicated athlete.

2. The word "working" here means energy and efficiency and is only used to refer to superhuman power.[3] In this case, it is the power of Christ. When the minister has gone as far as he can, Christ steps in to infuse energy and power into his body—an energy and power that works in him mightily.

APPLICATION:

The minister who has truly labored to the point of exhaustion and experienced the energy and power of Christ knows how glorious the experience is. It is just tragic that there are too few who labor to the point that Christ has to step in with His energy and power. We seem to forget too easily:

⇒ as long as we have physical strength and energy left to labor, the energy and power of Christ are not needed.

COLOSSIANS 1:24-29

The only way we can experience the physical energy and power of Christ is to use all of our own strength. When we are completely empty, then Christ has to step in or else leave us, abandoning us and disregarding the promise of His Word. And this He will never do. Therefore, when we have no more strength to walk and labor, it is then that He infuses us with His own supernatural energy and power.

> **"Therefore, my beloved brethren, be ye stedfast, unmoveable, always abounding in the work of the Lord, forasmuch as ye know that your labour is not in vain in the Lord" (1 Cor.15:58).**

QUESTIONS:
1. Do you ever experience feelings of laziness in your spiritual walk? What kinds of things make you lazy? What must you do to overcome spiritual laziness?
2. What does this verse say about your spiritual condition apart from Christ?
3. Has there been a time when you noticed God's power increasing in your life? What things happened that led you to experience a greater increase of Christ's power?

SUMMARY:

Every true believer is a minister of God. Therefore, we must all be willing to work tirelessly for the church in proclaiming the Word of God, its hopes as well as its warnings. We must do all we can, drawing on Christ for the energy to continue on. We must all become...

1. A minister who will willingly suffer for the church.
2. A minister who has been chosen by God to proclaim the Word of God.
3. A minister who will share the great mystery of God—"Christ in you, the hope of glory."
4. A minister who will preach Christ and will warn and teach every man.
5. A minister who will labor and work—strive laboriously, depending upon Christ for energy.

PERSONAL JOURNAL NOTES:
(Reflection & Response)

1. The most important thing that I learned from this lesson was:

2. The area that I need to work on the most is:

3. I can apply this lesson to my life by:

4. Closing Statement of Commitment:

---

[1] *Selected.* Paul Lee Tan, *Encyclopedia of 7,700 Illustrations: Signs of the Times* (Rockville, MD: Assurance Publishers, 1985), p.190.
[2] *Dr. W.H. Griffith Thomas.* Walter B. Knight, *Knight's Treasury of 2,000 Illustrations*, p.280.
[3] Kenneth Wuest, *Word Studies in the Greek New Testament*, Vol.1, p.195.

	CHAPTER 2	3 In whom are hid all the treasures of wisdom and knowledge.	c. Comes from knowing that in Christ is all wisdom & knowledge
	B. The Distinguished Marks of a Mature Church, 2:1-7	4 And this I say, lest any man should beguile you with enticing words.	**3. Mark 3: Resisting seductive teaching**
1. Mark 1: A minister who struggles in prayer & concern for the church	For I would that ye knew what great conflict I have for you, and for them at Laodicea, and for as many as have not seen my face in the flesh;	5 For though I be absent in the flesh, yet am I with you in the spirit, joying and beholding your order, and the stedfastness of your faith in Christ.	**4. Mark 4: Maintaining military discipline: Order & stedfastness**
2. Mark 2: Possessing confidence & assurance a. Comes from being knit together in love b. Comes from knowing that what one believes about the mystery of God is accurate	2 That their hearts might be comforted, being knit together in love, and unto all riches of the full assurance of understanding, to the acknowledgment of the mystery of God, and of the Father, and of Christ;	6 As ye have therefore received Christ Jesus the Lord, so walk ye in him: 7 Rooted and built up in him, and stablished in the faith, as ye have been taught, abounding therein with thanksgiving.	**5. Mark 5: Walking in the Lord** a. Walk rooted & built up b. Walk as taught c. Walk overflowing with thanksgiving

Section III
THE NEEDS OF THE CHURCH
Colossians 1:24-2:7

Study 2: THE DISTINGUISHED MARKS OF A MATURE CHURCH

Text: Colossians 2:1-7

Aim: To anchor your faith in a consistent walk with the Lord.

Memory Verse:
   "As ye have therefore received Christ Jesus the Lord, so walk ye in Him" (Colossians 2:6).

INTRODUCTION:
Do you ever feel stagnant in your Christian faith? Like you are going nowhere? Just going through the same motions day after day, week after week, year after year? Everyone probably has felt like this at some point, even the strongest believer. But this should not be a way of life. Scripture tells us that there are certain things we must do to be mature as individuals and as a church body.

The first great need of the church, as you studied in Colossians 1:24-29, is a minister who will tirelessly labor for the church. The second great need of the church is for mature people, a people who are consistently growing in the Lord. The word *consistent* is key: a mature people are consistent in all they do. They are consistently growing in the Lord. One of the great tragedies of today's society is the lack of consistency. Few people are consistent in their daily walk with the Lord. This is the subject of this great passage: the marks of a mature people.

COLOSSIANS 2:1-7

OUTLINE:
1. Mark 1: a minister who struggles in prayer and concern for the church (v.1).
2. Mark 2: possessing confidence and assurance (v.2-3).
3. Mark 3: resisting seductive teaching (v.4).
4. Mark 4: maintaining military discipline—order and stedfastness (v.5).
5. Mark 5: walking in the Lord (v.6-7).

1. MARK 1: A MINISTER WHO STRUGGLES IN PRAYER AND CONCERN FOR THE CHURCH (v.1).

Remember Paul had never seen the Colossian church personally; he was not the minister on the field. (The pastor of the Colossian church was Epaphras.) This says something of enormous importance: ministers are to wrestle in prayer for believers and churches all over the world. In fact, churches can be mature in the Lord only as the ministers of the world wrestle in prayer for all the churches of the world. Picture the scene: imagine yourself hovering above the earth and looking down upon it—looking upon every church upon the earth. Imagine every Christian believer of the world wrestling in prayer for every church. Imagine every church being prayed for every day by every minister. Just imagine what would happen: the growth, the maturity, the ministry, the reaching out to save souls. This is what Paul was after, and it is the great challenge to us. A mature people must have ministers who struggle in prayer and concern for them. There is no other way they can mature. A half-hearted, half-committed minister can only produce half-hearted, half-committed people.

Note the word "conflict." It means to strive, agonize, struggle, and wrestle in prayer for the believers of the churches. It is the picture of an athlete exerting every ounce of energy he has in the struggle of the contest. The idea is that Paul labored hard, toiled, strove, agonized, struggled, and wrestled in prayer.

The ministers of the world are to labor and struggle in prayer for the believers and churches of the world, whether or not they know them or have seen them. Prayer is not easy; it is labor, demanding and difficult labor. The minister or believer who takes prayer seriously knows what it is to struggle in prayer; he knows what it is to face the interrupting attacks of...

- wandering thoughts
- imaginations
- strict schedules
- pride and lofty things that exalt themselves against the knowledge of God
- pressing matters
- demanding work
- thoughts that struggle against being obedient to prayer

But against all these, the minister must gain the victory. The minister must pray: agonize and struggle in prayer—work and toil in prayer—for all the believers and churches of the world. It is the example of Paul and our Lord, and it is the will of the Lord for us. In fact, it is His command.

APPLICATION:
Without doubt, our failure to toil and agonize in prayer for each other is the major reason so many believers and churches are immature in the Lord. The Lord reveals Himself and blesses only those who pray and are bathed in prayer. Prayer—communion and fellowship with Him—is the primary channel through which He has chosen to bless His people. The duty to pray is ours.

"Ask, and it shall be given you; seek, and ye shall find; knock, and it shall be opened unto you" (Mt.7:7).

COLOSSIANS 2:1-7

ILLUSTRATION:

Are your personal prayer times like a sprint or a marathon? In other words, how fast do you pronounce the benediction in order to move on to other busy parts of your day? Here is a story about a man who is known as "Praying Hyde"—and for good reason.

> "Dr. Wilbur Chapman wrote to a friend: 'I have learned some great lessons concerning prayer. At one of our missions in England the audiences were exceedingly small; but I received a note saying that an American missionary was going to pray God's blessing down on our work. He was known as Praying Hyde.
>
> "Almost instantly the tide turned. The hall became packed, and at my first invitation fifty men accepted Christ as their Saviour. As we were leaving I said, 'Mr. Hyde, I want you to pray for me.' He came to my room, turned the key in the door, and dropped on his knees, and waited five minutes without a single syllable coming from his lips. I could hear my own heart thumping, and his beating. I felt hot tears running down my face. I knew that I was with God.
>
> "Then, with upturned face, down which the tears were streaming, he said, 'O God.' Then for five minutes at least he was still again; and then, when he knew that he was talking with God there came from the depths of his heart such petitions for me as I had never heard before. I rose from my knees to know what real prayer was. We believe that prayer is mighty and we believe it as we never did before.'"[1]

Before we can pray God's will, we must be able to hear His heart.

QUESTIONS:
1. What needs to be done in order to help you make prayer a focal point of your life?
2. Where and when can you get alone to wrestle in prayer for the church and for the believers of the world?
3. What kinds of things should you be praying for the church and the believers of the world?
4. How can you effectively pray for churches you have never seen or even heard of?
5. What things can you do to be better informed about the needs of the churches on the other side of town or on the other side of the world?

2. MARK 2: POSSESSING CONFIDENCE AND ASSURANCE (v.2-3).

The word "comforted" means to be strong, strengthened, established and braced.[2] It means to be encouraged. It is the kind of strength...
- that stirs confidence and assurance.
- that braces a person to withstand the onslaught of false teaching, trials, and temptations.
- that comforts and builds assurance and confidence in life, both now and eternally.

The human heart aches for such strength, for this kind of confidence, assurance, and comfort. Where does such strength come from? Where is the spring from which such confidence and assurance flow?

1.   Strong hearts come from *love*—from being knit together with others in love. Think of the people (and the times we ourselves have felt)...

• all alone	• neglected	• disfavored
• without friends	• by-passed	• unloved
• left out	• overlooked	• uncared for
• ignored		

A person who feels these emotions seldom feels strong, confident, or assured. On the contrary, he feels weak, unacceptable, and incapable of handling situations. He feels insecure, which either causes him to withdraw or react in a superior and boastful attitude. We have all seen such reactions.

The point is this: the answer to a strong, confident, assured heart is love—being knit together in love with others. This is the task of the church and its believers: to love each other—to build love among themselves—to build love among everyone, not neglecting, overlooking, or ignoring a single person. When our hearts are knit together in love, then the hearts of every believer will be strong, encouraged, braced, assured, confident, and comforted.

APPLICATION:

Note that strong hearts do not come from religion, ceremony, ritual, laws, or rules and regulations. Strong hearts come from love—hearts knit together in love.

2.   Strong hearts come from knowing that what one believes about God is accurate. Most people are not sure about God. They are not sure...
* that God really exists.
* that God really looks after their welfare.
* that God is really interested in their daily lives.
* that they can really know God in a personal way.
* that eternal life really exists.
* that they can really know there is life after death.

a.   Note the phrase "mystery of God." To most people God is a mystery. But this is not what mystery means in the Bible. "Mystery" means *a secret*, a secret of God's that He has now revealed. The critical fact is that it is *now revealed*: it not only *can* be known, but it is known by many persons. The point is this: a strong heart—assurance and confidence—comes from knowing the secret of God, from knowing that what one believes about God is accurate.

What is the great secret of God that has now been revealed? Note exactly what the verse says: "the mystery of God...even [kai] Christ." Jesus Christ is the mystery of God. It is Jesus Christ who reveals God to men.
⇒   When people look at Jesus Christ, they see God.
⇒   When people come to know Jesus Christ personally, they come to know God personally.

Once a person approaches God through Jesus Christ, God places His Spirit within the person's heart. And God's Spirit infuses strength, both assurance and confidence, within the believer's heart. God's Spirit gives absolute assurance that we truly know God and are adopted as His dear sons and daughters. We know with absolute assurance that what we believe about God is accurate. The Spirit of God instills that confidence within our hearts.

"For ye have not received the spirit of bondage again to fear; but ye have received the Spirit of adoption, whereby we cry, Abba, Father. The Spirit itself beareth witness with our spirit, that we are the children of God" (Ro.8:15-16).

b.   Note the words "understanding" and "acknowledgment." When a person understands and acknowledges Jesus Christ, then it is that he gains "full assurance" of God. He gains "full assurance" that his knowledge of God is accurate. Common sense tells us this fact: if we could be absolutely sure that our knowledge of God was accurate, then our hearts would be strong. And this is the glorious declaration of Scripture: we can be sure. In fact, we can have full assurance of understanding—through Jesus Christ—for Jesus Christ Himself is the revealed secret of God. Jesus Christ is the revelation of God, our assurance and confidence of God.

COLOSSIANS 2:1-7

"For our gospel came not unto you in word only, but also in power, and in the Holy Ghost and in much assurance; as ye know what manner of men we were among you for your sake" (1 Th.1:5).

QUESTIONS:
1. What emotions fill your heart when you are confident that God will see you through a crisis?
2. What difference does it make when you know that God loves you unconditionally, even when you fail?
3. What are some of the natural results when a person has no assurance of God's love?

A CLOSER LOOK: WISDOM & KNOWLEDGE (v.3).

A mature people know that all the treasures of wisdom and knowledge are hid in Christ.

1. Men seek for wisdom and understanding. The word "wisdom" means the ability to use the truth once the truth is known; it is using the truth wisely just as it should be used. It is knowing how to confront day to day problems and handle them wisely. It is practical wisdom, knowing how to apply the great truths of life to everyday living. The word "understanding" is the ability to grasp the facts and the truth. It means the ability to see and know the truth. It is seeing and knowing what to do. It grasps the great truths of life. It sees the answers to the problems of...
- life and death
- good and evil
- time and eternity
- God and man
- health and disease
- comfort and suffering

2. Note where the great treasures of wisdom and understanding are: they are hid in Jesus Christ. What does this mean?
   a. Jesus Christ is the very embodiment of all wisdom. He is the One Person who *lived out* the truth, who lived and never sinned. He is the Person who confronted every trial and problem in life and solved it—who lived exactly as all men are to live. The wisdom of life—of how to live life—is seen in Jesus Christ and in Him alone. In Him are all the treasures of wisdom, all the treasures of practical day to day living.
   b. Jesus Christ is the very embodiment of understanding. He is the Creator and Sustainer of the universe; therefore, all the truth and facts of the universe are found in Him. (This is bound to be true, for when anything is made, the facts of its nature are found in the person who created it.) In Jesus Christ is the understanding of creation, the universe, good and evil, time and eternity, health and disease, comfort and suffering, and God and man.

   All the *treasures of understanding* are bound up in Christ. Man can *understand* himself and his world only in Christ Jesus. Any approach to understand the world apart from Christ leads to false conclusions and a world of corruption, discrimination, strife, division, and all the other evils that exist within the world.

3. Note that wisdom and understanding are "hid" in Jesus Christ. This does not mean that they are hidden from us, but rather *for us*.[3] They are there for us to seek and search out in order to honor Christ as the Source and Substance of our hearts and lives.

"O the depth of the riches both of the wisdom and knowledge of God! how unsearchable are his judgments, and his ways past finding out! For who hath known the mind of the Lord! or who hath been his counsellor? Or who hath first given to him, and it shall be recompensed unto him again! For of him, and through him, and to him, are all things: to whom be glory for ever" (Ro.11:33-36).

3. MARK 3: RESISTING SEDUCTIVE TEACHING (v.4).

The word "beguile" means to mislead, delude, deceive, cheat, seduce, and lead someone astray. Note how the seduction takes place: by "enticing words," that is, by words that are persuasive, appealing, eloquent, flowery, and attractive.

1. Believers can be seduced by the persuasive and eloquent words of false teaching. People are easily influenced by...

*   eloquence
*   reasoning
*   persuasiveness

*   arguments
*   logic
*   thought processes

Therefore when some idea, position, philosophy, religion, doctrine, or belief is presented in a reasonable and eloquent fashion, people are persuaded. They are beguiled, deceived, and led astray from Christ. It may be an argument against...

*   the creation of the world by God.
*   man's being personally responsible to God.
*   the virgin birth or the incarnation of God in human flesh.
*   the perfect, sinless life of Christ.
*   the substitutionary death of Christ.
*   the resurrection of Jesus Christ from the dead.
*   salvation by grace through faith.
*   the coming again of the Lord Jesus Christ.
*   the bodily resurrection of the dead.
*   eternal judgment and eternal death.
*   the destruction of the world by fire and the making of a new heavens and earth.
*   the existence of believers face to face with God, worshipping and serving Him throughout all eternity.

The argument can be against any of the major teachings of Scripture. If they are persuasive enough, some persons are led astray. They begin to question the truth and to wonder and doubt.

Note the words "this I say." The very reason Paul has proclaimed that all wisdom and knowledge exist in Christ is to protect believers against false teaching. Believers are to know that all truth is in Christ, and they are to seek all truth in Christ.

2. Believers can be seduced by the enticing and appealing words of those who live after the lusts of the flesh. Human nature is easily influenced by...

*   appearance
*   attractiveness
*   charisma
*   thoughts

*   insinuations
*   suggestions
*   imaginations
*   desires

Therefore, when some idea is made in an appealing way, people are enticed and led astray from Christ. Again, the truth and the wise course of behavior for the believer is found in Christ. The course of wisdom is to turn away from the seduction of enticing words and suggestions. Christ Himself—the life of righteousness which He lived and the way of sinlessness which He walked—is the path of wisdom for the believer.

"Now I beseech you, brethren, mark them which cause divisions and offenses contrary to the doctrine which ye have learned; and avoid them. For they that are such serve not our Lord Jesus Christ, but their own belly; and by good words and fair speeches deceive the hearts of the simple" (Ro.16:17-18).

ILLUSTRATION:

What makes false teaching so attractive to so many people? If it is so destructive, how can it be so appealing to people? Rick Green writes:

> "A former policeman...told me about being on duty during an ice storm. The ice was a half-inch thick on every tree in the area. He was called to a site where the ice and falling branches had caused a power line to come down; his duty was to keep people away from the area.
> "'There was a small tree near the fallen power line,' he said, 'the kind with a short trunk and lots of long thin branches. While that fallen power line was crackling and popping with electricity, it was throwing out sparks through the branches of that small tree. The sparks would reflect off the ice-covered branches sending out a rainbow of glimmering colors. I stood there and watched, and wondered how anything so beautiful could be so deadly"[4]

Like any other sin, false teaching can look good and sound good. But a mature, believer (one whose faith is grounded in God's Word) is able to see beyond the outer appearance and discern the truth.

QUESTIONS:
1. What types of things appeal to the ears of immature believers?
2. Are you comfortable with your knowledge of the Bible? Are you able to resist being seduced by false teaching? In what areas do you need to become stronger?
3. What characteristics would you see in the content of false teaching?
4. Why is there a tendency to think that something must be true if it is on television or written in a book?

4. MARK 4: MAINTAINING MILITARY DISCIPLINE: ORDER AND STEDFASTNESS (v.5).

⇒ The word "order" means to maintain military discipline, array, and arrangement; to hold a solid front[5]; to hold the military line unbroken and intact[6].

⇒ The word "stedfastness" means to stand fast and persevere; to be immovable, steady, and unyielding; to never crack, give in, or back up. This, too, is a military word. A.T. Robertson says that it is "the solid part of the line which can and does stand the attack" of the seduction.

Note that the believers of the Colossian church were being attacked by false teaching even as Paul was writing to them. But they were responding like a victorious army. They were maintaining their discipline, holding their order and standing fast. Note also the importance of the minister's encouragement: Paul says that he was with them *in spirit*, joying and watching them gain the victory over the false teachers.

"Therefore, my beloved brethren, be ye stedfast, unmoveable, always abounding in the work of the Lord, forasmuch as ye know that your labour is not in vain in the Lord" (1 Cor.15:58).

"Be sober, be vigilant; because your adversary the devil, as a roaring lion, walketh about, seeking whom he may devour: whom resist stedfast in the faith, knowing that the same afflictions are accomplished in the world" (1 Pt.5:8-9).

1. Have you had an experience this past week where you had to resist false teaching? If you could go back to that time, what would you do differently?
2. As you think about false teaching, what are your biggest concerns for believers who are ignorant of the truth?
3. What are some ways you can help others gain the victory over false teachers?

5. MARK 5: WALKING IN THE LORD (v.6-7).

This means at least two things. First, believers walk just as they have received Christ—by faith. They received Christ by faith, so they are to walk and continue with Christ by faith. When they received Christ, they trusted His righteousness and death to cover their sins and to make them acceptable to God. Therefore, they are *to walk continuing to trust* His righteousness and death. It is His righteousness and death that continue to cover their sins, making them acceptable to God. They have nothing within themselves to earn, merit, deserve, or make God accept them. They can do nothing and they can possess nothing that will secure the approval of God. The believer's only acceptance before God is Christ, trusting the righteousness and death of Christ.

> **"For we walk by faith, not by sight" (2 Cor.5:7).**
> **"But if we walk in the light, as he is in the light, we have fellowship one with another, and the blood of Jesus Christ his Son cleanseth us from all sin" (1 Jn.1:7).**

Second, believers received Christ as *Christ Jesus the Lord*. That is, when believers received Him, they accepted Him as the true Messiah and Lord from heaven; they accepted Him as the *Lord of their lives*. Therefore, believers are to walk before Him as Lord; they are to continue walking and serving Him as the Lord of their lives.

> **"Therefore we are buried with him by baptism into death: that like as Christ was raised up from the dead by the glory of the Father, even so we also should walk in newness of life" (Ro.6:4).**

There are three things in particular the believer is to do.
1. The believer is to be rooted and built up in Christ. There are two pictures in this statement.
   ⇒ The picture of being rooted is that of a tree. The believer is to be like a towering tree that has its roots deeply planted in the ground. The ground provides strength against wind and storms as well as nourishment for life. The believer is to draw his nourishment and strength from Christ.
   ⇒ The picture of being built or constructed is that of a building. Jesus Christ is the foundation for life, the only sure foundation. Therefore, the mature believer is a person who has built his life upon Christ.

The point to note is this: the emphasis upon a strong attachment and a flow of nourishment and life from Christ to the believer. That is, the believer is to walk in a continuous, unbroken communion and fellowship with Christ. His life and mind are to focus upon Christ without interruption, drawing all nourishment and strength from Him. This is critical, for there is no other *permanent* nourishment or strength—not that lasts forever and imparts eternal life to the human soul.

> **"Therefore whosoever heareth these sayings of mine, and doeth them, I will liken him unto a wise man, which built his house upon a rock: and the rain descended, and the floods came, and the winds blew, and beat upon that house; and it fell not: for it was founded upon a rock. And every one that heareth these sayings of mine, and doeth them not, shall be**

likened unto a foolish man, which built his house upon the sand" (Mt.7:24-26).

2.   The believer is to walk established in the faith just as he has been taught. The word "established" means to be firm, stable, holding fast and not letting go. This shows the utter necessity for strong teachers in the church. When believers have strong teachers, they are to learn all they can about the faith and hold fast to it. They are not to let it go. William Barclay points out,

> "There are certain beliefs which remain the foundation of all belief, and they do not change...the unchanging and unchangeable truth that Jesus Christ is Lord."[7]

Mature believers are established in the faith, and they are to stand fast in the faith just as they have been taught.

> "Now to him that is of power to stablish you according to my gospel, and the preaching of Jesus Christ, according to the revelation of the mystery, which was kept secret since the world began" (Ro.16:25).

3.   The believer is to walk overflowing with thanksgiving. Christ Jesus the Lord has done so much for the believer—so much that flows on and on, never ceasing, not even for one moment of any day. Therefore, the believer is to learn to walk in an unbroken spirit of thanksgiving—a thanksgiving that overflows in praise to the Lord moment by moment throughout the day.

> "Rejoice in the Lord always: and again I say, Rejoice....Be careful for nothing; but in every thing by prayer and supplication with thanksgiving let your requests be made known unto God" (Ph.4:4, 6).

ILLUSTRATION:

Does your walk with Christ appeal to those who are close to you? H.G. Bosch shares this story about walking in the Lord:

> "Dr. Charles Weigle (the composer of 'No One Ever Cared For Me Like Jesus') visited Pasadena, California. Early that morning he had an opportunity to walk through some of the famous rose gardens when the full fragrance of the flowers filled the air.
> "Later in the day he arrived at the hotel where a Bible conference was being held. As he took his seat, a man turned to him and said, 'Dr. Weigle, I know where you've been. You toured one of our lovely gardens, for I can smell the pleasing aroma on your clothing.' 'My prayer is that I may walk so closely with the Lord that the fragrance of His grace will pervade my being. I want them to know by my words, actions, and songs that I have been with Jesus.'"[8]

QUESTIONS:
1.   What kind of fragrance do you emit? Can people tell by your words, your actions, and your attitude that you have a close walk with Jesus?
2.   If someone asked your friends if you were a believer, what would they say? Would they give a favorable response?
3.   What can you do in order to improve your "fragrance," or the kind of impression you give people.
4.   What specific actions do these verses require of you?
5.   Are you failing to grow spiritually? What barriers do you need to overcome in order to grow?

SUMMARY:

What kinds of things have you put your trust in as you journey with Christ? Paul has presented the need for you to be consistent and mature. This will be possible if you adhere to these five marks:

Mark 1: struggle in prayer and concern for the church.
Mark 2: possess confidence and assurance.
Mark 3: resist seductive teaching.
Mark 4: maintain military discipline—order and stedfastness.
Mark 5: walk in the Lord.

PERSONAL JOURNAL NOTES
(Reflection & Response)

1. The most important thing that I learned from this lesson was:

2. The area that I need to work on the most is:

3. I can apply this lesson to my life by:

4. Closing Statement of Commitment:

---

[1] *Gospel Herald.* Walter B. Knight, *Knight's Master Book of 4,000 Illustrations*, p.493.

[2] Marvin R. Vincent. *Word Studies in the New Testament*, Vol.3 (Grand Rapids, MI: Eerdmans Publishing Co., 1969), p.482).

[3] Matthew Henry. *Matthew Henry's Commentary*, Vol.5 (Old Tappan, NJ: Fleming H. Revell Co.), p.756.

[4] Craig B. Larson, Editor, *Illustrations for Preaching & Teaching*, p.257.

[5] The Amplified New Testament. (Scripture Quotations are from the Amplified New Testament, Copyright 1954, 1958, 1987 by the Lockman Foundation. Used by permission.)

[6] A.T. Robertson, *Word Pictures in the New Testament*, Vol.4 (Nashville, TN: Broadman Press, 1930), p.489.

[7] William Barclay, *The Letters to the Philippians, Colossians, and Thessalonians*, p.159.

[8] Paul Lee Tan, *Encyclopedia of 7,700 Illustrations: Signs of the Times*, p.1570.

	IV. THE CONTRAST BETWEEN CHRIST & FALSE TEACHING, 2:8-23	losophy and vain deceit, after the tradition of men, after the rudiments of the world, and not after Christ.	a. It is only tradition b. It deals only with the elements of the world c. It is empty delusion
		9 For in him dwelleth all the fulness of the Godhead bodily.	2. **Christ is the Source of reality & truth**
	A. Christ vs. False Philosophy & Astrology, 2:8-10	10 And ye are complete in him, which is the head of all	a. He is the fulness of God b. He is the completion of man
1. Beware of false philosophy	8 Beware lest any man spoil you through phi-	principality and power:	c. He is the head of all power

Section IV
THE CONTRAST BETWEEN CHRIST & FALSE TEACHING
Colossians 2:8-23

Session 1: CHRIST VS. FALSE PHILOSOPHY AND ASTROLOGY

Text: Colossians 2:8-10

Aim: To stand guard against false teaching.

Memory Verse:
> "Beware lest any man spoil [captivate] you through philosophy and vain deceit, after the tradition of men, after the rudiments of the world, and not after Christ" (Colossians 2:8).

INTRODUCTION:
What happens to a church when the Light of the world (Jesus Christ) is hidden? Darkness in the form of false teaching seeps its way into the hearts of people. Are you doing your part to warn the world of the consequences of rejecting Christ?

> *"Several years ago [there was] a terrible accident in which several youth were killed when their car was struck by a train. At the trial the watchman was questioned: 'Were you at the crossing the night of the accident?' 'Yes, your Honor.' 'Were you waving your lantern to warn of the danger?' 'Yes, your Honor,' the man told the judge.*
> *"But after the trial had ended, the watchman walked away mumbling to himself, 'I'm glad they didn't ask me about the light in the lantern, because the light had gone out'"[1]*

God has called the Christian believer to be a "watchman." The challenge is to make sure our lights do not go out but shine brightly as beacons of truth. The importance of this passage is clearly seen in the title of the subject: "Christ vs. False Philosophy and Astrology."

OUTLINE:
1.   Beware of false philosophy (v.8).
2.   Christ is the Source of reality and truth (v.9-10).

COLOSSIANS 2:8-10

1. BEWARE OF FALSE PHILOSOPHY (v.8).

The word "beware" means to take heed, look out, guard yourself. Why? "Lest any man spoil you through philosophy." The word "spoil" means to lead into captivity or slavery.

⇒ Some men are in a genuine search for truth and reality. They seek to learn the truth and reality of the universe and the problems that face them, but they limit themselves to the universe. This approach has one terrible flaw that leads either to incomplete or erroneous conclusions. This flaw will be discussed in a few moments.

⇒ Other persons have novel ideas or philosophies about truth and reality, but they become more interested in their position than the truth. They need others to accept their positions or else their ideas die. Therefore, they have to present and persuade people of their ideas and philosophies whether they are sound or not.

Believers must, therefore, beware and guard against worldly philosophies and ideas lest they become ensnared and enslaved.

What is meant by *worldly philosophy*? Paul tells us exactly what he means.

1.   Worldly philosophy is philosophy that follows the very same traditions that men have followed down through the ages.

2.   Worldly philosophy is philosophy that searches for reality by using the rudiments or elementary knowledge of this world. The word "rudiments" means...

- the elementary principles, the ABC teachings of the universe.
- the rudimentary teachings (Heb.5:12).
- the crude notions of the universe.
- the elements or materials of the universe (2 Pt.3:10-12).

Worldly philosophy uses only human knowledge and worldly tradition to search for the reality and truth of the world and life. The only source worldly philosophy uses is the world and its elements or materials.

3.   Worldly philosophy is philosophy that deals only with the elements and materials of this world (universe). Men have always tried to find the answers to life and the world within the world itself. Men want to know...

- What is the origin of the universe and life?
- Who is man and where did he come from? Why is man here, and where is he going?
- Where did evil come from? Can it be controlled? Or better yet, abolished?
- Is there a God? How can we know?
- Is life upon this planet all there is? Is there life after death?

The questions could go on and on. The point to see is this: worldly philosophy tries to find the answers to these questions *only in the world* (universe). Worldly philosophy looks only at the elements or materials of this world when seeking the answers to life. The consequence is tragic, for everything in the world—every element of it—passes away. Therefore, if a philosophy bases itself upon the elements of the world, there is no *permanent answer or solution* to life. Why? Because man and his world will die and cease to exist, for the universe itself is physical and wasting away—granted, much slower than man—nevertheless it is still wasting away. (Actually, it will be destroyed, however, not by man, but by God. But this is a discussion for another time. Cp. 2 Pt.3:3-18, esp. 10-13.) The point is this: a philosophy based upon the world is useless in finding permanent answers and solutions to life. The very best that a worldly philosophy or science can ever do is...

- make life more comfortable.
- make life safer and last longer.

But this is not permanent or eternal comfort and safety. It is not permanent truth or reality. Man and his world need something much more than a worldly philosophy, a philosophy that offers only *temporary and short term answers* to life.

"Professing themselves to be wise, they became fools" (Ro.1:22).

"For the wisdom of this world is foolishness with God. For it is written, He taketh the wise in their own craftiness. And again, The Lord knoweth the thoughts of the wise, that they are vain" (1 Cor.3:19-20).

Since man needs something more than worldly philosophy, what is it that He needs? What is it that can meet the needs of man better than the sharpest thinking and sciences of men? Keep in mind that man needs life—true life, real life, a life that is abundant and eternal—that does not become diseased and suffer accident and death. Man needs a real world that does not suffer under the weight of corruption, decay, and deterioration and does not explode in natural disasters.

⇒ Man needs a true world, not a world that seems to be false, as though it is a mistake.

⇒ Man needs a real world, not a world that only fades away as an illusion.

⇒ Man needs a genuine world, not a world that is only an appearance as though it is counterfeit.

⇒ Man needs a purposeful world, not a world that is only chance without any lasting permanent meaning.

How can man secure such a world? How can man find permanent and eternal life? The answer is simple: he cannot. If such a world does not exist, man can never find it, for it is not there to be found.

But, what if a *permanent world* does exist in a *spiritual dimension* of being? How then can man find it? He cannot. If a *spiritual world* exists, man cannot find it, for he is physical, that is, material substance. And the physical or material cannot penetrate or move over into the spiritual, regardless of what some persons may claim or think.

⇒ The corruptible cannot move over into the world of the incorruptible, for it is already corruptible.

⇒ The dishonorable cannot move over into the world of glory, for it is already dishonorable (short of glory or perfection).

⇒ The weak cannot move over into the world of infinite and perfect power, for it is already weak (short of infinite power).

⇒ The natural cannot move over into the world of the spiritual, for it is already natural.

⇒ The mortal cannot move over into the world of the immortal because it is already mortal.

⇒ The dying (the process of death) cannot move over into the world of life because it is already dying (in the process of dying—even a body is in the process of dying).

Man is just totally incapable of penetrating or moving over into the spiritual world or spiritual dimension. He cannot know the spiritual world because he and his world are physical and material (corruptible and dishonorable, weak and natural, mortal and dying).

This means a critical point: there is only one way man can ever know the spiritual world and dimension. The spiritual world must *reveal* itself to the physical world. God must *reveal* Himself to man. This is exactly what God has done in Christ, and this is the startling and glorious message of the next point.

APPLICATION:

The "rudiments" (elements or materials) of the universe also refer to the signs and spirits of the stars and planets. The idea that these determine the fate of man has, of course, been with man from the earliest times. *Astrology and the signs of the zodiac* are to be guarded against as much as any other worldly philosophy. The stars and planets are as much a part of the material universe as men are. They are of the physical world and dimension of being the same as man is. In fact, they are inanimate objects, possessing even less ability and power than man. They are even less capable of penetrating and moving over into the spiritual world or dimension than man is.

ILLUSTRATION:

Do you "glance" at the horoscopes in your daily paper—just for the fun of it? Have you ever "dabbled" in the occult? Be warned! Listen to this man's testimony:

"A minister paid an expensive fee to have a horoscope cast for himself, with [the] purpose of trying to prove it wrong and that astrology is nothing but ignorance and superstition.

"So, he waited confidently. BUT he was astonished to find his prophecies coming true, even to the smallest details. As [the] years [went] by, he [became] uneasy and tried to find a rational explanation for this.

"Finally, he concluded that he had sinned in the experiment—becoming a victim of evil spirit powers through the horoscope. He immediately repented and renounced all connections with astrology!"[2]

QUESTIONS:
1. What does this verse say about your spiritual condition apart from Christ? How does this verse help you prevent a life of compromise with worldliness?
2. What did Paul mean when he mentioned "worldly philosophy"? What safe-guards do you have in your life to prevent you from being consumed by the philosophy of this world?
3. What types of things would be called "the traditions of men"? Do any of these have a grip on your life?
4. Has someone you know been caught in the snare of the occult? How does trusting Christ help a person to break free of the power of the occult?

2. CHRIST IS THE SOURCE OF REALITY AND TRUTH (v.9-10).

Note: reality and truth—the answers to the world and life—are not found in a philosophy nor in human ideas. They are found in a Person, the Person of the Lord Jesus Christ.

Think for a moment: if a Person (God) really created the world, then the answer to life and creation (truth and reality) are bound to be wrapped up in Him, not in the world He made. He is the Source to understanding the world; the world is not the source to understanding Him. True, we can look at the world to learn some things about God but not all that we need to know. For example, the world cannot tell us how to conquer evil and death, not perfectly. Therefore, if we seek the truth only in the world, we are left short and incomplete and unfulfilled and in error. Thus, we must seek truth and the answer to all things in the Person who made all things. He alone knows the whole story.

The glorious message of the gospel and of this passage is that God does exist. He truly exists and He has revealed Himself in Christ. Christ is the revelation of God, of truth and reality, of life itself in all its origin, purpose, meaning, and destiny. Note three wonderful truths.

1. Christ is the fulness of God. Christ is God Himself who came to earth. Note the verse: "In Christ dwells *all the fulness of the Godhead*." All that God is dwells in Christ.
   ⇒ Christ is God in an absolute, full, and perfect sense.

Jesus Christ has the full nature and being of God just as God the Father has the full nature of God. God the Father and God the Son have the same being and nature, that of God. The word "fulness" means that not a single part of God's nature is lacking in the nature of Christ.

The word "dwells" means to be at home, to be permanently settled and present. This tells us that...
- the fulness of God has always dwelt in Christ, even before He came to earth (Jn.1:1, 18; 17:5, 24; Ph.2:6).
- the fulness of God dwelt in Christ when Christ was walking upon earth in a human body (Jn.1:14, 18; 1 Jn.1:1-3).
- the fulness of God was not just a temporary gift to Christ.

What does all this mean to us in practical day-to-day living? It means two wonderful things.
   a. First, God is not far off in outer space someplace. God is not unconcerned with the world. God has not just created the world and wound it up, leaving it on its own to fly throughout space with man making out the best he can. God is interested and

concerned with the world—so much so that He has come to earth to show how vitally concerned He is.

b. God is love, not evil. Only a God of evil would leave man in the dark where he would have to grope and grasp and stumble about in order to find God. A God of love would reveal Himself and show man...
- the way to God.
- the truth of God, man, and his world.
- the life that man is to live (Jn.14:6).

> "He that seeth me seeth Him that sent me" (Jn.12:45).
> "If ye had known me, ye should have known my Father also: and from henceforth ye know him, and have seen him" (Jn.14:7).

2. Believers are complete in Christ. The word "complete" means to be made full. The Greek actually says, "In Him you are full." When a person truly believes and partakes of Christ, he receives the fulness of Christ. Just what is the fulness of Christ which believers receive? Scripture describes it in several ways.

a. Believers receive wisdom, righteousness, sanctification, and redemption.

> "But of him are ye in Christ Jesus, who of God is made unto us wisdom, and righteousness, and sanctification, and redemption" (1 Cor.1:30).

⇒ *Wisdom* means that we understand God, the world, and man: the origin, purpose, and end of creation.
⇒ *Righteousness* means that we understand the evil in the world, both sin and death, and that we know the only way to attain righteousness is through Christ.
⇒ *Sanctification* means that we have set our lives apart unto God to live for Him and to serve Him.
⇒ *Redemption* means that we have been saved from corruption and death and given eternal life.

b. Believers receive the fulness of Christ's nature. The divine nature of God is actually placed in believers, and they become new creatures in Christ.

> "Whereby are given unto us exceeding great and precious promises: that by these ye might be partakers of the divine nature, having escaped the corruption that is in the world through lust" (2 Pt.1:4).

QUESTIONS:
1. In Christ *dwells* all the fulness of God (v.9). What does "to dwell" mean? Why is this important for you to understand?
2. What is the fulness of Christ's nature? How do you receive this in your life?
3. What is your role in experiencing the fulness of God's presence in your life?
4. Can you 'lose' the presence of Christ in your life?

c. Believers receive fulness of life now. From the time believers receive Christ, they should lack nothing. If a believer ever lacks anything—any fulness of life—it is be cause he has taken his eyes off Christ and has slipped away. When dealing with day to day living...

- the believer receives an abundance of life.

> **"I am come that they might have life, and that they might have it more abundantly" (Jn.10:10).**

- the believer receives fulness of joy.

> **"These things have I spoken unto you, that my joy might remain in you, and that your joy might be full" (Jn.15:11).**

- the believer receives all the necessities of life including food, clothing, and shelter (cp. Mt.6:24-34).

> **"But seek ye first the kingdom of God, and his righteousness; and all these things shall be added unto you" (Mt.6:33).**

- the believer receives the fulness of God's Spirit, of God Himself.

> **"But the fruit of the Spirit is love, joy, peace, longsuffering, gentleness, goodness, faith, meekness, temperance: against such there is no law" (Gal.5:22-23).**

d.   Believers receive the fulness of life eternal.

> **"And this is life eternal, that they might know thee the only true God, and Jesus Christ, whom thou hast sent" (Jn.17:3).**

e.   Believers receive the fulness of the knowledge of God's will.

> **"For this cause we also, since the day we heard it, do not cease to pray for you, and to desire that ye might be filled with the knowledge of his will in all wisdom and spiritual understanding" (Col.1:9).**

APPLICATION:

Note that the fulness of life and the answers to truth and reality do not come from a philosophy but from a Person, Jesus Christ.

3.   Christ is the Head of all principality and power; that is, no rule, authority, or power stands between God and man. Nothing, absolutely nothing, stands between God (ultimate Truth and Reality) and man...

- no force
- no power
- no energy
- no person
- no science

- no law of the universe
- no zodiac sign
- no sign or spirit of the stars and planets
- no astrological energy

The explanation and fate of man and his world are found in Jesus Christ and in Him alone. He is the only Intermediary between God and man. Man can approach God only through Christ. No one else—person or force—can present us to God and make us acceptable to God. God accepts only those persons who come to Him by Christ.

COLOSSIANS 2:8-10

"For God so loved the world, that he gave his only begotten Son, that whosoever believeth <u>in him</u> should not perish, but have everlasting life" (Jn.3:16).

ILLUSTRATION:

Our God is a rock to the Christian believer, a rock that resists the crashing waves of false teaching.

"A vessel was wrecked one stormy night off the coast of England. All were drowned except an Irish boy. The waves swept him onto a great rock. In the morning he was rescued. 'Lad, didn't you tremble out there on the rock during the night?' 'Sure I trembled, but the rock didn't tremble once all night long!'"[3]

As you live day by day, are you clinging to the solid rock? Or are you floundering around on your own, losing ground and losing strength?

QUESTIONS:

1. What is the relationship between reality and its source? Between truth and its source? Why does the world have such a difficult time distinguishing truth from fiction?
2. What does the Christian believer lack if he is *complete* in Christ? (Look closely at verses 8-10.)
3. What things are lacking in your relationship with Jesus Christ? What steps do you need to take in order to correct this?

SUMMARY:

There is an on-going conspiracy to pollute your mind with false teaching. Its success will be measured by putting out your light and making your witness to the world powerless. Remember the major points of this lesson:

1. Beware of false philosophy.
2. Christ is the Source of reality and truth.

PERSONAL JOURNAL NOTES:
(Reflection & Response)

1. The most important thing that I learned from this lesson was:

2. The area that I need to work on the most is:

3. I can apply this lesson to my life by:

4. Closing Statement of Commitment:

---

[1] Paul Lee Tan, *Encyclopedia of 7,700 Illustrations: Signs of the Times*, p.1640.
[2] Ibid., p.913.
[3] Walter B. Knight, *Knight's Treasury of 2,000 Illustrations*, p.183.

	B. Christ vs. False Religion, 2:11-12
1. False religion: Stresses ritual & outward form 2. True religion: Stresses Christ & the spiritual 　a. A cutting away of sins 　b. A burial in baptism & a resurrection to a new life 　c. An operation of God by faith	11 In whom also ye are circumcised with the circumcision made without hands, in putting off the body of the sins of the flesh by the circumcision of Christ: 12 Buried with him in baptism, wherein also ye are risen with him through the faith of the operation of God, who hath raised him from the dead.

Section IV
THE CONTRAST BETWEEN CHRIST AND FALSE TEACHERS
Colossians 2:8-23

Study 2:   CHRIST VS. FALSE RELIGION

Text: Colossians 2:11-12

Aim: To draw a clear line between true and false religion.

Memory Verse:
> **"But God commendeth His love toward us, in that, while we were yet sinners, Christ died for us" (Romans 5:8).**

INTRODUCTION:
Do you feel that Jesus Christ's love for you is *conditional*? That you have to earn God's love? That you have to work and work at being good in order to make God love you? That you have to pile up good work upon good work in order to make yourself acceptable to God? That you have to earn your way into heaven? Is God's acceptance of you based upon *your* performance? If you have answered yes to any of these questions, you have passed through the door called "false religion."

A false religion is any religion not based upon the love of God and Jesus Christ for the world.

> **"For God so loved the world, that He gave His only begotten Son, that whosoever believes in Him should not perish, but have everlasting life" (Jn.3:16).**
> **"But God commendeth his love toward us, in that, while we were yet sinners. Christ died for us" (Ro.5:8).**

Common sense tells us this: if God loved the world so much that He gave His only Son for its salvation, then the only way to approach God is through His Son. The only way He would accept us is through His Son.

God is not a God of indifference and hate, a God who has left us in the dark, trying to grope and grasp after God, seeking to discover the way to Him. God is love; He cares for man, deeply loves man. In fact, God loves man with an infinite, eternal love—a love so great that He sent His Son into the world to reveal the truth to us, to bear the judgment of our transgressions against God. The point is this: any religion that *focuses upon anything* other than God's love and God's Son is not of God—not of the only living and true God. It is a false religion.

The problem of false religion had seeped into the Colossian church. Some were teaching that a ritual was necessary for salvation, the ritual of circumcision. This Scripture gives us an excellent discussion of a false religion that stresses ritual over God's love and God's Son, the Lord Jesus Christ.

OUTLINE:
1. False religion: stresses ritual and outward form (v.11).
2. True religion: stresses Christ and the spiritual (v.11-12).

1. FALSE RELIGION: STRESSES RITUAL AND OUTWARD FORM (v.11).

Some in the Colossian church were stressing the ritual of circumcision. They said that a man had to be circumcised to be saved, that God would not accept him unless he was circumcised. Giving his heart and life to Jesus Christ was not enough. Even if he trusted Christ and gave all he was and had, God would not accept him unless he was circumcised. There was a reason for this belief. Circumcision was the ritual of faith to the Jews. It symbolized two things.

⇒ First, circumcision symbolized the faith of a man and his family in God. When a man trusted God, he was circumcised as a sign or testimony of his faith in God. His circumcision declared to the world that he and his family were going to follow God.

⇒ Second, circumcision also symbolized the cutting away of the "body of sins" that were in the flesh. When the foreskin was cut off and removed, it was a picture of sin—the whole body or package of sin—being cut off and removed from the man.

This was the true picture of circumcision, what God had intended until Christ came. Very simply, a man was to trust God, surrendering his heart and life to God; then, as a sign or symbol of his faith, he was to be circumcised. But what happened was exactly what happens so often with spiritual things: man corrupted God's purpose for circumcision. Man began to say that a person became acceptable to God...

- not because he trusted God
- but because he was circumcised.

No matter how much a man trusted God, he was not acceptable to God unless he was circumcised. Circumcision was his badge of being admitted into God's presence, and without it he could not gain entrance into God's presence.

The parallel with other false teachings is clearly seen. Down through the centuries, some have stressed that a person could not be saved—no matter how much he believed and gave his life to Christ—unless he...

- joined the church
- was confirmed
- was baptized
- kept the law

False teachings and religions have always tended to *add to* Christ in order to be saved. A person could believe and trust Christ with his whole heart, surrendering all he was and everything he had to Christ, but that was not enough. The person had to do something else in order to make himself acceptable to God.

> **"For I bear them record that they have a zeal of God, but not according to knowledge. For they being ignorant of God's righteousness, and going about to establish their own righteousness, have not submitted themselves unto the righteousness of God. For Christ is the end of the law for righteousness to every one that believeth" (Ro.10:2-4).**

1. What kinds of rituals do some Christians practice which lack Biblical support? What kinds of things do you do?
2. Why is it important for you to base your Christianity upon the Bible and not upon some outward form? What happens to a person whose dependence and faith is based upon some outward form or ritual?
3. Give an example of how you quit or changed some outward form or ritual and began living according to the Scripture? How did trusting Christ help you to do this?

2. TRUE RELIGION: STRESSES CHRIST AND THE SPIRITUAL (v.11-12).

True religion stresses Christ and Christ alone. Real religion is spiritual, not physical; and it is wrought by Christ, not by the hands of men. Note three critical points.

1. Real religion is undergoing the circumcision of Christ, letting Christ cut away the body of sins out of our flesh. Think for a moment: What man has the power to cut sin out of our lives? Where is a man who can take the sin of our flesh and remove it so that our bodies will stand perfect before God? Is there such a man? Has there or will there ever be such a man upon earth? Any thinking and honest person knows that no man can remove the sin from another person—not even one single sin, much less the whole body of sin. There is only one way that sin can be cut out and removed from our flesh—by Jesus Christ. How does Christ cut away sin from us? By death.

When Jesus Christ died, He died *for our sins*. That is, He bore the guilt and punishment for our sins. He hung upon the cross...
- as the guilty sinner for us: in our place, as our substitute.
- as the Person who would bear the judgment and punishment of sin *for us*.

Therefore, when we really believe and trust Christ—that He died for us—God removes our sin from us. He cuts away both the sin and the guilt and throws it away. This means a most wonderful thing: we stand before God without sin. Imagine standing before God sinless, completely and totally forgiven—accepted by God as perfect. But never forget why: it is because of Christ alone, not a ritual nor any other man-made or religious thing. We are acceptable to God because of Christ, His dear Son, and not because of anything else. True religion is not *Christ plus something else*; true religion is *Christ alone*. Christ alone can cut away sin. True circumcision—true religion...
- is the "circumcision made *without hands*."
- is "putting off the *body of sins* of the flesh by the *circumcision of Christ*."

> **"Knowing this, that our old man is crucified with him, that the body of sin might be destroyed, that henceforth we should not serve sin" (Ro.6:6).**

ILLUSTRATION:
"A good story is told of old Thomas K. Beecher, who could not bear deceit in any form. Finding that a clock in his church was habitually too fast or too slow, he hung a placard on the wall above it, reading in large letters: 'Don't blame my hands—the trouble lies deeper.'

"That is where the trouble lies with us when our hands do wrong, or our feet, or our lips, or even our thoughts. The trouble lies so deep that only God's miracle power can deal with it. Sin indeed goes deep; but Christ goes deeper"[1]

Thank God! Jesus has the power to remove the grossness of sin from our hearts by cutting it out.

2. Real religion is being baptized and raised with Christ. What does baptism refer to here? Does it mean Jesus' baptism of death or the baptism of water which the believer undergoes? Christ had said:

"But I have a baptism to be baptized with [death]; and how am I straitened till it be accomplished!" (Lk.12:50).

Commentators are split over the meaning. However, the meaning of the passage is the same no matter which interpretation is held. When a person believes in Christ, really believes, God takes his belief and...

- counts the person as having been buried with Christ in the baptism of His death.
- counts the person as having been raised with Christ when He arose.

When a person is baptized, the same message is proclaimed. The act of baptism proclaims to the world that the person has trusted Christ, His death and resurrection. Therefore...

- when the person is placed *under the water*, he is declaring that God counts him as buried with Christ.
- when he is raised up from the water, he is declaring that God counts him as risen with Christ.

The point to see is that the whole religious act is based upon and focused upon Christ—what Christ has done. Christ is the one who died and rose again. Therefore, it is Christ that man *believes in and trusts*, not the ritual of baptism. Christ alone can save: only His death can stand for the death of man; only His resurrection can stand for the resurrection of man.

⇒ No man shall ever escape death unless he truly trusts the death of Christ to stand for his death.

⇒ No man shall ever conquer death and live eternally unless he truly trusts the resurrection of Christ to stand for his resurrection.

Real religion focuses upon Christ, His death and resurrection, and nothing else. God saves and accepts a person because he focuses upon His Son and focuses upon Him alone.

"Know ye not, that so many of us as were baptized into Jesus Christ were baptized into his death? Therefore we are buried with him by baptism into death: that like as Christ was raised up from the dead by the glory of the Father, even so we also should walk in newness of life" (Ro.6:3-4).

3.   Real religion is an operation of God alone. The word "operation" means energy, power, working. God has to perform the operation or work upon a person if the person is to be acceptable to God. No person can operate upon any other person and make him acceptable to God. God alone has the ability and power to make a person acceptable to Him. Note two points.

a.   How does God operate on us to make us acceptable to Him? By faith in Christ. It is a fact:

⇒ Christ died and was raised from the dead.

As stated in the previous point, when a person really believes in Christ, God takes that person's *faith* and counts it as the death and resurrection of Christ. That is, God looks upon the person as being *in Christ*—as having died and been raised with Christ. Therefore, the person never has to die because he has already died and been raised from the dead—*in Christ*. The person lives before God and is acceptable to God—all because he is *in Christ*.

b.   How do we know that God actually does this, that God actually saves us this way? Because He raised Christ from the dead. Note that this is exactly what this verse declares:

"Buried with him in baptism [death], wherein also ye are risen with him through the faith of the <u>operation of God, who hath raised him from the dead</u>" (v.12).

The resurrection of Christ proves that God has the power to do what He declares. He has the power to count us as *being in Christ* and the power to *raise us up from the dead*. The proof is that He has already raised up one Person, Christ Jesus.

And look at who He was: the Person who was bearing *all the sins* of the world. The guilt and punishment for every sin ever committed was being borne by Him. If God would and could raise Him up, He can and will raise us up—if we will only believe and trust His Son.

True religion is the religion that is of God, that is created by the energy, power, working, and operation of God. True religion is of God and God alone.

"And he [Abraham] believed in the LORD; and he counted it to him for righteousness" (Gen.15:6).

"For all have sinned, and come short of the glory of God; being justified freely by his grace through the redemption that is in Christ Jesus" (Ro.3:23-24).

ILLUSTRATION:

How much of the power needed to live the Christian life do you attempt to provide? Even when you get creative and give it your <u>best</u> shot, failure is inevitable.

"In a seminary missions class, Herbert Jackson told how, as a new missionary, he was assigned a car that would not start without a push.

"After pondering his problem, he devised a plan. He went to the school near his home, got permission to take some children out of class, and had them push his car off. As he made his rounds, he would either park on a hill or leave his car running. He used this ingenious procedure for two years.

"Ill health forced the Jackson family to leave, and a new missionary came to that station. When Jackson proudly began to explain his arrangement for getting the car started, the new man began looking under the hood. Before the explanation was complete, the new missionary interrupted, 'Why Dr. Jackson, I believe the only trouble is this loose cable.' He gave the cable a twist, stepped into the car, pushed the switch, and to Jackson's astonishment, the engine roared to life.

"For two years needless trouble had become routine. The power was there all the time. Only a loose connection kept Jackson from putting the power to work.

"J.B. Phillips paraphrases Ephesians 1:19-20, 'How tremendous is the power available to us who believe in God.' When we make firm our connection with God, His life and power flow through us."[2]

QUESTIONS:

1. What characteristics define true religion?
2. Are there any areas of your life that Christ needs to cut away? What area does He need to change in you?
3. What circumstances tempt you to supply your own power in place of God's? How will you plug into God's power in the future?

SUMMARY:

Do you now know the difference between true and false religion? Knowing the difference will help keep you true to God. It will help guard you against false beliefs and false religion. As a reminder of our session:
1. False religion: stresses ritual and outward form.
2. True religion: stresses Christ and the spiritual.

PERSONAL JOURNAL NOTES
(Reflection & Response)

1. The most important thing that I learned from this lesson was:

2. The area that I need to work on the most is:

3. I can apply this lesson to my life by:

4. Closing Statement of Commitment:

---

[1] *Christian Witness.* Walter B. Knight. *3,000 Illustrations for Christian Service*, p.368.
[2] Craig B. Larson, Editor. *Illustrations for Preaching & Teaching*, p.182.

	C. Christ's vs. Man's Idea of Sin, the Law, & Evil Spirits, 2:13-15	14 Blotting out the handwriting of ordinances that was against us, which was contrary to us, and took it out of the way, nailing it to his cross;	2. Point 2: Christ's vs. man's idea of the law a. Man's idea of the law b. Christ has nailed the charges against man to His cross
1. Point 1: Christ's vs. man's idea of sin & death a. Man's idea of sin & death b. Christ quickens man, forgiving his sins	13 And you, being dead in your sins and the uncircumcision of your flesh, hath he quickened together with him, having forgiven you all trespasses;	15 And having spoiled principalities and powers, he made a show of them openly, triumphing over them in it.	3. Point 3: Christ's vs. man's idea of evil forces & evil spirits a. Man's idea of evil spirits b. Christ conquered all

Section IV
THE CONTRAST BETWEEN CHRIST AND FALSE TEACHING
Colossians 2:8-23

Study 3:   **CHRIST'S VS. MAN'S IDEA OF SIN, THE LAW, AND EVIL SPIRITS**

Text: Colossians 2:13-15

Aim: To accept God's ideas (not man's ideas) about sin, the law, and evil spirits.

Memory Verse:
> "Blotting out the handwriting of ordinances that was against us, which was contrary to us, and took it out of the way, nailing it to his cross" (Colossians 2:14).

INTRODUCTION:
All of you have probably heard how a frog can be boiled alive in a pot without fully realizing the danger he is in. By increasing the temperature of the water in the pot gradually, the frog has no sense to jump out and save himself. Mankind has found itself in the same pot of hot water. Unsaved man is not in touch with his environment and the danger around him. In ignorance, he lives as though <u>he</u> is a god unto himself. Man's attempts to get out of the pot only increase the heat. What is the solution? How has God provided a way out of the pot of boiling water?

This passage discusses three basic concepts or ideas about man and his world. It pits man's concepts against God's. It shows how weak man's ideas are in comparison to what God has done for man in Christ.

OUTLINE:
1.   Point 1: Christ's vs. man's idea of sin and death (v.13).
2.   Point 2: Christ's vs. man's idea of the law (v.14).
3.   Point 3: Christ's vs. man's idea of evil forces and evil spirits (v.15).

1. POINT 1: CHRIST'S VS. MAN'S IDEA OF SIN AND DEATH (v.13).

1.   Man's concept of sin and death is far different from what the Bible teaches. When man thinks of sin, he does not see it as a violation of God's law nor as rebellion against God. Man sees sin as...

- a human error
- a personal slip
- a moral flaw
- a physical failure
- an unpreventable error
- psychological immaturity

- philosophical misunderstanding
- an evaluating mistake
- semantic mislabeling
- social irresponsibility
- educational shortcoming
- character defect

Just what a person calls sin depends upon where he is standing—upon his environment, training, heritage, and beliefs. Few persons are willing to submit to God and confess that sin is basically a violation of God's law or will, rebellion and insurrection against Him and the way He has told man to live.

Man's view of death also varies according to a person's background and beliefs. Man's concepts and views of death differ as much from the Biblical concept as night differs from day. When men look at death, they think of it as...

- ceasing to exist.
- passing into oblivion.
- some semi-conscious, sleepy-eyed existence.
- reincarnation into another form of life on earth.
- moving on into another world and being given another chance to work one's way into heaven, that is, into being acceptable to God.

Man's idea of death involves either the denial of a life hereafter or else the giving of another chance to work oneself into the favor of God.

Note the critical point: man's idea of conquering death is *man-centered*. It *focuses upon man's ability*...

- to deny a life hereafter and hope that his denial causes life hereafter not to exist.
- to work his way into heaven—into God's acceptance when God gives him another chance.

Man's concept of sin and death is based upon man—his ability, energy, and power to make himself acceptable to God. The point is this: there were those in the Colossian church who were teaching that people secured the approval of God by their own efforts and work: they had to be circumcised, to undergo the basic religious ritual in order to be acceptable to God. They had to trust God *plus* be circumcised. They believed in the Biblical concept of sin and death, and they believed in Christ. But they added the religious ritual of circumcision to Christ.

APPLICATION:

    This proclaims a forceful point to us: it is not enough to be biblically sound if we fail to approach God exactly as He says. It is not enough to say that we do not take anything away from God's Word; we must not add to God's Word. Men sin and men die, and there is a hereafter; but God is love, and He has provided the way for men to become acceptable to Him and be given the right to live in the hereafter. It is absolutely critical that we pursue the way He has provided and that we pursue it exactly as He says.

2.   Christ stands opposed to man's idea of sin and death. Jesus Christ would have never come into the world if sin and eternal death were not realities. If there were not life hereafter—if sin and death were not keeping men out of life hereafter—Jesus Christ would have never come to earth. God would have never sent His Son into the world to die for man's sins and to conquer death if sin and death were not realities. Let no person ever fool himself: God would have never let Christ hang upon the cross unless men were sinners and doomed to eternal death. Note two points.

a. This verse says: "You, being dead in your sins and the uncircumcision of your flesh." Man is said to be already dead because of sin and because he is uncircumcised; that is, sin has not been cut out of his flesh by God. The emphasis is upon death—the fact that man is *already dead*. True, man is what he calls living, yet he is in the process of death. He is aging, deteriorating, decaying, and dying at every given moment. There is not a moment when man is not in the grip of death: even from the moment of conception man begins the process of dying; and while he is growing and maturing, he is still in the process of dying. He is living in what may be called a *world of death*, a *realm of death*, a *dimension of death*. Every hour that passes sees man age, deteriorate, and die one more hour.

> **"Verily, verily, I say unto you, He that heareth my word, and believeth on him that sent me, hath everlasting life, and shall not come into condemnation; but is passed from death unto life"** **(Jn.5:24).**

b. God quickens the believer with Christ. The word "quicken" means to make alive, to bring to life. The believer is brought to life *from the dead*. How?
    ⇒ By being *"together with Christ."*

What does this mean, to be "together with Christ"? Simply this: when we trust Christ—really trust Him—God takes our trust and identifies us with Him. God places us *together with Christ*. This means a most wonderful thing: it means that we were with Christ in His death and resurrection.

Therefore, when Christ died for our sins, we died with Him. God identifies us with Him; consequently, we never have to die for our sins. The penalty for our sins has already been paid; Christ paid for them. Christ bore the guilt, judgment, condemnation, and punishment for our sins. Consequently, we are *forgiven all trespasses*.

APPLICATION:
This is the true concept of sin and death, the only conceivable way we can ever be forgiven and delivered from death. Honest thought tells us this, for there is nothing else that can deliver man from sin and death...

- no person
- no force
- no ability or talent
- no material substance

- no science
- no energy
- no physical thing
- no magic

No matter how long or how much we search, nothing will ever be discovered that can give eternal life to man. We may discover ways to extend life and make it more comfortable, for long, long ago men did live to be hundreds and hundreds of years old. The Bible tells us this. But men will never conquer death completely and perfectly. Life eternal—the approval and acceptance of God—comes only through the quickening power of Jesus Christ.

> **"Jesus answered and said unto him, Verily, verily, I say unto thee, Except a man be born again, he cannot see the kingdom of God" (Jn.3:3).**
> **"Put on the new man, which is <u>renewed</u> in knowledge after the image of him that created him" (Col.3:10).**

2. POINT 2: CHRIST'S VS. MAN'S IDEA OF THE LAW (v.14).

1. Man's concept of the law is twofold.
   ⇒ Some men see the law as a list of rules that God has led great religious men to write down in either the Bible or other religious books.
   ⇒ Other men see the laws of God as unwritten laws that are rooted in the nature of man and the world. Man just instinctively senses what is right and wrong, and he is to live as his instinct tells him (cp. Ro.2:14-15).

Man just senses the handwriting of laws against him—laws that condemn him when he goes contrary to what they say or what he senses. Note the word "handwriting." It actually means a legal note or debt, what William Barclay calls *a charge list* or a list of charges against man.[1] The point is this: man senses the list of charges against him. And he should sense the wrong he has done, for it is his violation of God's law that condemns him to eternal death. Only as he senses and acknowledges his transgressions will he ever turn to God to save him.

APPLICATION:
Think how many people are defeated, discouraged, and whipped by the guilt of their sins and failures. How many are humiliated, low and depressed, feeling unworthy and unacceptable before God? How many are crushed because they feel they have just failed God so much? No matter how much they have tried to keep the law—to do good—they have failed. Therefore, God would never accept them, or so they feel.

2. Christ stands opposed to man's idea of the law. It is true, man shall face God *in his own righteousness* and be judged by the law. If that is the way he chooses to face God, he will be allowed to stand before God in his own righteousness. Man can claim a *righteousness by law*. In fact, there are only two ways to face God, and law or self-righteousness is one of the ways. But note: no person can ever be acceptable to a *perfect*, sinless God unless the person is perfect and sinless. And no honest and thinking person is going to claim to be perfect and sinless. Therefore, no person will ever be acceptable to God by law or self-righteousness. However, this is the glorious message of this verse. God has provided a way for the law and the list of charges against us to be removed. That way is Jesus Christ.

Jesus Christ has taken the law or list of charges against us and nailed them to His cross. This means two things.
   a. Christ "took the law out of the way" for man. How? Christ kept and fulfilled the law perfectly. He lived a sinless life as a Man upon earth. By so doing, He became the standard or the higher law for man. Man is now to look to Jesus Christ and follow Him as the standard of life. The law is set aside out of the way. Christ has now fulfilled the law and become the standard for men.
   b. Christ "nailed the law to the cross." That is, Christ bore the judgment and punishment passed down by the law upon man. Christ took the judgment of the law upon man and paid the penalty Himself. How was He able to do this? By keeping the law

perfectly. In obeying the law perfectly, Christ became the Pattern and Ideal for all men. As the Ideal Man, He embraced and covered all men. It is His righteousness that is the *ideal righteousness*; therefore, His righteousness covers all men. It is His death that is the *ideal death* or the ideal bearing of judgment; therefore, His death covers all men. It is His life that is the *ideal life*; therefore, His life covers all men. (cp. Mt.5:17-18.)

When a person trusts Jesus Christ as his Savior, God removes the list of charges against the person. How? By Christ—by the cross of Christ. When Christ died upon the cross, He actually bore the guilt and condemnation of the charges for the person. Therefore, the person stands guiltless and sinless before God—all because Christ took the list of the charges and nailed them to the cross with Him when He died.

> **"Think not that I am come to destroy the law, or the prophets: I am not come to destroy, but to fulfil" (Mt.5:17).**

ILLUSTRATION:
Do you live the "perfect" Christian life? Nobody does, but a lot of us try by living according to "the rules"—and fail and fall into defeat and condemnation. This is not God's best for the Christian believer. J. Vernon McGee shares this nugget of truth with us:

"You can't...keep the law today in your own strength...the law was given to discipline the old nature. But now the believer is given a new nature, and the law has been removed as a way of life.

"...A man once came to me and said, 'I'll give you $100 if you will show me where the Sabbath day has been changed.' I answered, 'I don't think it has been changed. Saturday is Saturday, it is the seventh day of the week, and it is the Sabbath day. I realize our calendar has been adjusted and can be off a few days, but we won't even consider that point. The seventh day is still Saturday and is still the Sabbath day.'

"He got a gleam in his eye and said, 'Then why don't you keep the Sabbath day if it hasn't been changed?' I answered, 'The day hasn't changed, but I have been changed. I've been given a new creation. We celebrate the first day because that is the day He rose from the grave.'

"That is what it means when he says that the ordinances which were against us have been nailed to His cross."[2]

QUESTIONS:
1. Do you ever experience feelings of failure in trying to keep every point of the law? Do you need a change of behavior or a change of attitude?
2. Why do some people think that God will only accept them if they can keep the law? What things could you share with this kind of person?
3. What does this verse say about your spiritual condition apart from Christ?
4. Have you thanked Christ for nailing the legal charges against you to His cross? How can you praise Him for what He did for you?

3. POINT 3: CHRIST'S VS. MAN'S IDEA OF EVIL FORCES AND EVIL SPIRITS (v.15).

Man's idea of the universe is that all kinds of forces exist within the universe.
⇒ Some persons view the forces as natural energies and powers within the universe such as gravity.
⇒ Other persons view the forces as living beings such as angels, among which some are good and some are bad.

Men have always recognized forces, energies, powers, or principalities within the universe. Men either see natural forces or supernatural spirits behind the stars and planets and life within the universe—either natural forces or supernatural spirits that control the lives and destinies of both man and his world. Just think of the millions down through the centuries who have looked to the signs or spirits of the planets or stars in astrology and the signs of the zodiac.

The point to see is this: the Bible declares without hesitation or equivocation that there are other forces within the universe. In fact, the Bible teaches that there is at least one other world in another dimension of being—another dimension other than the physical dimension. That world is the spiritual dimension of being. And there are living beings in that dimension, both good and bad, just as there are good and bad beings or men in this world.

The glorious declaration of this verse (v.15) is that Christ has spoiled all principalities and powers, no matter who they are or what their force or energy is. The word "spoiled" means to disarm and strip the evil forces of all their power.

William Barclay describes the scene well:

> "[The evil forces] were hostile, malicious, malignant to men. Jesus conquered them for ever. He stripped them: the word that is used is the word for stripping the weapons and the armour from a defeated foe. Once and for all Jesus broke their power. He put them to open shame and led them captive in His triumphant train. The picture is the picture of the triumph of a Roman general. When a Roman general had won a really notable triumph, he was allowed to march his victorious armies through the streets of Rome, and behind him there followed the wretched company of the kings and the leaders and the peoples he had vanquished and conquered. They were openly branded as his victims and his spoils. Paul thinks of Jesus as a triumphant conqueror, enjoying a kind of cosmic triumph; and in His triumphal procession are the powers of evil, beaten for ever, for every one to see."[3]

The point of this verse is to declare that Christ has defeated Satan and his evil spirits—all the forces and energies, power and principalities of the universe. Christ has triumphed over Satan and his evil forces, broken their power and destroyed their works. Christ has triumphed over evil by four acts.

1. He conquered evil spirits and forces by never giving in to the devil's temptations (Mt.4:1-11) and by never sinning (2 Cor.5:21; Heb.4:15; 7:26; 1 Pt.1:19; 2:22). Christ lived a perfect life; he was perfectly righteous. Therefore, He became the Perfect Man, the Ideal Man, the Ideal Righteousness...
   - whom all men are to trust.
   - whom all men are to follow.
   - whom all men are to use as the *pattern* for their lives.

Satan was defeated in that an Ideal Righteousness was now provided for man. Man could now become acceptable to God by putting on the righteousness of Christ *through faith* (2 Cor.5:21; Eph.4:23-24).

2. He conquered evil spirits and forces by dying *for man*, bearing all of man's guilt and punishment for sin. In behalf of man, Christ took all of man's sins upon Himself and bore the judgment of God against sin. He is the *Ideal Man*, so His death becomes the Ideal Death. Just as His *Ideal Righteousness* stands for and covers every man, so His Ideal Death stands for and covers every man. Thus, the penalty and punishment for sins has now been paid. Man no longer has to die and be separated from God. The way to live forever in the presence of God is now open. Satan's power is broken and destroyed.

"Forasmuch then as the children are partakers of flesh and blood, he also himself likewise took part of the same; that through death he might destroy him that had the power of death, that is, the devil; and deliver them who through fear of death were all their lifetime subject to bondage" (Heb.2:14-15).

3. He conquered evil spirits and forces by being raised from the dead. Again, as the Ideal Man, Christ's resurrection becomes the *Ideal Resurrection*. His resurrection stands for and covers every man. Note two facts.

    a. It was the *perfect spirit of holiness* (perfect righteousness) that raised Christ from the dead. Death could not hold perfection, for death is the result of sin. Christ, being perfect, was bound to arise.

    b. When Christ arose, He triumphed over Satan, openly showing that death is the work of Satan. Death is not to be the natural experience of man. Death was never the purpose of God; life is the purpose of God. The resurrection of Christ openly shows this.

> **"God, who hath raised him from the dead...and having spoiled principalities and powers, he made a show of them openly, triumphing over them in it" (Col.2:12, 15).**

4. He conquered evil spirits and forces by His Incarnation, that is, by coming into the world and being revealed as the Son of God. Think about it: the fact that the Son of God came into the world destroys the works of the devil. As soon as the Son of God appeared on the scene, His coming meant that the works of the devil were to be destroyed.

> **"For this purpose the Son of God was manifested, that he might destroy the works of the devil" (1 Jn.3:8).**

ILLUSTRATION:

Are your steps restrained by the Adversary (the devil)? If he has bound you, be warned: he plays for keeps!

> *"Spurgeon told of a wicked king who wished to impoverish and destroy one of his subjects, a blacksmith. He ordered him to make a chain of a certain length. When he was finished, he ordered him to make it longer, and after that still longer. Finally, the blacksmith had no more money to buy metal. Then the wicked king commanded that he be bound with the chain."*[4]

The devil is like this evil king: he draws us in a little at a time and then snatches us into his firm grip to enslave us. But praise God—Jesus came to destroy the works of the devil. The enemy has <u>already</u> been disarmed and has been made a public display. The victory is yours through Christ, through His finished work on the cross. Calvary <u>does</u> cover our sin and death. But you must <u>choose</u> to accept Christ and His victory. You must choose Christ to be saved from sin and death. You can conquer and be victorious only through Christ.

QUESTIONS:

1. In what ways has Satan's power over your life been broken by Christ?
2. In what ways does Satan have you in bondage? How meaningful is this verse in your effort to be set free?
3. How can you guard against being made a captive of Satan's ploys?
4. What things did Jesus do in order to set you free from a life of captivity?

PERSONAL JOURNAL NOTES:
(Reflection & Response)

1.   The most important thing that I learned from this lesson was:

2.   The area that I need to work on the most is:

3.   I can apply this lesson to my life by:

4.   Closing Statement Of Commitment:

[1] William Barclay. *The Letters to the Philippians, Colossians, and Thessalonians*, p.170.
[2] J. Vernon McGee. *Thru The Bible, Vol.5*, p.351-352.
[3] William Barclay. *The Letters to the Philippians, Colossians, and Thessalonians*, p.172.
[4] Walter B. Knight. *Knight's Treasury of 2,000 Illustrations*, p.107.

	D. Christ vs. Rules, Ritual, & Spiritism, 2:16-19		

1. Christ vs. rules & ritual
  a. The false approach to God: Through the shadows of rules & rituals & judging others by them
  b. The true approach to God: Through Christ, the only acceptable body
2. Christ vs. spiritism
	16 Let no man therefore judge you in meat, or in drink, or in respect of an holyday, or of the new moon, or of the sabbath days:
	17 Which are a shadow of things to come; but the body is of Christ.
	18 Let no man beguile
		you of your reward in a voluntary humility and worshipping of angels, intruding into those things which he hath not seen, vainly puffed up by his fleshly mind,
		19 And not holding the Head, from which all the body by joints and bands having nourishment ministered, and knit together, increaseth with the increase of God.
			a. The false approach to God: Spiritism-- through the worship of angels or spirits & visions
			
			b. The true approach to God: Through Christ who is the Head
			  1) He alone supplies & nourishes life
			  2) He alone binds life together

Section IV
THE CONTRAST BETWEEN CHRIST AND FALSE TEACHING
Colossians 2:8-23

Study 4: CHRIST VS. RULES, RITUAL, AND SPIRITISM

Text: Colossians 2:16-19

Aim: To break free from the rituals that keep you from a true worship of Christ.

Memory Verse:
> **"Let no man therefore judge you in meat, or in drink, or in respect of an holyday, or of the new moon, or of the sabbath days" (Colossians 2:16).**

INTRODUCTION:
What tools does the devil use to destroy your relationship with God? Throughout the ages, Satan has used the tools of rules, ritual, and spiritism on Christians and tragically proven to be highly successful. As you will see by studying the Scriptures in this session, God has provided the tools that the Christian believer needs to counteract the devil's work.

This passage pits Christ against two false teachings that have hounded people down through the ages, false teachings that are constantly infiltrating the church as well as attacking people out on the street.

OUTLINE:
1.   Christ vs. rules and ritual (v.16-17).
2.   Christ vs. spiritism (v.18-19).

1. CHRIST VS. RULES AND RITUAL (v.16-17).

Every thinking person knows that we have to have rules and laws in order to live a controlled and just life. But when we adopt a rule, at some point we fail to keep it. Somehow, some way, we just fail and come short of keeping the rule perfectly. This means something of critical importance: we can never approach God and become acceptable to God through rules or laws or rituals or through anything else we might undertake by our own efforts. Why? Because God is perfect, and to approach God we have to be perfect. But this is the very problem of human life: we are already imperfect and can never be perfect because we have already failed. How then can we ever become acceptable to God whose very nature demands perfection? There is only one way: through the love of God. We have to trust that God loves us enough to provide a way that He can count and consider us perfect. We are not perfect, so we have to believe that He will provide a way for us to be credited with perfection. This is the glorious gospel of His Son, Jesus Christ. When we trust the righteousness and perfection of Jesus Christ, then God counts our trust in His dear Son as righteousness. When we focus upon God's Son, that is, honor Christ with our trust and our lives, God honors us for honoring His Son. God honors us by counting us righteous and perfect *in the righteousness of Christ*.

Note: the emphasis of the present passage is upon focusing and concentrating upon Christ, God's Son. God the Father loves His Son with an eternal love, the greatest love in existence. Therefore, God accepts any person *in His Son* and no person *out of His Son*. He honors any person who *completely trusts* His Son, and no person who comes short of *complete trust*. Now, note the points of these two verses.

1. Rules and rituals were the problem that had seeped into the Colossian church. Some believers were reverting back to rules and rituals and judging others by them. Some false teachers were diverting the attention of some believers away from Christ. They were saying...

- that rules and rituals were to be the *focus of man's attention and life*.
- that man *became acceptable to God* by keeping certain rules and rituals.
- that man *pleased God* by eating and drinking the right foods and by keeping certain religious rituals and holy days.

Note how this teaching led a person to focus upon rules and rituals instead of upon Christ. This emphasis found its roots in the false teaching of Gnosticism which had seeped into the Colossian church.

APPLICATION:

People tend to approach God by keeping rules that discipline their body, minds, and spirit. A person feels that God will accept him if he can present himself to God with...

- a body that is clean and moral.
- a spirit that is religious and that keeps the rituals and holy days of religion.
- a life that serves and gives.

2. The true approach to God is through Christ. Rules and rituals are only shadows in approaching God; Christ is the real body that enables us to approach God and to please Him. The point is this: Christ was the perfect Son of God; that is, He kept all the rules of the law and never broke a single rule. He was sinless, the perfect Man. Therefore, He stands before the human race as the Ideal Man, the Pattern to whom every man is now to look. We no longer have just rules and rituals to lead us to God; we have a human life, the very body of Christ Himself— a body that lived life just like God wants life to be lived. Therefore, we are no longer to approach God through rules and rituals, but through Christ. Christ is to be the *focus and concentration* of our lives. We are to *live and move and have our being* in Him, following the Ideal life and pattern He has set before us.

⇒ Christ is our only approach to God.
⇒ Christ is our only acceptance by God.
⇒ Focusing upon Christ is the only way we can please God.

Note: rules and rituals were shadows that were used by God before Christ came. They were used by God to teach men that nothing could provide real life, not the real substance of life that satisfies and gives absolute assurance of living forever with God. Rules and rituals never satisfy the human heart, not permanently. Only the presence of God living within the human heart can satisfy man. This is where Christ comes in: Christ dwells within the lives of believers, actually lives within the bodies of believers in the person of the Holy Spirit. Therefore, the believer experiences the satisfaction and assurance of being acceptable to God and of living forever with God.

The point is this: no rule and no ritual can give life and assurance to man. Rules and rituals are only inanimate, lifeless objects. But not Christ. He is a living Person who can relate and infuse the very life and assurance of God into the heart of a person. Rules and rituals may point us toward God, but they are not the real substance of life. Christ is the real substance of life—the only substance, body, and life that can bring us to God and present us as acceptable to God.

> **"But now the righteousness of God without the law is manifested, being witnessed by the law and the prophets; even the righteousness of God which is by faith of Jesus Christ unto all and upon all them that believe: for there is no difference"** (Ro.3:21-22).

APPLICATION:

We must always remember something when dealing with this issue. When a person follows Christ, he is to live as Christ lived. That is...

- he is to eat as Christ ate, eating only what he needs and what is good for His body.
- he is to worship faithfully as Christ worshipped.
- he is to live soberly, righteously, and godly as Christ lived.

The list could go on and on. The point is that Christ fulfilled the law to give us a pattern of how life is to be lived through the fulness of God's Spirit. He did not fulfill the law to turn us loose to live in the indulgence and license of sin. He, the very Son of God, is now a Pattern. We now have more than just written laws and rituals, more than just ink on paper. We have the life of Christ to follow.

ILLUSTRATION:

Do you attempt to approach God on your own terms? Listen closely to this story:

> *"The captain of the ship looked into the dark night and saw faint lights in the distance. Immediately he told his signalman to send a message: 'Alter your course 10 degrees south.'*
>
> *"Promptly a return message was received: 'Alter your course 10 degrees north.'*
>
> *"The captain was angered; his command had been ignored. So he sent a second message: 'Alter your course 10 degrees south—I am the captain!'*
>
> *"Soon another message was received: 'Alter your course 10 degrees north—I am seaman third class Jones.'*
>
> *"Immediately the captain sent a third message, knowing the fear it would evoke: 'Alter your course 10 degrees south—I am a battleship.'*
>
> *"Then the reply came: 'Alter your course 10 degrees north—I am a lighthouse.'*
>
> *"In the midst of our dark and foggy times, all sorts of voices are shouting orders into the night, telling us what to do, how to adjust our lives. Out of the darkness, one voice signals something quite opposite to the rest—something almost absurd. But the voice happens to be the Light of the World, and we ignore it at our [own] peril."*[1]

Whose rules do you follow? Whose voice do you listen to—the god and false teachings of this world or the God of heaven?

QUESTIONS:
1. What are some rituals practiced by some churches that shift the focus away from Christ?
2. Have you failed to keep your focus on Christ? What rules or rituals tend to distract you from Him? What steps do you need to take in order to regain your focus?
3. What is God's intent for rules and rituals? Why do some people fail to understand His intent? What happens to a Christian believer when he loses his focus on Christ?

2. CHRIST VS. SPIRITISM (v.18-19).

Note the word "beguile." It means to rob, to defraud, to cheat a person out of his reward. It is possible for believers to be cheated out of their reward by false teachers. How? By following those who teach that there is another approach to God other than Christ. Christ is God's appointed way to approach Him, and there is no other way. Note the points of these verses.

1. The false approach to God now being discussed is spiritism, the worship of God through angels or spirits and visions. Again, the Colossian church had been heavily influenced by the Gnostic teaching of intermediaries or mediators between God and man. Note the words "intruding into those things which he hath not seen." This is a reference to visions, seeing into the spiritual realm, into a world other than the physical world. Some of the believers were claiming all kinds of visions—visions of spiritual beings and of angels. And, as so often happens when people have deep spiritual experiences, the Colossians began to focus upon the visions and angels whom they claimed were appearing to them: they focused upon the spirits instead of upon Christ.

Men tend to feel God is far off in outer space someplace or in some unreachable dimension of being, at least unreachable to the common person. They feel too sinful and unworthy to approach God or to secure God's interest and care. Therefore, they feel the need for intermediaries to stand between them and God—intermediaries who can present them and their lives and situations to God. As a result, men tend to look and pray to lesser beings such as angels or spirits of departed saints. Others turn to seeking visions or deep spiritual experiences in order to know God and secure His help in life.

Note another fact as well: there is false humility in this approach to God. A person who approaches God through visions and spirits is claiming that he is unworthy to approach God himself. He needs others to appear before God for him. But note: this is false humility, for the person claims to have visions of angels or spirits which other people do not have. Some in the Colossian church were claiming that they possessed special gifts and that they had experienced special visions, yet they were unworthy of such experiences. There was a voluntary (self-imposed) air of humility about them that really came across as being more spiritual than other believers. Paul says that they were deceived and that they were in danger of losing their reward. They were "puffed up" by a fleshly mind.

The point is this: spiritism focuses attention upon the spiritual experience—the angels, spirits, and visions—not on God's appointed way to approach Him, which is Christ. Christ is relegated to a lower position in the person's life than the spirits and visions. The person seeks to have visions of the spirits more than he seeks Christ.

What William Barclay says at this point stands as a warning to all believers, even to those who walk faithfully and know what it is to have deep experiences with the Lord:

> "No one will deny the visions of the mystics, but there is always a danger when a man begins to think that he has attained a height of holiness which enables him to see what common men—as he calls them—cannot see; and the danger is that men will so often see, not what God sends them, but what they want to see."[2]

ILLUSTRATION:
For good reason, God warns us against dabbling in the world of spiritism, in the world of the devil and his horde of evil spirits.

> "Marlowe's drama, <u>Dr. Faustus</u>, tells the story of the man who sold his soul to the devil, signing the contract with his own blood, in return for which he was to have everything he wants in this life. During the twenty-four years, Faustus had a big time, gratifying every wish for wealth, power, wisdom, and pleasure....At last the time was up. Still not satisfied, Faustus hoped he may have an eleventh hour repentance, but it was not to be. As the clock struck twelve a horde of devils came to carry off the screaming victim.
> "Alas, many are selling out for much less than Dr. Faustus did."[3]

2. The true approach to God is Christ. Christ is the Head, the only mediator who can stand before God and...

- secure the approval and acceptance of God for man.
- secure the love and care of God for man.

No spirit—no angel or vision—can do what Christ can do. Christ alone has access into God's presence *in behalf of man*. Christ alone stands before God as the representative or *Head of man*. No other person or being can stand before God in behalf of men. Why? Because the body has only one head, not two. The answer is found in the analogy or picture of the human body. A body has only one head. And God's people are a body of people—a body of people who live under the *will and control of the Head* who is Christ. Note two things about the Head, who is Christ.

a. The head is the part which supplies and nourishes the body. So it is with Christ. Christ alone can supply and nourish the body of believers, the church. Christ alone can give men the strength and nourishment of God to help them as they walk day by day through life.

b. The head is that which knits the body together making it function as it should. So it is with Christ. He alone...

- can knit a person together—all the thoughts, emotions, and other things that are needed to make him a whole person.
- can knit all people together as one body in love, joy, and peace—worshipping, serving, and living for God like they should.

APPLICATION:

The point is well made. Man cannot approach God nor receive the help of God through any means other than His Son, the Lord Jesus Christ. No spirit nor angel nor vision can bring the knitting or nourishing power of God to men. Only Christ, God's appointed Head, can knit and nourish men throughout life.

"He that cometh from above is above all: he that is of the earth is earthly, and speaketh of the earth: he that cometh from heaven is above all" (Jn.3:31).

COLOSSIANS 2:16-19

SUMMARY:

The devil is always busy trying to lure us away from Christ. You have to make a clear choice: either you allow the devil to work his sinister work in you, or else you work at frustrating the devil's plans for you. Remember the two main points from this passage:

1. Christ vs. rules and ritual: Christ is to be the focus of our worship—not rules and rituals.
2. Christ vs. spiritism: Christ is the only way to approach God—not through spiritism.

PERSONAL JOURNAL NOTES:
(Reflection & Response)

1. The most important thing that I learned from this lesson was:

2. The area that I need to work on the most is:

3. I can apply this lesson to my life by:

4. Closing Statement of Commitment:

---

[1] Craig B. Larson, Editor, *Illustrations for Preaching & Teaching*, p.134
[2] William Barclay, *The Letters to the Philippians, Colossians, and Thessalonians*, p. 175.
[3] Paul Lee Tan, *Encyclopedia of 7,700 Illustrations; Signs of the Times*, p.920.

	E. Criticisms of Worldly Philosophy & Man-Made Approaches To God, 2:20-23	not; handle not; 22 Which all are to perish with the using;) after the commandments and doctrines of men?	enslave & subject men to the rules & teachings of men
1. Believers are dead with Christ to man's crude notions about God & the world	20 Wherefore if ye be dead with Christ from the rudiments of the world, why, as though living in the world, are ye subject to ordinances,	23 Which things have indeed a show of wisdom in will worship, and humility, and neglecting of the body; not in any honour to the satisfying of the flesh.	3. Man-made approaches are based upon the works & efforts & pride of men 4. Man-made approaches profess humility before the world, but the humility is false
2. Man-made approaches	21 (Touch not; taste		

Section IV
THE CONTRAST BETWEEN CHRIST AND
FALSE TEACHING Colossians 2:8-23

Study 5:   **CRITICISMS OF WORLDLY PHILOSOPHY AND MAN-MADE APPROACHES TO GOD**

Text: **Colossians 2:20-23**

Aim: To learn why you must reject man-made approaches to God.

Memory Verse:
> "Wherefore if ye be dead with Christ from the rudiments of the world, why, as though living in the world, are ye subjects to ordinances?" (Colossians 2:20).

INTRODUCTION:
Most of us are familiar with the children's story about the three little pigs and the big bad wolf. The first little pig's house was built with straw. After huffing and puffing, the big bad wolf blew it down. He then moved on to the second little pig's house which was built out of wood. As before, the wolf huffed and puffed and blew this house down also.

By this time, the big bad wolf was feeling pretty confident in his ability to blow down houses built by pigs. Filled with pride, he approached the next house—the one made of bricks. Once again, he huffed and he puffed but nothing happened. So he huffed and he puffed and he huffed and he puffed and...he failed to blow down this house. He had been deceived by his previous experiences.

In the same way, man has acted just like the big, bad wolf. He has deceived himself by thinking that he can huff and puff and blow down the walls that keep him from approaching God. But Scripture declares that man has no power to approach God.

"But doesn't huffing and puffing count for something?" you might ask. "I go to church; I'm a good person; I do good things for people. Isn't that the basis for approaching God?" No! As you will see in this study, man-made approaches are totally inadequate.

This passage closes the study on the contrast between Christ and false teaching. It stands as a mighty fortress against false teaching. It gives three strong criticisms against worldly philosophy or man-made approaches to God.

OUTLINE:
1. Believers are dead with Christ to man's crude notions about God and the world (v.20).
2. Man-made approaches enslave and subject men to the rules and teachings of men (v.21-22).
3. Man-made approaches are based upon the works and efforts and pride of men (v.23).
4. Man-made approaches profess humility before the world, but the humility is false (v.23).

1. BELIEVERS ARE DEAD WITH CHRIST TO MAN'S CRUDE NOTIONS ABOUT GOD AND THE WORLD (v.20).

1.   The rudiments or the "basic principles of the world" mean the crude notions of men about the universe—that is, about God, reality, and truth. It is man's ideas and philosophies: their elementary or rudimentary teachings; their ABC understanding of God and the universe, reality, and truth. When men think of God, they come up with all kinds of ways and laws to reach Him and to secure His approval and acceptance. However, there are three basic problems with man's approach to God.

      a. First, we cannot keep rules and laws—not in a perfect sense. No matter what way we choose to reach God, we cannot walk a straight path to Him. We cannot stay on the path—not every moment and not perfectly. This poses an insurmountable problem, for God is perfect and we are not. Therefore, we are not acceptable to Him; we are automatically rejected because of our imperfection. Imperfection cannot live in the presence of a perfect God. This is the first problem with trying to keep rules and laws in order to be good enough for God.

      b. Second, once we have broken a rule or law, we stand guilty before God. Therefore, we must be judged, condemned, and punished for having broken the law. A law-breaker is guilty and unacceptable and the punishment must be borne. Therefore, rules and laws cannot make us acceptable to God, and they can only lead to guilt and condemnation.

      c. Third, we die; we do not live forever. And there is no law or force on this earth that can give us the energy and power to live forever. If there were, there would be all kinds of people laying hold of and obeying that law. Rules and laws only condemn us when we break them. They have no power to save us from death nor to give us eternal life. Because of this, rules and laws cannot be the way to approach God.

         How then can we approach God? If the best thinking of men about the universe and God are not the way to approach God, what is the way? The answer will be discussed in a moment, but first look at the second meaning of the word rudiments.

2.   Rudiments mean the basic elements or materials of the universe, the things that men say lie behind the universe or at the very base of reality. Down through the centuries men have posed all kinds of forces, energies, powers, principalities, spirits, angels, and beings as standing behind the universe and life. As a result, men have committed their lives and worshipped all sorts of creatures and forces or elements and materials. However, there is a critical problem with this approach to God, a problem that dooms all who seek truth and approach God through the elements of this universe or through the spirits of the spiritual world.

      a. First, there is the problem of corruption. Everything in the universe is corruptible, aging, dying, deteriorating, and decaying. Therefore, there is nothing in the universe that can save man, for the way of all things—all elements and all materials—is the way of death.

      b. Second, the problem with seeking truth and God through the spirits or angels of a spiritual world is a twofold problem.

        ⇒ First, man cannot penetrate the spiritual world. He is physical, and the physical just cannot move over into the world of the spiritual no matter what any person claims. If the spiritual world is ever to be known, then the spiritual has to reveal itself to us.

        ⇒ Second, those who claim to have been given visions or revelations by the spiritual world still have the same problems that everyone else has: the problems of imperfection (unrighteousness), death, and eternal life. No angel, spirit, or any other intermediary has ever taken care of the problem of sin and death and of eternal life for us. We have already sinned, and we are already imperfect. Therefore, someone, someplace must bear our sin or punishment for us, or else we have to pay for it ourselves. And, on top of that, someone has to go through the experience of death and conquer it to tell us how to do the same or else we are going to die and never reach God.

This is the glorious message of the gospel. God is love, eternal and infinite love, so He has done all this for us. He did it through His Son, Jesus Christ.

> **"For God so loved the world, that he gave his only begotten Son, that whosoever believeth in him should not perish, but have everlasting life" (Jn.3:16).**

QUESTIONS:
1. What are "rudiments" or "the basic principles of the world"?
2. What are the basic problems with man's approach to God?
3. Can any combination of man-made approaches gain us salvation or eternal life?

God's Son, Jesus Christ, has secured righteousness for us. He came to earth and lived a sinless and perfect life. Therefore, He stood before God and the world as the Ideal and Perfect Man. As the Ideal and Perfect Man, He could take our sins upon Himself and die for them. And this He did: Christ actually took our judgment and bore the punishment for our imperfections or sins. Then He arose from the dead, conquering death.

Now note the verse: "...if ye be dead with Christ from the rudiments of the world...." The death of Christ is the way God has established for us to approach Him. A person is to...

- repent and turn from the rudiments of the world, that is, from man's approaches to God.
- believe that God loves the world, that He is not far off, leaving man in the dark having to grope and grasp after the truth and God.
- to believe that God's Son died for him, bearing his punishment and death.

If Christ has done this for us, then we are free from having to seek after God through rules, laws, angels, spirits, and through the forces and energies of the universe. How? By believing in Christ. When we believe in Christ, we are trusting the Ideal Man. Therefore, His death and resurrection can stand for us. That is, when He died, He was dying as the Ideal Man; and when He arose from the dead, He arose as the Ideal Man. This simply means that the Ideal, Perfect Man stands for all other men. Everything He did stands for man. When He died, He died for us; and when He arose to live with God forever, He arose for us. Therefore, when we believe in Christ, we are accepted by God in the righteousness of Christ. And being accepted by God, we are freed from having to use any other approach to reach Him. Christ has freed us from all other approaches.

Simply stated, God loves us; therefore, He has taken care of the problems of imperfection (sin) and death. He has provided the way and given us the right to approach Him face to face—through His Son. In Christ we are free from the corruptible and insufficient approaches to God, from the elements and materials of the universe, and from the crude notions and ideas of men about how to approach and please God.

> ⇒ If you are dead with Christ, then you are free from having to approach God through the rudiments of the world.

QUESTIONS:
1. Why do some people place their trust in a worldly philosophy and not God's Word? Is it important to study the Bible and learn what God says? Do you also think it is important to understand the worldly philosophies being followed in one's own generation? Why or why not?
2. What advantages are offered to the Christian believer according to this verse?
3. What things would attract a believer to be subject to the religious ordinances, laws, or rituals of the world again?

2. MAN-MADE APPROACHES ENSLAVE AND SUBJECT MEN TO THE RULES AND TEACHINGS OF MEN (v.21-22).

Some in the Colossian church were returning to the rules and regulations of men as a means to please God. They returned to the idea...

- that man can please God by controlling the defilement and weaknesses of the flesh—that man can secure God's approval by presenting a clean and pure body to God. Therefore, they began to come up with all the rules necessary to eat the right foods, to take care of their bodies, and to live a clean life. Note how simply Paul puts it: they were saying "touch not; taste not; handle not."

There is no question, discipline and control and a clean body are wise, and every person should develop the healthiest, most moral body he can. But this is not what makes us acceptable to God. This approach to God has two critical flaws.

⇒ First, a person can have the healthiest, most pure body in the world, but that person is still imperfect and still dies. Health and morality, no matter how undiseased and pure, do not keep us from aging and dying. We are still corruptible and are still going the way of all flesh—the way of death and separation from God.

⇒ Second, the approach to God by rules and discipline forces us to focus upon the rules instead of Christ. We have to keep our minds upon the rules, or else we break them before we know it. Contrary to pleasing God, this displeases God. God wants our lives focused upon His Son, Jesus Christ.

The point is this: the philosophies and ideas of men enslave us: they force us to commit our lives to them and to focus upon them, and then they leave us enslaved to the bondage of death. Man-made ideas do not free us; they can carry us no higher than the man who made up the idea, and that height is not a height at all. It is a depth, the depth of death to which all men go.

The question is this: If you are dead with Christ and never have to die again—if you are in union with Christ—if you are already acceptable to God...why then are you still trying to become acceptable to God? Your task is not to become acceptable to God. Your task is to focus upon God's Son, Christ, who has given you so much in His death and resurrection. Your task is...

- to study His life and will.
- to follow and pattern your life after His life.
- to serve Him in His mission, giving all you are and have to reach all men with the gospel of eternal life.

Life in Christ is not slavery; it is freedom. Life in Christ is a life freed from corruption and death—a life which is already acceptable to God and which has already been given eternal life by God. Life in Christ is enslaved by nothing—it is set free from all the elements and materials of this world including death—it is set free to live and move and have its being face to face with God Himself. Not because we are worthy or merit it but because of Christ and what He has done. God loves Christ so much that He accepts anyone who comes to Him acknowledging and praising Christ for what He has done in dying for man.

Since you are dead with Christ, why are you returning to the ideas and rules of men and now trying to please God by your own works and efforts? Man is to please God, yes! But he is to please God by being enslaved to Christ and following Him, not by being enslaved to the rules and religions, philosophies and ideas of men. Man is to focus upon Christ, not upon the enslaving elements and materials of this world, and he is certainly not to focus upon man's fluctuating notions of God and how to approach Him.

> **"Not every one that saith unto me, Lord, Lord, shall enter into the kingdom of heaven; but he that doeth the will of my Father which is in heaven" (Mt.7:21; cp. 1:Jn.3:23).**

ILLUSTRATION:

What motivates you in your faith? A genuine love for Christ? Or a list of rules and regulations?

Mike grew up in a home where he was taught that the only way to please God was to be in church every time the doors were open. From his parents, he learned by example the art of saying "yes" to every opportunity to get involved in religious work.

As Mike became an adult, he quickly rose up through the ranks of church leadership. One day, his pastor asked him for permission to place his name in nomination for chairman of the board. Mike thought about it for awhile and measured the pros and cons. "Becoming chairman of the board would be great for my insurance business. My client base should increase as they see me at work in the church. It would be a real honor. Just think: God, the preacher, and me! It will mean more time away from my wife and children, but I'm sure they'll understand."

His wife and children did not understand. They never did see much of him after he became the chairman. His excuse was, "I'm doing it for God. Quit being so selfish." Who was being selfish? Mike or his family? In the book Toxic Faith, the authors make this appropriate statement:

> "Churchaholics have embraced a counterfeit religion. God is not honored, and the relationship with Him in not furthered. Work is the focus of everything. It—and not God—allows the person to feel safe. Rather than retreat to the loving arms of God, they literally bury themselves in their compulsive acts. The harder they work, the better they feel because they convince one another that God is applauding their efforts. They are so entangled in the world of the church that they no longer have time for the family. They are trying to work their way to heaven or pay the price for their guilt. Without intervention, they lose all sense of reality and rarely come to understand God as He really is."[1]

QUESTIONS:
1. In what ways can you relate to Mike? What advice would you give to him? To his family?
2. Are you sometimes guilty of being a "churchaholic"? What is the first thing you need to do to tackle your own problem?
3. What is it that makes you acceptable to God? What is your basis for believing this?
4. What makes some people want to please God with their own works and efforts? What difference does it make when you know what God expects from you?

3. MAN-MADE APPROACHES ARE BASED UPON THE WORKS, EFFORTS, AND PRIDE OF MEN (v.23).

Very simply, the most that man can come up with in saving himself is a religion of works which is nothing more than a religion of pride. Note: Scripture admits that man can have a worldly wisdom and a strong will. The rules and ideas of man "show wisdom in will worship," that is, in self-made worship. Men are very capable in...

- thinking
- reasoning
- intelligence
- controlling
- disciplining
- acting

But there are critical flaws existing in men that man cannot solve. These flaws need to be closely heeded.
⇒ Man's wisdom and will cannot destroy sin in the life of men. Man cannot keep from sinning through wisdom and will—no matter what he does.
⇒ Man's wisdom and will cannot destroy death. A man cannot keep from dying.

Therefore, no matter how wise and how much man controls his body and life--no matter what kind of values and morality he follows; no matter what kind of self-made religion he worship--

man still sins and still dies. He is still unacceptable to God. Therefore, when man uses his own wisdom and will to create ways to approach God...

- he is only exalting himself and his own wisdom and discipline.
- he is by-passing and ignoring God and the approach God has provided and established.
- he is following a way that is totally meaningless and utterly inadequate, for nothing man-made can end up any place other than as decayed matter.
- he is totally incapable of destroying sin and death in man.

> **"And the Lord said unto him, Now do ye Pharisees make clean the outside of the cup and the platter; but your inward part is full of ravening and wickedness. Ye fools, did not he, that made that which is without, make that which is within also?" (Lk.11:39-40).**
>
> **"Professing themselves to be wise, they became fools" (Ro.1:22).**

ILLUSTRATION:

For a person with natural gifts and abilities, the temptation is to think more highly of himself than he should. Listen closely to this fable:

> *"A woodpecker was pecking away at the trunk of a dead tree. Suddenly lightning struck the tree and splintered it. The woodpecker flew away, unharmed. Looking back to where the dead tree had stood, the proud bird exclaimed, 'Look what I did!'"*[2]

If you are like the woodpecker, who are you trying to fool? Certainly not God!

QUESTIONS:

1. What is your greatest talent or ability? What must you do in your heart to ensure that God receives the credit in your life?
2. Why do you think God was so careful to tell us how He wanted us to approach Him?
3. Why does God hate pride? What sort of attitude are you to have concerning the pride in your life?

4. MAN-MADE APPROACHES PROFESS HUMILITY BEFORE THE WORLD, BUT THE HUMILITY IS FALSE (v.23).

⇒ When a person follows a set of rules or of religion, he is confessing a need—either a need for something more than what he has or for something higher than himself. The confession of need is a sign of humility—of lacking something.

But note a significant point: when he begins to follow the rules and rituals of his religion—begins to control and discipline his life by the rules—he is showing his ability to control and discipline, to make himself acceptable to God. Therefore, his humility is contradictory; it is a false humility. The only true humility is to confess total inadequacy—total depravity—and the utter necessity for God Himself to save us. When God saves us, we can be saved by no higher person, and we are saved by no merit or work of our own. Therefore, God and God alone is praised, not us. True humility is focusing totally upon God as the Savior of the world and never seeing man as having any part in salvation. As Paul says: there is no "honor to the satisfying of the flesh"—not in true humility and salvation.

> **"Two men went up into the temple to pray; the one a Pharisee, and the other a publican. The Pharisee stood and prayed thus with himself, God, I thank thee, that I am not as other men are, extortioners, unjust, adulterers, or even as this publican. I fast twice in the week, I give tithes of all that I possess. And the publican, standing afar off, would not lift up**

so much as his eyes unto heaven, but smote upon his breast, saying, God be merciful to me a sinner. I tell you, this man went down to his house justified rather than the other: for every one that exalteth himself shall be abased; and he that humbleth himself shall be exalted" (Lk.18:10-14).

APPLICATION:

Throughout the ages, men have tried to come to God in their own ways. One extreme example can be seen in the religion "Jainism." In order to be a good Jain, a follower must adhere to these five doctrines:
1. A vow not to injure any life (including bugs).
2. A vow to always speak the truth (although, for them all truth is relative, not absolute).
3. A vow to refrain from taking anything not given to them.
4. A vow to renounce sexual pleasures (for them, the flesh is evil. This is the kind of gnosticism that Paul addressed to the Colossians.)
5. The vow to renounce all attachments (including family and possessions).

As a Christian believer, you might look at this religion and say to yourself, "I would never do that." But really? Do you believe in the absolute truth of the Bible? Are you so legalistic that you brand certain things as evil when God has not said so? Are you so "committed" to the cause of Christ that your other responsibilities (such as family) are suffering from lack of attention?

God hates a false humility. Thankfully, He expects us to approach Him on much firmer terms—by His grace!

QUESTIONS:
1. Do you believe God gives points to His children who do good? Why do some believers feel this way?
2. What does God want your role to be in approaching Him? What is His role?
3. What does true humility focus on? What things can you do to sharpen your focus on Christ instead of self?

SUMMARY:

As you conclude this study, remember that there is a clear distinction between Christ and false teaching. Without His involvement in our lives, we will ultimately fail every test that comes our way. God's challenge to us is to pass the test on His terms.

> "Steve Winger...writes about his last college test—a final in a logic class known for its difficult exams:
> "To help us on our test, the professor told us we could bring as much information to the exam as we could fit on a piece of notebook paper. Most students crammed as many facts as possible on their 8-1/2 x 11 inch sheet of paper.
> "But one student walked into class, put a piece of paper on the floor, and had an advanced logic student stand on the paper. The advanced logic student told him everything he needed to know. He was the only student to receive an 'A.'
> "The ultimate final exam will come when we stand before God and He asks, "Why should I let you in [into heaven]?" On our own we cannot pass that exam. Our creative attempts to earn eternal life fall far short. But we have Someone who will stand in for us."[3]

The major points of this study are:
1. Believers are dead with Christ to man's crude notions about God and the world.
2. Man-made approaches enslave and subject men to the rules and teachings of men.
3. Man-made approaches are based upon the works and efforts and pride of men.
4. Man-made approaches profess humility before the world, but the humility is false.

PERSONAL JOURNAL NOTES
(Reflection & Response)

1. The most important thing that I learned from this lesson was:

2. The area that I need to work on the most is:

3. I can apply this lesson to my life by:

4. Closing Statement of Commitment:

---

[1] Stephen Arterburn & Jack Felton, *Toxic Faith: Understanding & Overcoming Religious Addiction* (Nashville, TN: Oliver- Nelson Books, 1991), p.120.

[2] Walter B. Knight, *Knight's Treasury of 2,000 Illustrations*, p.299.

[3] Selected from *Leadership*, Fall 1994, Vol.XV, number 4, p.43.

CHAPTER 3	which are above,	risen with Christ
	where Christ sitteth on	2. The believer's new
V. THE DEMANDS	the right hand of God.	life is a life that seeks
OF THE BELIEV-	2 Set your affection	the things above—in
ER'S NEW LIFE:	on things above, not	heaven, where Christ is
GREAT CHAR-	on things on the earth.	a. The meaning: Set
ACTER, 3:1-17	3 For ye are dead, and	your mind on
	your life is hid with	things above, not
A. The Basis of the	Christ in God.	on things on earth
Believer's New	4 When Christ, who is	b. The reason: You are
Life, 3:1-4	our life, shall appear,	dead & hid with Christ
	then shall ye also ap-	c. The reward: You
1. The believer's new	If ye be risen with	pear with him in	shall appear in
life is a life that is	Christ, seek those things	glory.	glory with Christ

Section V
THE DEMANDS OF THE BELIEVER'S NEW
LIFE: GREAT CHARACTER Colossians 3:1-17

Study 1:   THE BASIS OF THE BELIEVER'S NEW LIFE

Text: Colossians 3:1-4

Aim: To strongly focus on your new life in Christ.

Memory Verse:
"**If ye then be risen with Christ, seek those things which are above, where Christ sitteth on the right hand of God**" (Colossians 3:1).

INTRODUCTION:
How many times have you heard the expression: "Don't put the cart before the horse"? This is a clever saying telling us to do things in the right order. There are many Christians who put the cart before the horse in their relationship with Christ. They work *towards* the cross of Christ instead of working *away* from it.
This kind of mindset boils down to this simple formula:

My work (my obligation to God)
+ God's provision for me (His grace)
= The basis of Christianity

This is a false basis for Christianity. This kind of life is simply based upon works. God has a better plan for life than this. The basis of the believer's new life is this:

God's provision for me (through His work on the cross)
+ My gratitude (I serve Him)
= The true basis of the believer's new life.

Are you ready for a change? Are you willing to put things in the proper order? Do you want to know how it is done in practicality and in truth? If your heart is echoing "yes" to these questions, then answers from this great passage are waiting to be discovered. And in the end, you will find for yourself the basis of the believer's new life.

OUTLINE:
1. The believer's new life is a life that is risen with Christ (v.1).
2. The believer's new life is a life that seeks the things above—in heaven, where Christ is (v.1-4).

1. THE BELIEVER'S NEW LIFE IS A LIFE THAT IS RISEN WITH CHRIST (v.1).

God loves His Son, Jesus Christ—loves Him with an eternal and perfect love. Therefore, when a person believes, really surrenders his life to Christ, God forgives the person's sins, accepting Him *in Christ*. God actually *identifies the person* with Christ in His death and resurrection. God begins to *consider the person* as having died and risen with Christ. The new believer was not bodily present when Christ died and arose, but God considers the believer to have been there. God reckons, credits, and counts it so.

Remember: God does this for us because He loves His Son, Jesus Christ, so much. He loves Him so much that when we believe in Christ, God does *exactly what we believe*. He does this because our belief *focuses upon and honors Christ*. And because it honors God's Son, God counts our belief as the real thing. He counts us as having actually died and risen with Christ.

This means a most wonderful thing. It means that we are in union with Christ; we are identified with Christ. Our faith *in Christ* has placed us *in Christ*. Therefore, whatever Christ experienced we experienced. When He arose from the dead, we arose with Him. His resurrection means...

- that we have risen with Him.
- that we have conquered death.
- that we are raised to a new life.
- that our old life in this sinful world is over; it no longer has a claim upon us. We are, as stated, raised to a *newness of life*.
- that we are walking in newness of life, living a life that is dead to sin, but alive to God—alive to righteousness and holiness.

> **"But if the Spirit of him that raised up Jesus from the dead dwell in you, he that raised up Christ from the dead shall also quicken your mortal bodies by his Spirit that dwelleth in you" (Ro.8:11).**

ILLUSTRATION:
What does it mean to be risen with Christ? It means to be alive! Author and pastor Warren Wiersbe shares a graphic story from World War II.

> *"It is possible to be alive and still live in the grave. During World War II, several Jewish refugees hid in a cemetery, and a baby was actually born in one of the graves. However, when Jesus gave us His life, He lifted us out of the grave and set us on the throne in heaven! Christ is seated at the right hand of God, and we are seated there 'in Christ.'"*[1]

Because of Christ, up from the grave _we_ arose!

QUESTIONS:
1. Practically, what does it mean to be in union with Christ?
2. What advantage does the Christian believer have over the non-Christian, according to this verse?
3. Do you have a responsibility to share this advantage with the lost? What are some things you can do?

2. THE BELIEVER'S NEW LIFE IS A LIFE THAT SEEKS THE THINGS ABOVE—IN HEAVEN—WHERE CHRIST IS (v.1-4).

Note three significant points.

1. Note the meaning of the charge: "...seek those things which are above." The meaning is clearly and pointedly explained in two statements:

⇒ First, seek those things above, where Christ sits on the right hand of God. That is, seek heavenly things, the things of heaven.

⇒ Second, set your "affection," your mind on things above and not on things on the earth. The word "affection" means mind; to set and focus your mind constantly upon heavenly things, not upon earthly things.

Very simply, the things of Christ and of heaven are to consume the believer's life and mind. But for the believer to keep his mind upon the things of Christ, he must know what those things are. Therefore, the question naturally arises: What are the things of Christ and the things of heaven which are to consume our thoughts?

> **"For they that are after the flesh do mind the things of the flesh; but they that are after the Spirit the things of the Spirit. For to be carnally minded is death; but to be spiritually minded is life and peace" (Ro.8:5-6).**

The resurrection of Christ tells us what the things of Christ and of heaven are. It is His resurrection that allows us to be *"risen with Christ."* Remember: we actually take part and participate in the resurrection of Christ. This is a *positional relationship* to God. As stated in the former note, when we accept Christ, God places us in Christ positionally. He begins to see us *in Christ, already seated in the heavenlies and perfected forever* (cp. Eph.2:4-7). It is because of this glorious position which God has given us that we should seek the things of Christ and of heaven. The resurrection of the Lord Jesus Christ has done at least seven wonderful things for us. These seven things should consume not only our thoughts and minds but also the praise and prayers of our lips.

a. The resurrection of Christ shows and guarantees that Christ is the Son of God. Our thoughts should focus upon this glorious fact: that God has sent His Son into the world to save us.

> **"Concerning his Son Jesus Christ our Lord, which was made of the seed of David according to the flesh; and declared to be the Son of God with power, according to the spirit of holiness, by the resurrection from the dead" (Ro.1:3-4).**

Jesus Christ claimed that He was the Son of God, that He possessed God's very own nature, that He was One with the Father (Jn.10:30-33, 36). He claimed time and again that God was His Father. When God raised Jesus Christ from the dead, He set His seal to Christ's claim. And by the resurrection, God declares that Christ is His own dear Son.

b. The resurrection of Christ saves and justifies us. The glorious truth of salvation and justification should consume our thoughts and praise all through the day.

> **"[Christ] who was delivered for our offenses, and was raised again for our justification" (Ro.4:25).**

QUESTIONS:
1. What does justify mean?
2. Do we deserve justice?
3. Can we earn justification or salvation?
4. How do we obtain justification?

c. The resurrection of Christ gives us or raises us up to a new life—a life that is abundant and eternal. It is the only way we can keep from walking after the flesh.

> "Therefore we are buried with him by baptism into death: that like as Christ was raised up from the dead by the glory of the Father, even so we also should walk in newness of life" (Ro.6:4).
>
> "For though we walk in the flesh, we do not war after the flesh: (For the weapons of our warfare are not carnal, but mighty through God to the pulling down of strong holds;) casting down imaginations, and every high thing that exalteth itself against the knowledge of God, and bringing into captivity every thought to the obedience of Christ" (2 Cor.10:3-5).

QUESTIONS:
1. Do you have the power on your own to fight the flesh and its temptations?
2. What was your life like before you became a believer?
3. Has there been a change for the better?
4. What brought the change about?

d. The resurrection of Christ gives us power to live victoriously over the sins and trials of this world and to bear the fruit of God's Spirit as we walk throughout this world.

> "Wherefore, my brethren, ye also are become dead to the law by the body of Christ; that ye should be married to another, even to him [Christ] who is raised from the dead, that we should bring forth fruit unto God" (Ro.7:4).
>
> "But if the Spirit of him that raised up Jesus from the dead dwell in you, he that raised up Christ from the dead shall also quicken your mortal bodies by his Spirit that dwelleth in you. Therefore, brethren, we are debtors, not to the flesh, to live after the flesh. For if ye live after the flesh, ye shall die: but if ye through the Spirit do mortify the deeds of the body, ye shall live " (Ro.8:11-13).

Imagine living a life of power, bearing the fruit of God's Spirit as we walk day by day—conquering the sins and walking through the trials of life victoriously. It is through our union with Christ that we *receive the power* [energy] to triumphantly walk day by day (cp. Jn.15:1-5 for an excellent description of our union with Christ).

e. The resurrection gives us a living hope, the hope of glory. Our minds and praise should focus upon the glory of heaven which shall be ours when either God takes us home or Christ returns.

> "Blessed be the God and Father of our Lord Jesus Christ, which according to his abundant mercy hath begotten us again unto a lively hope by the resurrection of Jesus Christ from the dead, to an inheritance incorruptible, and undefiled, and that fadeth not away, reserved in heaven for you" (1 Pt.1:3-4).

f. The resurrection guarantees our resurrection (cp. 1 Cor.15:12-58). Our thoughts and praise should center upon the wonderful praise of the new and glorious body God has promised us.

> "For if we have been planted together in the likeness of his death, we shall be also in the likeness of his resurrection" (Ro.6:5).

1. If Christ had not risen from the dead, how could you have assurance of being raised?
2. Would God give abundant and eternal life to you, a sinner, if He had not done it for His own Son?

g. The resurrection assures that God will judge the world by Christ. Our minds and prayers should be focused upon evangelism and the terrible fact that judgment is coming. Every person will have to give an account to Christ, and all those who have rejected Him will be eternally separated from God.

> **"Because he hath appointed a day, in the which he will judge the world in righteousness by that man whom he hath ordained; whereof he hath given assurance unto all men, in that he hath raised him from the dead"** (Acts 17:31).

Christ claimed that God had committed all judgment to Him: that He is the One whom God has appointed to judge the world. God stamped His approval to what Christ said by *raising Him* from the dead. Christ Himself shall judge the world. Judgment is coming: the resurrection of Christ proves it.

QUESTIONS:
1. Do the things of Christ and of heaven consume your life and mind? How is something like this measured?
2. Why is the resurrection of Christ such an important belief for you?
3. Considering the fact that all men will be judged by Christ, what should be your focus while you are here on earth?

2. Note the two reasons why we are to seek the things of Christ and of heaven: because we are dead, and our lives are *hid with Christ* in God.
a. The believer is dead. He is not actually dead; he still lives upon earth. But God *counts the believer dead* in the death of Christ. When Christ died, the believer died--right along with Christ *in God's mind*. God counts it so, and whatever God counts so is a fact. Therefore, the believer is actually dead in God's mind. This means a significant fact: a dead man cannot sin, for a dead man no longer lives for this earth. He lives for the next world.

b. The believer is *hid with Christ*. What does this mean? It means that God counts the believer *hid* in the resurrection and life of Christ. When Christ arose, He arose to a new life not to His *old life*. He had just died to the old life once for all. Therefore, when the believer is said to be *hid* in Christ, it means that God counts the believer risen with Christ. God counts the believer as risen to a new life. God sees the believer *hid* in Christ day by day. God sees him walking *in* Christ and in Christ's righteousness. And because he is in Christ, the believer sets his mind upon things above, upon the things of Christ and of heaven. He sets his mind and life upon things that please Christ.

ILLUSTRATION:
An excellent illustration of what it means to be *"hid with Christ"* is this: take the index finger of your right hand and wrap your left hand around it. Say that the index finger represents you and the left hand represents Christ. Where are you (the index finger)? *In Christ.* You are hid in Christ. When God looks at you, He sees you *hid in Christ!*

APPLICATION:

When you are hid in Christ...

- Christ is the only life that God sees as living. Christ is your life in the eyes of God, the life in which you live.
- you live, move, and have your being in the life of Christ. You are hid in His life. Christ is the only life, the only body, that is seen by God and that is to be seen by the world.

Just think how surrendered and given over to Christ we are to be—so given over that Christ's life is all that is seen. How is this possible?

⟹ By seeking those things which are above, where Christ sits.

⟹ By setting our minds on things above, not on things on earth. By working to cast down imaginations and every high thing that exalts itself against the knowledge of God, even to the point of captivating every thought for Christ.

In practical day-to-day living, turn the television off; set aside the magazines and books. Get into the Word of God; meditate and pray through the Word, and memorize and live out the Word. In addition, get alone and pray—at least every morning and evening—and learn to silently whisper a prayer every few minutes. Surrender your life totally to Christ; present your body as a *living* sacrifice to God: to know, to believe, to understand Him and to make Him known. You are His witness—do it!

"Ye are my witnesses, saith the LORD, and my servant whom I have chosen: that ye may know and believe me, and understand that I am he: before me there was no God formed, neither shall there be after me" (Is.43:10).

There is no way to know Him apart from setting our minds upon Him. Therefore, let us do it and do it now by getting to our secret places of prayer and seeking His face with a renewed commitment.

⟹ Our lives are hid with Christ.

⟹ We live, yet not us, but Christ lives in us (Gal.2:20).

⟹ We are always delivered unto death for Jesus' sake that the life of Jesus might be made manifest in our flesh (2 Cor.5:15).

⟹ For us to live is Christ, and to die is gain (Ph.1:21).

⟹ We know this: we have passed from death unto life—therefore, let us live for Christ (1 Jn.3:14).

3.   Note the reward for being hid in Christ and for seeking the things of Christ and of heaven: the reward is that of appearing with Christ in glory. Think for a moment: God sees us *hid with Christ*; therefore, we are risen with Christ. This means that being risen from the dead, we never have to die. Christ already lives in the presence of God. Since God sees us *hid with Christ*, God sees us in His presence. He has already accepted us as being in His presence forever and ever—all because we are there *"hid with Christ."*

Now, in practical terms we are still on earth. God has left us here to be witnesses for Him. But when He is ready to take us home to heaven, what happens is this: when we confront death—in the last second, in the last moment, right before we are to leave this world for the next—God shall fix our minds upon Jesus and immediately transport us into His heavenly kingdom. God will give us a *fixation of mind,* and we will never taste or experience spiritual or eternal death (cp. Jn.8:51-52; Heb.2:9).

Note that the verse has to do with the return of Christ. When Christ returns, we shall appear or return with Him *in glory*. There is to be a new heavens and earth where Christ is to reign forever and ever, and we are to reign in glory with Him.

"Then shall the righteous shine forth as the sun in the kingdom of their Father. Who hath ears to hear, let him hear" (Mt.13:43).

"For our light affliction, which is but for a moment, worketh for us a far more exceeding and eternal weight of glory" (2 Cor.4:17).

ILLUSTRATION:

Are you bilingual (the ability to speak more than one language)? Have you ever thought about what language is spoken in heaven? Will you know how to communicate when you get there? This illustration was taken from an unnamed tract.

> *"There...is a man who tells you he intends to be in Heaven some day; but he has no wish whatever to talk on Heavenly subjects. He enjoys the world and the things of the world. His heart is set upon earthly things. Yet he tells you he has a hope of Heaven. Vain, delusive hope! They that are on their way to Heaven are cultivating an experimental acquaintance with the language and ways of a Heavenly people. Let me ask, is this the case with you?"*[2]

QUESTIONS:

1. Are you expecting to go to heaven to enjoy all the benefits of a true believer without living the life of a true believer here on earth?
2. A worldly affection focuses upon the things of this earth. What kinds of things would be included in a worldly affection?
3. What areas of your life need to be changed in order to show that your true affection is set upon Christ?
4. What "things" is Christ referring to in verses 1 and 2? What will help you to keep looking up?
5. What does this verse teach you about God's provision for you? What is your obligation to God?

SUMMARY:

The Christian believer experiences a great sense of freedom when he understands one basic truth: life is to be lived on the basis of all that God has done through Christ—not on what we have done. In response to this great provision, our thankful hearts should compel us to serve Him with all that we are and have.

The major points show you that:

1. The believer's new life is a life that is risen with Christ, not in the grave.
2. The believer's new life is a life that seeks the things above—in heaven, where Christ is, not on earth where man is.

COLOSSIANS 3:1-4

1.   The most important thing that I learned from this lesson was:

2.   The area that I need to work on the most is:

3.   I can apply this lesson to my life by:

4.   Closing Statement of Commitment:

---

[1] Warren W. Wiersbe, *The Bible Exposition Commentary, Vol.2*, p.133.
[2] Walter B. Knight. *3,000 Illustrations for Christian Service*, p.338.

	B. The Violent Demands of the New Life, 3:5-11	off all these; anger, wrath, malice, blasphemy, filthy communication out of your mouth.	**is violent: Strip off the sins that enslave the emotions & tongue**
1. The first demand is violent: Put to death all sins that enslave the body & its members	5 Mortify therefore your members which are upon the earth; fornication, uncleanness, inordinate affection, evil concupiscence, and cov-	8 Lie not one to another, seeing that ye have put off the old man with his deeds;	a. The sins listed b. The reasons
a. The sins listed	etousness, which is idolatry:	9 And have put on the new man, which is renewed in knowledge after the image of him	1) We have put off the old man 2) We have put on the new man
b. The reasons 1) Such sins bring down the wrath of God upon man 2) Such sins belong to the old life	6 For which things' sake the wrath of God cometh on the children of disobedience: 7 In the which ye also walked some time, when ye lived in them.	that created him: 10 Where there is neither Greek nor circumcision nor uncircumcision, Barbarian, Scythian, bond nor free: but Christ is all,	3) We are all *one body* in Christ
2. The second demand	8 But now ye also put	and in all.	

Section V
THE DEMANDS OF THE BELIEVER'S NEW LIFE: GREAT CHARACTER
Colossians 3:1-17

Study 2:   THE VIOLENT DEMANDS OF THE NEW LIFE

Text: Colossians 3:5-11

Aim: To free yourself from the grip of sin.

Memory Verse:

"**Mortify therefore your members which are upon the earth; fornication, uncleanness, inordinate affection, evil concupiscence, and covetousness, which is idolatry" (Colossians 3:5).**

INTRODUCTION:
The good things in life seldom come easy. Unfortunately, many of us settle for a life of spiritual mediocrity—failing to break free from sin's deadly grip. Many believers have become comfortable with sin; they are at peace with sin in their lives. But this is the peace of accommodation and compromise. And accommodation and compromise open the floodgates for the enemy's aggression.

Living the Christian life is difficult, but the difficulty intensifies when we give in to our old sinful nature. Our old nature—the sinful nature—must be put to death, violently! This is not a task for the spiritually squeamish as Jesus reminds us:

"**And he said to them all, if any man will come after me, let him deny himself, and take up his cross daily, and follow me" (Lk.9:23).**

This is a violent passage of Scripture, a passage that attacks many persons right where they live. But it is a passage that is desperately needed by us all. It covers the violent demands of the believer's new life in Christ.

OUTLINE:
1. The first demand is violent: put to death all sins that enslave the body and its members (v.5-7).
2. The second demand is violent: strip off the sins that enslave the emotions and tongue (v.8-11).

1. THE FIRST DEMAND IS VIOLENT: PUT TO DEATH ALL SINS THAT ENSLAVE THE BODY AND ITS MEMBERS (v.5-7).

The word "mortify" means to put to death or to act as though the body is dead. The believer is to take the various parts of his body and put them to death in so far as sin is concerned. How does a believer do this? He considers his body to be *hid in the death of Christ*. He acts as though his body is dead with Christ. And remember: a dead man cannot sin; a dead man can do nothing. Therefore, the believer is dead to sin.

The point is this: it is all an act of the mind or spirit. If a person wants to live for God, he looks at his body and at sin. The person has to live as though his body has no part in sin, and sin has no part in his body. But note: this life is possible only in Christ. Christ alone—through the Holy Spirit—can work within the human heart to give it the energy and power to conquer sin *permanently and eternally*. Some men can discipline themselves to overcome some sin, but not *all sin, not permanently and not eternally*. This can be done only through Christ. There is an enormous difference between human discipline and godly control, and that difference is Jesus Christ.

What sins are to be mortified or put to death? The Bible is very specific, for there are some very specific sins which tend to enslave the human body. In fact, note the term "children of disobedience" (v.6). These particular sins are not only terrible *acts of disobedience* to God, they are sins that can enslave the human body so much that they make a *child of disobedience* out of a person. They cause a person to actually become a *child of disobedience*. Shocking!

1. What are the sins that enslave the human body so much?
   a. There is the sin of *fornication*. *Fornication* is a broad word including all forms of immoral and sexual acts. It is pre-marital sex and adultery; it is abnormal sex, all kinds of sexual vice.

   > **"Flee fornication. Every sin that man doeth is without the body; but he that committeth fornication sinneth against his own body" (1 Cor.6:18).**

   b. There is the sin of *uncleanness*. *Uncleanness* means moral impurity; doing things that dirty, pollute, and soil life.

   > **"But I say unto you, That whosoever looketh on a woman to lust after her hath committed adultery with her already in his heart" (Mt.5:28).**

   c. There is the sin of *inordinate affection*: passion, craving, strong desire, intense arousal, a driving lust. It is, of course, a desire and craving for the wrong things such as the second and third helping of food, alcohol, drugs, nudity, pornography, suggestive and filthy literature, illicit affairs, extra-marital sex, etc.

   > **"For this cause God gave them up unto vile affections: for even their women did change the natural use into that which is against nature: and likewise also the men, leaving the natural use of the woman, burned in their lust one toward another; men with men working that which is unseemly, and receiving in themselves that recompence of their error which was meet" (Ro.1:26-27).**

d. There is *evil concupiscence*: evil desire, a yearning and an aching for all kinds of evil. It is that within a person that pulls him to desire, grasp, grab, and take hold of all forms of evil that give pleasure to the body and its members. It is that which drives a man to keep on...

- looking
- feeling
- touching
- listening
- smelling
- seeking

> "But every man is tempted, when he is drawn away of his own lust, and enticed. Then when lust hath conceived, it bringeth forth sin: and sin, when it is finished, bringeth forth death" (Jas.1:14-15).

e. There is *covetousness*: craving, grasping, grabbing, desiring to have something. It is desiring to have something when it is not needed; it is desiring more than what we should have. Note that covetousness is idolatry. If a person looks at something so much that he covets it, he has set it up as a god which he pursues with the energy and effort of his mind and body.

> "Thou shalt not covet thy neighbour's house, thou shalt not covet thy neighbour's wife, nor his manservant, nor his maidservant, nor his ox, nor his ass, nor any thing that is thy neighbour's" (Ex.20:17).

QUESTIONS:
1. What are some of the things people set up as gods in society?
2. Do believers sometimes get caught up in the materialistic world, desiring more than they need and more than they should have? What causes a person to covet something someone else has? How can we learn to turn to God for our needs instead of materialistic possessions?

2. There are two strong reasons for putting to death the sins that enslave the body.
a. It is such sins that shall bring down the wrath of God upon man. The word "wrath" means anger, but it is not the outburst of anger that quickly blazes up, not the anger that arises solely from emotion. Rather, it is a decisive and a deliberate anger. It is an anger that comes from a thoughtful decision, an anger that comes from the mind because someone has done something evil and hurtful. It is an anger that judges and condemns sin and evil, violence and slaughter, immorality and injustice. It is an anger that hates sin and evil and that metes out a just revenge and equal punishment.

> "But when he saw many of the Pharisees and Sadducees come to his baptism, he said unto them, O generation of vipers, who hath warned you to flee from the wrath to come?" (Mt.3:7).
> "For the wrath of God is revealed from heaven against all ungodliness and unrighteousness of men, who hold the truth in unrighteousness" (Ro.1:18).

b. It is such sins that were common to our old life. We used to walk and live in such sins, but not now. What is the difference? Christ. We are *hid in Christ*. He has saved us from the sins that bring down the wrath of God upon us. To turn back and to begin walking in those sins again would be to deny Christ. And this we must not do...

- lest we break the heart of God by abusing the death of His dear Son.
- lest we bring down the wrath of God upon us.

"And you hath he quickened, who were dead in trespasses and sins; wherein in time past ye walked according to the course of this world, according to the prince of the power of the air, the spirit that now worketh in the children of disobedience" (Eph.2:1-2).

ILLUSTRATION:

Surely, Paul must be addressing non-believers! What kind of believer would practice these kinds of sins? The answer: not a very good believer! Warren Wiersbe adds his insight:

"Do believers in local churches commit such sins? Unfortunately, they sometimes do. Each of the New Testament epistles sent to local churches makes mention of these sins and warns against them.
"I am reminded of a pastor who preached a series of sermons against the sins of the saints. A member of his congregation challenged him one day and said that it would be better if the pastor preached those messages to the lost. 'After all,' said the church member, 'sin in the life of a Christian is different from sin in the lives of other people.'
"'Yes' replied the pastor, 'it's worse!'"[1]

Wow! That really hits where it hurts! But, tragically, how true. Sins in the life of a believer are worse than sins in the life of a non-believer. Why? Because as believers we know the truth, and we know the power of God to help us overcome sin. A non-believer has neither the knowledge of God nor access to the power of God!

QUESTIONS:
1. In what practical ways are you to mortify or put to death the members of your body?
2. Why does God require you to mortify or put to death the members of your earthly body? Why do we sometimes have so much trouble putting our members to death?
3. What can be expected of a person who refuses to put to death those sins listed in verse five?

2. THE SECOND DEMAND IS VIOLENT: STRIP OFF THE SINS THAT ENSLAVE THE EMOTIONS & TONGUE (v.8-11).

The picture is that of putting off or stripping off clothes.
1.   There are six sins that are to be stripped off. Note: all six have to do with either deep-seated emotions or else the tongue—reactions and feelings against another person.
   a.   There is the sin of *anger*. The believer is to strip away the garment of anger. Men do become angry: note that Scripture recognizes this. There are times when anger is called for, but we are to guard against sinning when we become angry. Anger causes us to either react, lash out and hurt others, or else it motivates us to right wrongs and correct injustices.
      1)   There is wrong anger or what may be called unjustified or selfish anger.
         a)   There is the anger that broods, that is selfish. It harbors malice; it will not forget; it lingers; it wishes revenge and sometimes seeks revenge.
         b)   There is the anger that holds contempt. It despises; it ridicules; it arrogantly exalts self and calls another person empty and useless. This is an anger that is full of malice. It despises and scorns. It arises from pride—a proud wrath (Pr.21:24). Such feelings or anger walk over and trample a person. They say that whatever ill comes upon a person is deserved.

    c)   There is the anger that curses. It seeks to destroy a man and his reputation morally, intellectually, and spiritually.

2)   There is right anger or what may be called justified anger. The believer must be an angry person—angry with those who sin and do wrong and who are unjust and selfish in their behavior. However, a justified anger is always disciplined and controlled; it is always limited to those who do wrong either against God or against others. The distinguishing mark between justified and unjustified anger is that a justified anger is never selfish; it is never shown because of what has happened to oneself. It is an anger that is purposeful. The believer knows that he is angry for a legitimate reason, and he seeks to correct the situation in the most peaceful way possible.

> **"Be ye angry, and sin not: let not the sun go down upon your wrath" (Eph.4:26).**

b.   There is the sin of *wrath*. *Wrath* is bursts of anger; indignation; a violent, explosive temper; quick-tempered explosive reactions that arise from stirred and boiling emotions. But it is anger which fades away just as quickly as it arose. It is not anger that lasts.

> **"Wherefore, my beloved brethren, let every man be swift to hear, slow to speak, slow to wrath: for the wrath of man worketh not the righteousness of God" (Jas.1:19-20).**

c.   There is the sin of *malice*: deep-seated feelings against a person, hatred that lasts on and on, intense and long-lasting bitterness against a person.

> **"Therefore let us keep the feast [the Lord's Supper], not with old leaven, neither with the leaven of malice and wickedness; but with the unleavened bread of sincerity and truth" (1 Cor.5:8).**

d.   There is the sin of *blasphemy*: speech that slanders, insults, hurts, injures, and shows contempt. It is railing at someone.

> **"But when the Jews saw the multitudes, they were filled with envy, and spake against those things which were spoken by Paul, contradicting and blaspheming" (Acts 13:45).**

e.   There is the sin of *filthy communication*. If a believer is to follow and imitate God, he has to be pure in speech and conversation; he has to keep his mouth or tongue clean. He cannot let his mouth become foul and polluted, filthy and vile.

f.   There is the sin of *lying*. Scripture gives one strong reason for believers to speak only the truth: they are members of one another. Every believer is a member of the great body of people which God is building, the body of Christ, that is, the church.

2.   There are three strong reasons why we are to strip off the sins of the emotions and tongue.

a.   We have put off the *old man*. The "old man" refers to what a man is *before he accepts Christ*. It is the very *nature of man*, the *natural*, corruptible seed which is passed on from generation to generation and leads to death. It is what is called the nature of Adam.

b.   We have put on the *new man*. A man *regenerated, renewed, born again* who has become spiritually minded. It is a *new man* created by Christ; he has been given a holy nature and an incorruptible life. It is opposed to the *old man* with a corrupt nature. It is a man who is...

- in fellowship with God.
- obedient to God's will.
- devoted to God's service.

c. We are all *one body* in Christ (v.11). Christ has made it possible for us to be adopted as children, sons and daughters, of God. We are all—everyone of us—children of God. We belong to the same family—the family of God. Therefore, there is no place for reacting against each other, no place for...

- anger
- wrath
- malice

- blasphemous, insulting, hurting talk
- filthy talk
- lying

Note how Scripture covers everything that could possibly cause feelings and divisions between us:

⇒ race and birth (Greek nor Jew)
⇒ religion and ritual (circumcision nor uncircumcision)
⇒ education and culture (Barbarian nor Scythian)
⇒ social class and wealth and property (bond and free)

> **"So we, being many, are one body in Christ, and every one members one of another" (Ro.12:5).**

ILLUSTRATION:

Have you heard the saying, "Sticks and stones may break my bones, but words will never hurt me"? That, of course, is a lie! The tongue has poisoned plenty of people that we know. Listen carefully to this story:

> *"One day a dog stole a Quaker's roast. Said the Quaker to the dog, 'I will not whip thee, or stone thee, but I will give thee a bad name!' As the dog ran away, the Quaker shouted, 'Bad dog! Bad dog! Bad dog!' Soon a group of people were chasing the dog and shouting, 'Mad dog! Mad dog! Mad dog!' A blast from a shotgun ended the dog's life.*
>
> *"How easily our words are twisted, sometimes to our embarrassment, but more often to the injury or even death of others!*
>
> *"If you would keep your lips from slips,*
> *Five things observe with care:*
> *To whom you speak, of whom you speak,*
> *And how and when and where."*[2]

QUESTIONS:

1. How can you guard your tongue from sinning against others?
2. What is the relationship between your tongue and sin? Why is it important to carefully measure your words?
3. Has anyone ever said things about you that hurt? How did you respond? Would you do anything differently today?
4. Have you ever said something that hurt someone else? What happened because of it? How could you have handled the situation differently?

SUMMARY:

Are you prepared for the fight of your life, the fight against sin? In your own strength, you'll be powerless, but the power of God is at your disposal as you put to death the power of sin in your life. God demands two violent things of you:

1. Put to death all sins that enslave the body and its members.
2. Strip off the sins that enslave the emotions and tongue.

COLOSSIANS 3:5-11

PERSONAL JOURNAL NOTES
(Reflection & Response)

1. The most important thing that I learned from this lesson was:

2. The area that I need to work on the most is:

3. I can apply this lesson to my life by:

4. Closing Statement of Commitment:

---

[1] Warren W. Wiersbe. *The Bible Exposition Commentary, Vol.2*, p.135.
[2] Walter B. Knight. *Knight's Treasury of 2,000 Illustrations*, p.413.

	C. The Clothing of the New Life, 3:12-14	13 Forbearing one another, and forgiving one another, if any man have a quarrel against any: even as Christ forgave you, so also do ye.	of humility, v.12
1. Believers, the elect of God, are holy & beloved	12 Put on therefore, as the elect of God, holy and beloved, bowels of mercies, kindness, humbleness of mind, meekness, longsuffering;		5. Put on the garment of meekness, v.12
2. Put on the garment of mercy			6. Put on the garment of patience
3. Put on the garment of kindness			7. Put on the garment of forbearance
4. Put on the garment		14 And above all these things put on charity, which is the bond of perfectness.	8. Put on the garment of forgiveness, v.13
			9. Put on the garment of love

Section V
THE DEMANDS OF THE BELIEVER'S NEW LIFE: GREAT CHARACTER
Colossians 3:1-17

Study 3:   THE CLOTHING OF THE NEW LIFE

Text: Colossians 3:12-14

Aim: To select the correct clothing for your new life.

Memory Verse:
> "And above all these things put on charity [love], which is the perfect bond of unity" (Colossians 3:14).

INTRODUCTION:
How would you respond if someone gave you a gift certificate for eight garments from your favorite clothing store and told you to select anything you wanted? As you enter the store, you gaze upon the racks of the latest fashions. "That would be nice...I would look great in that suit...Everybody will notice this outfit...Wow!"

With an entire inventory to choose from, how would you narrow your focus to eight items? What would govern your decision? Would you:
⇒ Be modest?
⇒ Look for quality?
⇒ Select gaudy styles?
⇒ Settle for poorly-made clothes?
⇒ Choose clothes that cause others to lust?

Life is full of opportunities to make decisions. Some are wise...some are not. Be careful as you choose your wardrobe. It must enhance your new life. Is the task too difficult for you to do alone? No need to worry—God has helped you by marking His choices for you to select and wear.

As seen in the former passage, the believer is to strip off the clothing of his old life, for the garments of his old life are unbecoming to his new life. Now, there are some garments that the believer is to put on, some garments that are becoming to his new life in Christ.

OUTLINE:
1.   Believers, the elect of God, are holy and beloved (v.12).
2.   Put on the garment of mercy (v.12).
3.   Put on the garment of kindness (v.12).
4.   Put on the garment of humility (v.12).
5.   Put on the garment of meekness (v.12).
6.   Put on the garment of patience (v.12).
7.   Put on the garment of forbearance (v.13).
8.   Put on the garment of forgiveness (v.13).
9.   Put on the garment of love (v.14).

1. BELIEVERS, THE ELECT OF GOD, ARE HOLY AND BELOVED (v.12-14).

⇒ Believers have been elected to be *holy*. The word "holy" means separated or set apart. God called believers out of the world and away from the old life it offered, the old life of sin and death. He called believers to be separated and set apart unto Himself and the new life He offers, the new life of righteousness and eternity.

⇒ Believers have been elected to be the *beloved* of God. God has called believers to turn away from the old life that showed hatred toward God, the old life that rejected, rebelled, ignored, denied, and constantly cursed in the face of God. God has called believers to be the beloved of God, the persons who receive His love in Christ Jesus and who allow Him to shower His love upon them.

The point is this: the elect of God, holy and beloved, are those who have really believed and trusted Jesus Christ as their Savior. It is these persons, the believers, who now have a *new life* in Christ. Therefore, this passage is for the believer. Note one other thing: the command "put on" is the picture of putting on clothing; the believer is to *clothe the new man*. The new man must not be left naked; he must be clothed. What are the garments to be put on? There are eight garments of clothing for the new man.

QUESTIONS:
1. What difference does it make in your life knowing that God has called you? What is the source of your assurance?
2. According to verses 12-14, what is your role in carrying out your new life? Is it easy doing all that these verses require you to do? What can you do to improve in this area?

2. THE GARMENT OF MERCY (v.12).

Mercy means compassion, pity, tender-heartedness. God has had so much mercy upon us; the one thing we should do is to show mercy to others. Compassion and pity should flood our hearts for the...

• lost	• hurting	• homeless	• empty
• wayward	• diseased	• hungry	• unclothed
• lonely	• poor	• aged	• aged

Of course, the list could go on and on. The point is that the believer no longer has the right to overlook the needy of the world. He is now a new man; a part of the clothing of the new man is the garment of mercy. The believer is to be clothed with mercy. He is to have compassion and reach out to meet the needs of the world—reach out with all he is and has, holding back nothing so long as a single need exists.

> **"Remember them that are in bonds, as bound with them; and them which suffer adversity, as being yourselves also in the body" (Heb.13:3).**

ILLUSTRATION:
Sometimes we can get so close to the forest that we fail to see the trees around us. Many times we pray for those around us, asking God to meet their needs. Perhaps we are that answer!

> *"A lady answered the knock on her door to find a man with a sad expression.*
> *"'I'm sorry to disturb you,' he said, 'but I'm collecting money for an unfortunate family in the neighborhood. The husband is out of work, the kids are hungry, the utilities will soon be cut off, and worse, they're going to be kicked out of their apartment if they don't pay the rent by this afternoon.'*
> *"'I'll be happy to help,' said the woman with great concern. 'But who are you?'*
> *"'I'm the landlord,' he replied"[1]*

In today's hectic, fast-paced society, we often get so wrapped up in our own lives that we fail to see the small ways in which we can help each other.

1. On a scale of 1 (I really don't care) to 5 (What can I do to help), rate yourself in the following situations. Do I care about and help...
   ...the poor in my community?
   ...the homeless who live downtown?
   ...single-parent households in my church?
   ...the elderly members of my church who are home-bound?
   ...the person who has hurt me and now I've got a chance to help him or her?
2. From the list above, what requires your immediate attention? What can you do in order to improve the quality of mercy in your own life?

3. THE GARMENT OF KINDNESS (v.12).

Being kind means being good, useful, helpful, gentle, sweet, considerate, and gracious through all situations no matter the circumstances. A person who is gentle does not act...
- hard
- indifferent
- harsh
- unconcerned
- too busy
- bitter

Gentleness cares for the feelings of others and feels with them. It experiences the full depth of sympathy and empathy. It shows care and gets right into the situation with a person. Gentleness suffers with those who suffer, struggles with those who struggle, and works with those who work.

⇒ God is kind.

> **"But love ye your enemies, and do good, and lend, hoping for nothing again; and your reward shall be great, and ye shall be the children of the Highest: for he is kind unto the unthankful and to the evil" (Lk.6:35).**

⇒ Believers are to be kind to one another.

> **"Be kindly affectioned one to another with brotherly love; in honour preferring one another" (Ro.12:10).**

1. Who is the kindest person you know? What qualities does this person have that you need to learn or practice?
2. When is it easiest for you to be kind to others? Why? When is it most difficult? Why?

4. THE GARMENT OF HUMILITY (v.12).

The garment of humility offers oneself as lowly and submissive; to walk in a spirit of lowliness; *to present* oneself as lowly and low-lying in mind; to be of low degree and low rank; not to be high-minded, proud, haughty, arrogant, or assertive.

Note: a humble person may have a high position, power, wealth, fame, and much more; but he carries himself in a spirit of lowliness and submission. He denies himself for the sake of Christ and in order to help others.

Men have always looked upon humility as a vice. A lowly man is often looked upon as a coward, a cringing, despicable, slavish type of person. Men fear humility. They feel humility is a sign of weakness and will make them the object of contempt and abuse, causing them to be shunned and overlooked.

Because of all this, men ignore and shun the teaching of Christ on humility. This is tragic.

COLOSSIANS 3:12-14

ILLUSTRATION:

The garment of humility is often overlooked in today's culture. We have been told that "the biggest is the best." "You are the show, so show off." And so, we find ourselves wearing pride instead of humility.

> Howard was a most talented church-choir leader. His life was filled with humble service to the Lord and to His church. He was truly a "glory-deflector"—one who was careful to always give God the glory.
>
> One afternoon before the Christmas cantata, a choir member approached Howard and said, *"Tonight, all of the men are going to wear colorful bow-ties to celebrate the season. Do you want to wear one also?"*
>
> In a very loving, but blunt response Howard said, *"I really do not want to do anything that would distract others from clearly hearing our message of the gospel."*

Is your humility helping others to clearly hear the gospel?

QUESTIONS:
1. Are you as humble as you can be? In what ways can you learn to be more and more humble?
2. Do you know anybody like Howard? How do you think people like Howard cultivate their humility? Are they just born that way?

5. THE GARMENT OF MEEKNESS (v.12).

Meekness means to be gentle, tender, humble, mild, considerate—but strongly so. Meekness has the strength to control and discipline, and it does so at the right time.

1. Meekness has *a humble state of mind*. But this does not mean the person is weak, cowardly, and bowing. The meek person simply loves people and loves peace; therefore, he walks humbly among men regardless of their status and circumstance in life. Associating with the poor and lowly of this earth does not bother the meek person. He desires to be a friend to all and to help all as much as possible.

2. Meekness has *a strong state of mind*. It looks at situations and wants justice and right to be done. It is not a weak mind that ignores and neglects evil, wrong-doing, abuse, and suffering.
   ⇒ If someone is suffering, meekness steps in to do what it can to help.
   ⇒ If evil is being done, meekness does what it can to stop and correct it.
   ⇒ If evil is running rampant and indulging itself, meekness actually strikes out in anger. However, note a crucial point: the anger is always at the right time and against the right thing.

3. Meekness has *strong self-control*. The meek person controls his spirit and mind. He controls the lusts of his flesh. He does not give way to ill-temper, retaliation, passion, indulgence, or license. The meek person dies to himself, to what his flesh would like to do, and he does the right thing—exactly what God wants done.

In summary, the meek man walks in a humble, tender, but strong state of mind; he denies himself, giving utmost consideration to others. He shows a control and righteous anger against injustice and evil. A meek man forgets self and lives for others because of what Christ has done for him.

QUESTIONS:
1. What specific things makes a person meek?
2. Why do some people tend to think that meekness is weakness, simply a lack of a strong backbone?
3. Do you know someone who is truly meek? Do you admire that quality in the person? What can you do to become more meek?

6. THE GARMENT OF PATIENCE (v.12).

The qualities of this garment are patience, bearing and suffering a long time, perseverance, being constant, stedfast, and enduring. Long-suffering never gives in; it is never broken, no matter what attacks it.

⇒ Pressure and hard work may fall upon us, but the Spirit of God helps us suffer long under it all.

⇒ Disease, accident, or old age may afflict us; but the Spirit of God helps us to suffer long under it.

⇒ Discouragement and disappointment may attack us, but the Spirit of God helps us to suffer long under it.

⇒ Men may wrong, abuse, slander, and injure us; but the Spirit of God helps us to suffer long under it all.

Two significant things need to be noted about long-suffering.

1. Long-suffering never strikes back. Common sense tells us that a person who is attacked by others could strike back and retaliate. But the Christian believer is given the power of long-suffering—the power to suffer the situation or person for a long, long time.

2. Long-suffering is one of the great traits of God. As pointed out in this verse, it is a fruit of God's very own Spirit, a fruit that is to be in the life of the believer.

⇒ God and Christ are long-suffering toward sinners.

> "Or despisest thou the riches of his goodness and forbearance and long-suffering; not knowing that the goodness of God leadeth thee to repentance?" (Ro.2:4).

ILLUSTRATION:

In the days of instant coffee and fast-food service, we have come to expect short waiting periods for things. We struggle with patience day by day; we get tied up in knots. Why? Because God is not on our schedule. We want to hurry up and wait while He wants us to be patient, to wait on Him.

William Carey, the father of a modern missions movement, had to be patient before the first Hindu convert was baptized in India. Did he wait for a few months? Was he patient for a year or two? The Lord gave him the grace to wait <u>seven</u> years until he could see the fruit of his labor.

The next time you have to wait for a "slow" traffic light to change, put on the garment of patience...and use the time to pray or think or plan. Make use of the time, patiently so; enjoy the wait!

QUESTIONS:

1. What is the secret to having patience?
2. Is there a time when God gave you a supernatural ability to wait?
3. What good things can come from learning to wait?

7. THE GARMENT OF FORBEARANCE (v.13).

Forbearing means to hold back; to put up with; to refrain; to bear with; to control.

Something is often forgotten: there are many things about everyone of us that people have to forbear. People have to put up with a great deal of things when dealing with us. Everyone of us is guilty of some...

- weakness
- unattractive behavior
- wrong behavior
- mistreatment

- neglect
- failure
- bad habit
- irritating behavior

There are things about everyone of us that just turn some people off. None of us can escape that fact. In addition, everyone of us does things that irritate some people. Again, there is no escaping the fact. Any person can be looked at and have his flaws and weaknesses picked out.

But note: this is not what the Scripture says to do. The Scripture says that the believer is to put on the clothing of forbearance. The believer is to forbear the flaws of others. He is to put up with and bear with the weaknesses of other believers.

> **"We then that are strong ought to bear the infirmities of the weak, and not to please ourselves" (Ro.15:1).**
> **"Bear ye one another's burdens, and so fulfil the law of Christ" (Gal.6:2).**

QUESTIONS:
1. Who is forbearing with you? Who puts up with your flaws and failures? Why do you think they put up with you?
2. How have you learned to live with the flaws of others?
3. How can you make yourself more tolerant of others?
4. What is the ultimate picture of forbearance?

8. THE GARMENT OF FORGIVENESS (v.13).

The believer must be forgiving. The word means to be gracious to a person; to pardon him for some wrong done against us. Note: a quarrel or some difference has taken place. A person has hurt us and brought pain to us. But no matter what he has done, we are to have a forgiving spirit clothing us. We are to be so clothed with the spirit of forgiveness that no difference or quarrel can shake us.

Note why: because Christ has forgiven us. No matter how much wrong a person has done against us, it cannot match the wrong we have done against Christ. Yet, Christ has forgiven us. Therefore, we are to forgive those who have done wrong against us—no matter how great the wrong is.

> **"And when ye stand praying, forgive, if ye have ought against any: that your Father also which is in heaven may forgive you your trespasses" (Mk.11:25).**

ILLUSTRATION:
Many of us remember the "Watergate" episode that nearly tore America apart in the early 1970's. President Richard Nixon had just resigned in disgrace and the new President, Gerald Ford, granted Nixon a free, full, and absolute pardon.

Many Americans struggled with that decision. President Ford did the very thing that God wants each of us to do when someone hurts us: we need to forgive the person and go on with our lives.

In a portion of Ford's statement he said, *"My conscience tells me clearly and certainly that I cannot prolong the bad dreams that continue to reopen a chapter that is closed. My conscience tells me that only I, as President, have the constitutional power to firmly shut and seal this book."*[2]

And so it is with the Christian believer. When we put on the garment of forgiveness, we have the power to set people free.

QUESTIONS:
1. Why are you supposed to forgive others?
2. Is there anyone whom you need to forgive for hurting you? What kinds of things can you do to set the person free?
3. Where does the power come from that allows you to forgive others?
4. How does trusting God help you to forgive others?
5. What are the benefits of forgiving others?

9. THE GARMENT OF LOVE (v.14).

Above all, the believer is to put on the garment of *love*. Note that love is to be the main garment of the believer's new life. It is called the *bond of perfection*; that is, love binds all the clothing or great qualities of the believer's life together. If the believer has put on love—if he really loves people—then he is always clothed with...

- mercy
- kindness
- humility
- meekness

- long-suffering
- forbearance
- forgiveness

"And Jesus answered him, The **first of all the commandments** is, Hear, O Israel; The Lord our God is one Lord: and thou shalt love the Lord thy God with all thy heart, and with all thy soul, and with all thy mind, and with all thy strength: this is the **first commandment**. And the second is like, namely this, Thou shalt love thy neighbour as thyself. There is **none other commandment** greater than these" (Mk.12:29-31).

QUESTIONS:

1. Why do you think some believers overlook the essential quality of love?
2. Are you loving and lovable to all people, or just to some people?
3. Who does God command you to love? Just your family? Your friends? Your neighbors?
4. You may have been raised in a family where love was not expressed or even felt. How can you learn to be loving? Who is to be the role model for showing love? What can you do that will help you feel comfortable in expressing love?

SUMMARY:

Just as you have a choice about the quality of clothing you will wear, you have a choice about the quality of your Christian life. Relate the good qualities of the clothes you would choose to the qualities of Christ. Relate the poor qualities of clothes that you would discard to the poor qualities of man that you would avoid. With Christ as your example, it is His garments, His qualities, that you as a believer should strive for.

1. You are the elect of God, holy and beloved.
2. Put on the garment of mercy.
3. Put on the garment of kindness.
4. Put on the garment of humility.
5. Put on the garment of meekness.
6. Put on the garment of patience.
7. Put on the garment of forbearance.
8. Put on the garment of forgiveness.
9. Put on the garment of love.

COLOSSIANS 3:12-14

1.   The most important thing that I learned from this lesson was:

2.   The area that I need to work on the most is:

3.   I can apply this lesson to my life by:

4.   Closing Statement of Commitment:

---

[1] Craig B. Larson, Editor,. *Illustrations for Preaching & Teaching*, p.161.
[2] Paul Lee Tan, *Encyclopedia of 7,700 Illustrations: Signs of the Times*, p.459.

1. A heart ruled by God's peace a. A choice: Let it rule b. The reason: One body c. The response: Be thankful **2. A heart rich with the Word of Christ**	**D. The Heart of the New Life, 3:15-17** 15 And let the peace of God rule in our hearts, to the which also ye are called in one body; and be ye thankful. 16 Let the word of Christ dwell in you richly in all wisdom;	dom; teaching and admonishing one another in psalms and hymns and spiritual songs, singing with grace in your hearts to the Lord. 17 And whatsoever ye do in word or deed, do all in the name of the Lord Jesus, giving thanks to God and the Father by him.	a. A choice: Let it dwell b. The reason: To teach & admonish one another in c. wisdom d. The evidence: A singing spirit **3. A heart that does all in the name of Christ** a. A choice: Do all b. The response: Give thanks

Section V
THE DEMANDS OF THE BELIEVER'S NEW LIFE: GREAT CHARACTER
Colossians 3:1-17

Study 4: THE HEART OF THE NEW LIFE

Text: Colossians 3:15-17

Aim: To develop a healthy, spiritual heart.

Memory Verse:

"Let the word of Christ dwell in you richly in all wisdom; teaching and admonishing one another in psalms and hymns and spiritual songs, singing with grace in your hearts to the Lord" (Colossians 3:16).

INTRODUCTION:

When Dr. Christian Bernard performed the first human heart-transplant, the medical world basked in the glow of human achievement. Sick and dying people were given hope that in receiving a brand new heart, their lives would be extended.

As great as this is, it pales in comparison to what God has done for His followers. He has been in the heart-transplant business for a much longer time and, unique to His surgery, His patients live forever.

When a new life enters the world, a new heart enters the world too. There is no life apart from a physical heart. So it is with the believer: the believer receives a new heart when he receives a new life. *The heart of the new life* is the subject of this great passage.

OUTLINE:

1. A heart ruled by God's peace (v.15).
2. A heart rich with the Word of Christ (v.16).
3. A heart that does all in the name of Christ (v.17).

1. A HEART RULED BY GOD'S PEACE (v.15).

The believer is to let the peace of Christ rule in all things. The best Greek texts read the "peace of Christ" instead of the "peace of God." The word "peace" means to be bound, joined, and weaved together. It means to be assured, confident, and secure in the love and care of God. It means to know that God will take care of us no matter the problem or circumstance. It means to be absolutely assured that God will allow nothing to swamp or defeat us. God will...

- strengthen
- encourage
- guide
- sustain
- deliver
- save
- provide
- give life both now and forever

But note the critical point: this peace is the peace of Christ, and He alone possesses it. Therefore, a person can experience true peace only as he comes to know Christ. Only Christ can bring real peace to the human heart, the kind of peace that brings deliverance and the assurance of deliverance to the human soul. Three significant things are pointed out about the peace of Christ.

1. The choice is up to the believer: the believer does not automatically experience the peace of Christ. He is supposed to, but he may not. This is a command, which means it demands obedience. The word "rule" means to be or to act as an umpire. Peace is to be the umpire, the deciding factor in all circumstances and situations of life.

⇒ Matthew Henry words it well: "Let this peace rule in your heart—prevail and govern there...as an umpire [let it] decide all matters of difference among you."[1]
⇒ William Barclay pointedly says: "Let the peace of God...be the decider [umpire] of all things within your heart."[2]

The point is this: the believer must make a choice—the decision is his whether he lets the peace of Christ rule or not. Scripture commands it, but the believer has to be willing to let the umpire of peace rule. He has to be willing to lay aside all the differences and circumstances—to be willing to give up differences and let Christ handle them through the rule of His peace.

> **"Peace I leave with you, My peace I give unto you: not as the world giveth, give I unto you. Let not your heart be troubled, neither let it be afraid" (Jn.14:27).**

2. The reason why believers are to let the peace of Christ rule is clearly stated: we are called to be *in one body*. We are not called to be *in two bodies* or *many bodies*, but in one. Any believer who stands *out there* in another body is not a genuine believer. There is only one body of Christ, only one body of believers, only one church. This means something significant: believers are to act as one. They are to live and behave as one body, as a body of people in union with each other. How? By letting the peace of Christ rule in their hearts. Peace is to be the deciding factor, the umpire in all relationships between believers.

APPLICATION:

Why is this exhortation (allowing the peace of God to rule in your heart) given? Because too often some person arises within the church who is...

- cantankerous and divisive
- critical and judgmental
- murmuring and grumbling
- gossiping and spreading rumors

Too often some person becomes a troublemaker, a person who stirs up trouble within the body of Christ, the church. He lets *differences* rule within his heart instead of Christ and His peace.

This is the reason for the exhortation. The exhortation is needed. Some persons desperately need to hear the challenge and demand of God: *Let the peace of God rule in your hearts...for you are called to live as one body in peace.*

> **"Acquaint now thyself with him, and be at peace: thereby good shall come unto thee" (Job 22:21).**
> **"Depart from evil, and do good; seek peace, and pursue it" (Ps.34:14).**

3. Believers are to respond to the demand for peace with thankfulness. Believers should always thank Christ for His peace...

- the peace He has brought to their own hearts personally.
- the peace He has brought to all men who trust Him.
- the peace He has brought within His body, the church.
- the glorious privilege which all men have to know His peace.

COLOSSIANS 3:15-17

"Giving thanks always for all things unto God and the Father
in the name of our Lord Jesus Christ; submitting yourselves one to
another in the fear of God" (Eph.5:20-21).

ILLUSTRATION:

What kind of respect do you give to the "umpire" in your heart? Do you tend to argue the call, going nose to nose with the umpire?

Years ago, there was a Major League Baseball manager by the name of Leo "the Lip" Durocher. He picked up his nick-name from newspaper writers who took notice of his brash and bullying conversations with the umpires. On more than one occasion, the umpire would grow weary of this onslaught and put Leo the Lip in his place—off the field and in the shower. His involvement in the game that day was finished.

How often does God send you to the showers? Notice the first phrase of verse 15: **"And let the peace of God rule in your hearts...."** Do you _let_ His peace work in your heart?

QUESTIONS:
1. Why is it important for God's peace to rule in your heart?
2. How do you know when you are lacking His peace in your heart?
3. What is the secret to keeping God's peace in your heart?

2. A HEART RICH WITH THE WORD OF CHRIST (v.16).

The believer is to let the Word of Christ dwell in his heart. Throughout Scripture this is the only time "the Word of God" is referred to as "the Word of Christ." The emphasis of Colossians is Christ; therefore, the Word of God becomes the *Word of Christ* in this great book. (Cp. 2 Cor.2:17; 4:2; 1 Th.1:8; 2:13; 4:15; 2 Th.3:1.)

Three significant points are made about the Word of Christ.

1. The choice is up to the believer: the Word of Christ does not naturally dwell within the believer's heart. The word "dwell" means to be at home or to make a home; to abide or dwell within. The believer must make room within his heart for the Word of Christ. He must let the Word of Christ enter his heart, making a home within his heart. He must let the Word of Christ dwell and abide in his heart. The believer must clean out all the old furnishings of his heart to let the Word of Christ settle down as the permanent resident within his heart.

Note the word "richly." It is important, for the Word of Christ must be allowed to dwell *richly* within our hearts. The believer is not to be satisfied with just a meager visit by the Word of Christ. He is to let the Word of Christ *dwell richly* within Him. The Word of Christ must be allowed to furnish the believer's heart with all the wealth of its commandments and promises, instructions and warnings.

"Therefore shall ye lay up these my words in your heart and in your
soul, and bind them for a sign upon your hand, that they may be as
frontlets between your eyes" (Dt.11:18).
"Thy word have I hid in mine heart, that I might not sin against thee"
(Ps.119:11).

2. The reason why believers are to let the Word of Christ dwell within them is clearly stated: believers are to teach and admonish one another in all wisdom. This is the believer's task, the very reason God has not yet taken us home to heaven: to teach and admonish one another. By teaching is meant the instruction of the Word and by admonition is meant the warning of Scripture. But how can we teach and admonish others if we do not...
- know the Word of Christ?
- let the Word of Christ dwell in us?

The answer is obvious: we can't. And note another fact: it is not enough to know the Word of Christ. We must be living the Word of Christ. Knowing the Word but not living it is hypocrisy.

Our very lives must be the home, the dwelling place, for the Word of Christ. When people look at us, they must immediately see that our lives are different and special, governed by the Word of Christ.

Something else should be pointed out as well. We can teach and admonish others in forbearance and not *in wisdom*. Worldly philosophy and teachings about reality, truth, God, and the universe are only the crude notions of men. The truth and wisdom of life are found in the *Word of Christ alone*.

> **"And they shall <u>teach</u> my people the difference between the holy and profane, and cause them to discern between the unclean and the clean" (Ezk.44:23).**

3. There is a way to tell whether or not the Word of Christ dwells in us: Are we teaching and admonishing one another in psalms and hymns and spiritual songs, singing with grace in our hearts to the Lord? As we walk throughout the day are we...

- talking about Christ?
- sharing the Word of Christ with each other?
- teaching each other?
- admonishing and encouraging and warning each other?
- singing to ourselves and with others?

APPLICATION:

What a contrasting picture to how so many of us live! The believer is to live and move and have his being in Christ, and he is to let Christ live and move and have His being in him. For the believer, to live is Christ. We are to walk all day long talking about and sharing Christ, teaching and admonishing others in the Word of Christ, singing the psalms of Scripture, the hymns of the church, and the spiritual songs that arise out of a heart filled with the joy of the Lord and His Word.

> **"And these words, which I command thee this day, shall be in thine heart: and thou shalt teach them diligently unto thy children, and shalt talk of them when thou sittest in thine house, and when thou walkest by the way, and when thou liest down, and when thou risest up" (Dt.6:6-7).**

ILLUSTRATION:

By dwelling in God's Word, we connect ourselves to "the Manufacturer's Handbook." Many car owners buy their car, get in, and drive away without taking the time to read through the owner's manual. In <u>Focus on the Family</u>, Rolf Zettersten writes:

> *"A good friend in North Carolina bought a new car with a voice warning system...At first Edwin was amused to hear the soft female voice gently remind him that his seat belt wasn't fastened...Edwin affectionately called this voice the 'little woman.'*
>
> *"He soon discovered his little woman was programmed to warn him about his gasoline. 'Your fuel level is low,' she said one time in her sweet voice. Edwin nodded his head and thanked her. He figured he still had enough to go another fifty miles, so he kept on driving. But a few minutes later, her voice interrupted again with the same warning. And so it went over and over. Although he knew it was the same recording, Edwin thought her voice sounded harsher each time.*
>
> *"Finally, he stopped his car and crawled under the dashboard. After a quick search, he found the appropriate wires and gave them a good yank. So much for the little woman.*
>
> *"He was still smiling to himself a few miles later when his car began sputtering and coughing. He ran out of gas! Somewhere inside the dashboard, Edwin was sure he could hear the little woman laughing."[3]*

If we attempt to live the Christian life, but unplug ourselves from God's Word, we too will find ourselves stranded on the side of the road!

QUESTIONS:
1. What practical things can you do in order to spend more quality time in ___ ___ Word?
2. What role are you to play according to verse sixteen? Which area needs your immediate attention? Why?
3. As you walk through the day, is Christ the focus of your conversation? What things tend to compete against Christ as you talk with others?

3. A HEART THAT DOES ALL IN THE NAME OF CHRIST (v.17).

Whatever a believer does in word or deed, he does all in the name of the Lord Jesus.

1. The believer has a choice. He is the one who speaks and acts; no one speaks and acts for him. Whether or not he speaks and acts for Christ is his choice. The command is there: "do all in the name of the Lord Jesus," but the choice as to what he talks about and does is his. He and he alone is responsible for his words and deeds.

2. The believer is to do all *in the name of the Lord Jesus*. What does this mean? It means that the believer knows something: the name of Christ is the only name that God accepts in His presence. Therefore, the only persons He accepts are those persons who come to Him in the name of Christ. There is no other name given among men whereby men may be saved. Therefore, the believer approaches God "in the name of Jesus Christ," that is, by surrendering his life to Christ and by living for Christ. This is the reason the believer does not dare speak or act outside the name of Christ. To do so would be evidence that he had not really approached God in Christ, that his profession was a false profession.

Again, what does it mean to do all in the name of the Lord Jesus? It means...

- to *live, move, and have our being* in the name of Christ.
- to *trust and depend* upon the name of Christ in all that we do.
- to *claim* the name of Christ in all that we say and do.
- to *represent* Christ in all that we say and do.

Simply stated, we must do nothing that dishonors Christ. Whenever we speak, Christ peppers and fills our conversation; and whenever we act, Christ is honored by our behavior.

We must always remember something: Christ hears every word and sees every deed. We love Him with all our hearts; therefore, we seek never to hurt or cause pain for Him by what we say or do. We diligently seek to bring only honor to His name.

> **"And whatsoever ye shall ask in my name, that will I do, that the Father may be glorified in the Son" (Jn.14:13).**

3. The believer's response is that of thanksgiving. God *the Father* has become the believer's Father through Christ. Therefore, the believer is constantly thanking God the Father. But note: even in thanksgiving and praise, the believer still approaches God only by and through Christ. God will accept no person apart from Christ, not even to offer thanksgiving and praise.

> **"Whether therefore ye eat, or drink, or whatsoever ye do, do all to the glory of God. Give none offense, neither to the Jews, nor to the Gentiles, nor to the church of God" (1 Cor.10:31-32).**

ILLUSTRATION:

If God's peace is ruling our hearts and His Word is dwelling richly in us, our ministry to others will be empowered by the Holy Spirit.

Pat Morley illustrates this point in his book, *I Surrender: Submitting to Christ in the Details of Life*:

> "When I am a good friend, I am a very good friend. But there are times when my friends would be better off without me.

COLOSSIANS 3:15-17

"One friend was sick for two weeks, and I didn't even call him on the phone. Another friend went through a divorce, and I wasn't there for him. Still another friend received a great honor, but I never congratulated him. A friend stopped by to see me, but I was tied up in a meeting, and I never tried to contact him later.

"Sometimes we are the weakest of friends. We disappoint. Then, when we see that friend again, we are embarrassed. We were not there for them when they needed us. We let them down. We do not know what to say.

"When we are not a good friend, it is possible that we are being a selfish, wicked-hearted person. But the far more likely answer is that we are weak, not filled with the power of the Holy Spirit."[4]

We must be filled with God's Spirit every day of our lives. And we must walk in God's Spirit all day long. It is then and only then that we will grab every opportunity to do good and to do it in the name of Christ.

QUESTIONS:
1. As you review the events of your life this week, for what things can you thank God?
2. Why do you think some Christians fail to be thankful to God for all that He has done for them?
3. How can you guard against not having a thankful heart to God?

SUMMARY:

If you were to have a "heart check-up" now, what would be the results? If you have given your life to Christ, He has given you a brand new heart. Are you taking good care of your heart? As the Great Physician, He has prescribed these instructions that will keep your heart healthy:

1. Let your heart be ruled by God's peace.
2. Let your heart be rich with the Word of Christ.
3. Let your heart do all in the name of Christ.

PERSONAL JOURNAL NOTES
(Reflection & Response)

1. The most important thing that I learned from this lesson was:

2. The area that I need to work on the most is:

3. I can apply this lesson to my life by:

4. Closing Statement of Commitment:

---

[1] Matthew Henry. *Matthew Henry's Commentary*, Vol.5, p.764.
[2] William Barclay. *The Letters to the Philippians, Colossians, and Thessalonians*, p. 190.
[3] Craig B. Larson, Editor. *Illustrations for Preaching & Teaching*, p.39.
[4] Patrick M. Morley. *I Surrender: Submitting to Christ in the Details of Life* (Dallas, TX: Word Publishers, Inc., 1990), p.137.

	VI. THE RESPON- SIBILITIES OF THE BELIEV- ER, 3:18-4:6	the Lord. 19 Husbands, love your wives, and be not bit- ter against them. 20 Children, obey your parents in all things:	2. Christian husbands: Love your wives & do not be bitter against them
	A. The Believer & His Family, 3:18-21	for this is well pleas- ing unto the Lord.	3. Christian children: Obey your parents
1. Christian wives: Submit to your hus- bands	18 Wives, submit your- selves unto your own husbands, as it is fit in	21 Fathers, provoke not your children to anger, lest they be dis- couraged.	4. Christian fathers or parents: Do not pro- voke your children

Section VI
THE RESPONSIBILITIES OF THE BELIEVER
Colossians 3:18-4:6

Study 1: **THE BELIEVER AND HIS FAMILY**

Text: **Colossians 3:18-21**

Aim: To adopt God's model for the Christian home.

Memory Verse:
> "Wives, submit yourselves unto your own husbands, as it is fit in the Lord. Husbands, love your wives, and be not bitter against them" (Col.3:18-19).

INTRODUCTION:
This is a critical passage of Scripture, no matter the generation. Every generation witnesses an attack upon the union of husband, wife, and family. The lust of man and woman for sensual pleasure is a driving threat to their faithfulness and commitment to one another—faithfulness and commitment that is demanded by God. Christ and Christ alone must be at the center of every family if it is to survive the attacks made against it. And it is not enough for one or two members of the family to be obedient to Christ—every member has to make Christ the center of his life. One disobedient and unfaithful member dramatically affects the union of the family, bringing trauma, pain, and often destruction to the family. This is the critical importance of this discussion on the Christian and the family.

OUTLINE:
1. Christian wives: submit to your husbands (v.18).
2. Christian husbands: love your wives and do not be bitter against them (v.19).
3. Christian children: obey your parents (v.20).
4. Christian fathers or parents: do not provoke your children (v.21).

1. CHRISTIAN WIVES: SUBMIT TO YOUR HUSBANDS (v.18).

This is the only fitting or right thing to do. Scripture pulls no punches: it tells the wife exactly what the Lord expects. The husband's turn comes in a moment, but for now the Lord's will for the wife is covered. His will involves two striking points.

1. First, Christian wives are to submit themselves to their husbands. The word "submit" means to subdue and subject in obedience.

In modern society this is strong; in fact, it is too strong for many. Many reject the idea of woman's subjection as archaic, outdated, and old-fashioned. Some even react in anger and hostility against the Word of God and those who preach the duty of wives.

Are they right? Has Scripture gone too far in declaring that wives should be subject to their husbands? Has God made a mistake within the order of the family? To the Christian, the answer is no. The problem is not in what God has said, but in our *understanding of what He has said* or in our rebellion against what He wills. Any wife who reacts to God's command is reacting either because she does not understand what God is saying or is just *unwilling to give her life to God and follow Him as He says*. What does God mean by subjection? God does not mean *dictatorial subjection...*

- that a wife is to subject herself to a tyrant.
- that a wife is to submit herself to the demands of a husband who acts like a beast.
- that a wife is to be a slave or footstool for the husband.
- that a wife is to serve her husband without restraint.
- that a wife is to be treated as inferior to her husband.

What God means by subjection is order, cooperation, relationship, partnership—the way a husband and wife are to walk together throughout life. Every body of people—even when the body is only two persons—must have a leader who takes the lead in plowing through the wilderness of the world and its trials and temptations and difficulties. Between the two, wife and husband, one of them has to be the primary leader. God's order for the two is that the husband take the lead.

2. Second, Christian wives must submit because it is the only fitting thing to do. The word "fitting" means the right thing to do. Why is it the only fitting and right thing to do? Not because the husband is superior and the wife is inferior as a human being. The reason is because the wife is *in the Lord*. She has surrendered her life to live in the Lord and to love and follow Him and to witness for Him by *living just as He says to live*. Therefore, when the Lord says that it is His will for her to submit to her husband, she submits. She submits because the Lord tells her that submission is the way He wants her to live with her husband. Again, submission is simply...

- God's order for the family.
- the relationship, cooperation, and partnership that is to exist between the wife and husband.

> **"Likewise, ye wives, be in subjection to your own husbands; that, if any obey not the word, they also may without the word be won by the conversation [behavior] of the wives" (1 Pt.3:1).**

ILLUSTRATION:

Does Biblical submission mean that the woman is to become a "doormat" and accept physical, emotional, or verbal abuse as God's will for her life? Of course not. Biblical submission is a partnership between the wife and husband. Stephen P. Beck writes:

> *"Driving down a country road, I came to a very narrow bridge. In front of the bridge, a sign was posted: 'Yield.' Seeing no oncoming cars, I continued across the bridge and [on] to my destination.*
> *"On my way back, I came to the same one-lane bridge, now from the other direction. To my surprise, I saw another 'Yield' sign posted.*
> *" 'Curious,' I thought. 'I'm sure there was one positioned on the other side.'*
> *"When I reached the other side of the bridge, I looked back. Sure enough, yield signs had been placed at both ends of the bridge. Drivers from both directions were requested to give the other the right of way. It was a reasonable and gracious way of preventing a head-on collision."*[1]

God never intended marriage to be a head-on-collision. Biblical submission keeps the traffic of life safe and steady. Without it, the marriage will become a wreck.

QUESTIONS:
1. Under what circumstances would you feel that submission would <u>not</u> be as God intended it to be?
2. Why is it important for the woman to submit herself to her husband?
3. Some believers and most non-believers have a difficult time embracing the idea of submission within a marriage. Why?

2. CHRISTIAN HUSBANDS: LOVE YOUR WIVES AND DO NOT BE BITTER AGAINST THEM (v.19).

This command destroys all opposition and reaction to the command of subjection given to the wives. How?

The word "love" is not only the love of affection and feelings, but the *agape love* of God Himself. The Christian husband is to love his wife just as much and in the same way that God has loved us. *Agape love* is...

- a selfless and unselfish love.
- a giving and sacrificial love.
- a love of the will as well as of the heart.
- a love of commitment as well as of affection.
- a love that works for the highest good of the wife.

Very practically, the husband does not seek to have his wife fill his needs, desires, comfort, and interests; but he seeks to meet, nurture, and nourish all these for his wife. It is God's will for the husband to totally sacrifice himself for his wife. And note: he is to do it without bitterness. Wives are just like husbands; they sometimes fail to submit; and when they fail, the husband tends to become bitter or resentful. It is the very nature of men to sense resentment or bitterness; therefore, the Christian husband must struggle and fight against the temptation. A husband is to love sacrificially even if the wife does not deserve to be loved and is utterly unworthy of being loved. Husbands are to obey Christ regardless. It is the will of Christ.

APPLICATION:

Think what an enormous difference would exist between husbands and wives who loved and submitted as Scripture says.

> **"Husbands, love your wives, even as Christ also loved the church, and gave himself for it" (Eph.5:25).**
>
> **"Likewise, ye husbands, dwell with them according to knowledge, giving honour unto the wife, as unto the weaker vessel, and as being heirs together of the grace of life; that your prayers be not hindered" (1 Pt.3:7).**

ILLUSTRATION:

William Bennett, the former U.S. Secretary of Education, has said that a divorce is like the death of a small civilization. Statistics tell us that about one out of every two marriages fail in America. How close has divorce come to wiping out your "small civilization," your marriage? If you have yet to do so, now would be a great time to plant some protective hedges around your marriage. Protecting your marriage is a wonderful way to love your wife.

In the excellent book, *Hedges: Loving Your Marriage Enough to Protect It*, author Jerry Jenkins shares this hedge with us:

> *"Evangelist Robert M. Abbott writes that, just as the fact that 'a certain percentage of people die annually through traffic accidents does not mean we stop searching for ways to remedy the situation,' neither should we be ready to shrug off moral impurity among our leaders.*
>
> *"Abbott continues, 'None of us plan[s] to have moral accidents, but we must also plan <u>not</u> to! Danger rides with us all the time.' He compares the moral danger to that of a driver pulling several tons of equipment behind his car. '[This] requires more braking power and a longer stopping time...Brakes! Thank God for brakes!'*

⇒ *"Abbott writes that '[we] must learn to keep plenty of space between us and sinful acts, so we can start braking soon enough to stop before it is too late.' He offers a list...when we might 'need to put on the brakes early and well.' Among them:*

⇒ *When you are so busy there is no time to be alone with God.*

⇒ *When you are too busy to spend at least one relaxed evening a week with your wife and family.*

⇒ *When you feel you deserve more attention than you are getting at home.*

⇒ *When you wouldn't want your wife [or a colleague] to see what you are reading or looking at.*

⇒ *When the romance in your marriage is fading.*

⇒ *When your charisma, appearance, and personality are attractive to women, and you are tempted to make the most of it.*

⇒ *When you enjoy fantasizing about an illicit relationship.*

⇒ *When a woman makes herself available by her behavior.*

⇒ *When some woman [not your wife] tells you how wonderful you are and how much she loves you.*

⇒ *When Scriptures concerning adultery are for others, not you.*

⇒ *When you start feeling sorry for yourself.*

⇒ *When you hope God isn't looking or listening."*[2]

God will provide the brakes...if you choose to use them. What do you need to start pumping the brakes for today?

QUESTIONS:
1. What kinds of hedges do you need to place in your marriage?
2. What sacrifices is the husband to make in the marriage for his wife?
3. What sacrifices is the wife to make in the marriage for her husband?
4. What is the secret for a happy marriage according to this verse? What sorts of things need to be taking place in your home in order to experience a healthy marriage?

3. CHRISTIAN CHILDREN: OBEY YOUR PARENTS (v.20).

The word "obey" means to follow the directions or instructions of some guide. When parents guide and direct a child, the child is to obey. And note: he is to obey "*in all things*." How about the terrible problem of sinful instructions sometimes given to children by abusive parents? This is not what Scripture is talking about. Scripture is talking about the normal day-to-day instructions and guidance which parents give to children. Children are to obey their parents *in all instructions*. What happens when older children have different opinions? They feel like they should be able...
- to have something
- to do something
- to go someplace
- to come in late

Differences always arise, yet God says that the child is to obey *in all* things. Does this mean the parent is always right? No. It means that the child has a unique opportunity to learn discipline, control, and order. When they go out to face life alone without their parents, they are going to be facing a world that is...
- self-centered
- demanding
- corrupt
- evil
- sinful
- powerful
- competitive
- threatening
- dangerous
- authoritative

The child has to be prepared, and one of the major preparations is that of discipline or control. When the child becomes an adult, he will have demands made upon him, some of which will be unjust and unfair. He will have to obey the demands in order to survive in this corruptible world.

It is up to the Christian children to learn to obey and follow instructions now—while they are still at home. They are to use the instruction of their parents as the training ground for the future—for their adulthood. The more obedient the child, the more disciplined, controlled, and prepared he will be to face life when he goes out to face the world.

Note one other point: the child's obedience pleases the Lord. The Lord has one primary objective for the child: to prepare him to be the most balanced and productive adult he can be. Therefore, when the child obeys his parent(s), the Lord sees the child's being disciplined and controlled; He sees the child's preparing himself to become a strong adult. Therefore, the child's obedience pleases the Lord.

> "For Moses said, Honour thy father and thy mother; and, Whoso curseth father or mother, let him die the death" (Mk.7:10).
> "Children, obey your parents in the Lord: for this is right" (Eph.6:1).

QUESTIONS:
1. Why is it important for children to obey their parents? What are some of the natural consequences to a child who fails to obey?
2. What is the relationship between discipline and love?
3. Why do some Christian parents fail to discipline their children?

4. CHRISTIAN FATHERS OR PARENTS: DO NOT PROVOKE YOUR CHILDREN (v.21).

Four things will provoke a child.

1. Failing to accept the fact that things do change. Time and generations do change. This does not mean that a child should participate nor be allowed to do everything that his generation does. But it does mean that parents need to be alert to the changes between generations, thus allowing the child to be a part of his own generation instead of trying to conform the child to the parent's childhood generation. The parent's childhood generation does not exist anymore, nor will it ever exist again.

What changes should and should not be allowed by a Christian parent? Three words provide a good guideline: *rebellion, immorality,* and *injustice.* Open defiance or resistance to authority and immorality and injustice are contrary to God's Word. Any change that involves rebellion, immorality or injustice needs to be dealt with and controlled by the parent. We are probably safe to say that any change not involving one of these areas should be allowed. Whether true or not, these three areas provide a good practical guideline.

The point is this: a parent must not resist normal and natural change that takes place between generations. If he resists and forbids his child to grow up in his own generation, the parent is asking for trouble. Most likely the child will be provoked to wrath—to react.

2. Overcontrolling a child will also provoke a child to wrath. Overcontrol ranges all the way from stern restriction and discipline to child abuse. Disciplining and restricting a child *too much* will either stifle the growth of a child or stir him to react and rebel, causing the child to flee from the parent. What is too much discipline? How much should a child be restricted? Should he be allowed to do everything he wants? No! There is a limit, and the limit must be placed upon the child with discipline being exercised when the limit is crossed. What Christian parents need to remember is this:

⇒ *Some parents allow their children* to participate in every function and activity offered to the child. They are usually the ones without *proper parental* guidance.

The point is this: there must be a balance between family life and the child's community life. The child should be allowed to do his own thing sometimes and should be required to share with the family at other times. As he grows older, he should, of course, be allowed to break away from the family more and more in order to prepare him for the day when he will step out into the world on his own. A child needs free time away from the parent and family as well as some family time in order to grow into a healthy person.

"Fathers, provoke not your children to anger, lest they be discouraged" (Col.3:21).

3.   Undercontrolling a child can provoke a child. It should be noted that this is the most prevalent problem in an industrialized society. There is a tendency for those with plenty or with wealth to pamper, indulge, and give a child everything imaginable—well beyond what a child needs and what is really best for him. Parents pamper and indulge children for five reasons.

⇒   A parent indulges and pampers—gives in to the child—in order to escape responsibility for the child: to keep a child from interrupting the parent's time or schedule or desires; to get a child out from under the parent's feet. The parent, of course, needs some free time; but too many parents live selfishly, wanting nothing interfering with their own desires and needs. Too many parents push their children out and away, allowing their children to run around too much. Too few sacrifice their own time and desires to look after their children as much as they should.

⇒   A parent indulges and pampers—gives in to a child—in order to gain social standing or to relive own childhood. The parent did not have and was not allowed to do what he wanted as a child; therefore, he sees to it that his child has everything and does everything that everyone else does. He is determined that his child will have everything no matter what it costs.

⇒   A parent indulges and pampers—gives in to a child—because he has a false understanding or philosophy of child-rearing. He gives in to ill behavior, whining, pouting, sulkiness, and temper tantrums just to secure peace and quiet.

⇒   A parent indulges and pampers—gives in to a child—because of misguided devotion and love: to keep from losing the loyalty, quietness, cooperativeness, and affection of the child.

⇒   A parent indulges and pampers—gives in to a child—because of insecurity and lack of purpose. For example, some pamper and cling to a child because they (the parents) are insecure in the world. Others cling and pamper because they lack any other purpose. The child fills the need for security and purpose. *Playing house* is lived to the limit: the parent plays house with his child, clinging and pampering to the limit.

"Chasten thy son while there is hope, and let not thy soul spare for his crying" (Pr.19:18).
"Foolishness is bound in the heart of a child; but the rod of correction shall drive it far from him" (Pr.22:15).

4.   Living an inconsistent life before a child can provoke a child. A parent who tells a child one thing and then turns around and does the opposite thing himself is full of hypocrisy and false profession. Yet, how common! How many children are doing things because their parents do them:

⇒   drinking alcohol
⇒   taking drugs
⇒   watching sexual scenes on television or movies
⇒   reading immoral stories
⇒   looking at magazines exposing the human body
⇒   eating too much
⇒   wasting time
⇒   dressing or exposing the body to attract attention
⇒   attending socials or parties that are loose on decency, morality, marital faithfulness, and on and on

Seeing an inconsistent life in a parent can provoke children.

"And he did evil in the sight of the LORD, and walked in the way of his father, and in the way of his mother, and in the way of Jeroboam the son of Nebat, who made Israel to sin" (1 Ki.22:52).

QUESTIONS:
1. If you are a parent, is it possible that God may want you to make some adjustments in your discipline of your children? If so, what would they be?
2. What types of things provoke children?
3. If you are a parent, do you worry about being too strict? What kinds of things bring a balance to Biblical discipline?

SUMMARY:

With so many worldly models for the family, it is crucial that the Christian believer be grounded in the truth found in God's Word. From the Scriptures, we find God's model for the Christian family. Do you want a family that is wholesome, loving, and faithful? As a reminder of how this can be achieved, here is God's plan:

1. Christian wives: submit to your husbands.
2. Christian husbands: love your wives and do not be bitter against them.
3. Christian children: obey your parents.
4. Christian fathers or parents: do not provoke your children.

PERSONAL JOURNAL NOTES
(Reflection & Response)

1. The most important thing that I learned from this lesson was:

2. The area that I need to work on the most is:

3. I can apply this lesson to my life by:

4. Closing Statement of Commitment:

---

[1] Craig B. Larson, Editor. *Illustrations for Preaching & Teaching*, p.249.
[2] Jerry B. Jenkins. *Hedges: Loving Your Marriage Enough to Protect It.* (Chicago, IL: Moody Press, 1989), p.81-83.

	B. The Believer & His Work, 3:22-4:1	ceive the reward of the inheritance: for ye serve the Lord Christ.	
1. The slave (employee)	22 Servants, obey in all things your masters according to the flesh; not with eyeservice, as menpleasers; but in singleness of heart, fearing God:	25 But he that doeth wrong shall receive for the wrong which he hath done: and there is no respect of persons.	2) Work will be judged by Christ
a. Obey your master (employer)--not only when he is watching			
b. Work--fearing God			
c. Work heartily, as you would work for the Lord	23 And whatsoever ye do, do it heartily, as to the Lord, and not unto men;	**CHAPTER 4** **M**asters, give unto your servants that which is just and equal; know-	2. **The master (employer)**
1) Work will be rewarded by Christ	24 Knowing that of the Lord ye shall receive	ing that ye also have a Master in heaven.	a. To give justice & equity b. Reason: He has a master

Study 2:   THE BELIEVER AND HIS WORK

Text: Colossians 3:22-4:1

Aim: To do all you can to build a godly atmosphere at work.

Memory Verse:
> "And whatever ye do, do it heartily, as to the Lord, and not unto men" (Colossians 3:23).

INTRODUCTION:

Do you think your faith should be seen where you work? Or is Christianity just meant for the inside walls of the church building? The Bible teaches us that the witness of the church is to touch every aspect of society—including where you work. Can you imagine what your workplace would be like if everyone based his relationship upon God's plan?

This passage is almost identical to the passage in Ephesians (Eph.6:5-9). It deals with the critical subject of the world's economy: slave and master, labor and management, employee and employer, workman and supervisor. It points out in no uncertain terms that the answer to the basic problems of the workplace is spiritual, not economic. Note that the discussion concerns slaves and their masters, but the instructions are applicable to every generation of workmen, no matter their status.

OUTLINE:
1.   The slave (employee) (v.22-25).
2.   The master (employer) (ch.4, v.1).

1. THE SLAVE [EMPLOYEE] (v.22-25).

The workman is to obey; that is, he is to follow the instructions of the person over him. Note that he is to obey "in all things." In the workplace there is to be no instruction that is not to be obeyed. This, of course, does not mean he is to obey orders that are contrary to the teaching of the Lord and damaging to His people and creation. However, it does mean that the Christian workman is to do what he is told to do when he has been given the privilege of a job, the privilege...

- to earn a livelihood and provide for himself and his family.
- to serve humanity through providing some needed product or service.
- to earn enough to help meet the desperate needs of the world and to carry the gospel to the world.

The attitude of the Christian workman is that the energy and effort he puts into his job is important to the Lord. Therefore, the Lord spells out several clear and unmistakeable instructions for the Christian workman.

1. The Christian workman is not to work with eyeservice, as a manpleaser; that is, he is not to work only when the boss is watching or standing around. The Christian workman is to work diligently all the time, doing exactly...

- what he has been instructed *and more*.
- what is expected of him *and more*.
- what he should produce *and more*.

The Christian workman should never do the average—never do just what he has been instructed. The Christian workman should always be the best at his job, going beyond the call of duty.

"For they loved the praise of men more than the praise of God"
(Jn.12:43).

2. The Christian workman is to work in *singleness of heart*. "Singleness of heart" means with purpose and focused attention, in sincerity and without any pretense or hypocrisy or slack. It means that the workman does not beat time; he is totally committed to his work. There is no *fakiness*, no pretending to be a good workman at all. The Christian workman is a good workman. His heart is single-minded and focused upon doing his job and doing it well. And note why: because he offers his labor *to the Lord*.

"For ye are bought with a price: therefore glorify God in your body,
and in your spirit, which are God's" (1 Cor.6:20).

3. The Christian workman is to work fearing the Lord. This is to be the very mark of the Christian workman. It is to be his fear and reverence for the Lord that stands out to those working around him. Every man is to be judged for what he does upon this earth, judged for the kinds of things he does and judged for how diligently he did the good things. The Christian workman knows...

- that God is watching his diligence.
- that God is going to reward him for his diligence.
- that the heavenly work that is to be awarded him is being delivered by his faithfulness and diligence upon earth.

Therefore, the Christian workman labors ever so diligently in the fear and reverence of the Lord—labors arduously lest he become a castaway and miss out on the best that God has.

"But I keep under my body, and bring it into subjection: lest that by
any means, when I have preached to others, I myself should be a casta-
way" (1 Cor.9:27).

4. The Christian workman is to work heartily—as he would work for the Lord and not for men. The word "heartily" means *out of the soul*. The Christian workman's labor is to arise out of his soul, from the innermost part of his being. He is not working for the men of this earth but for the Lord. He is working for the deepest reason possible: the Lord Jesus Christ has told him to work and to work diligently. The Lord Jesus is his Lord; therefore, the Christian workman does what his Lord says. But note: there are two other critical reasons why he works diligently.

   a. Diligent work will be rewarded by Christ. On earth the workman may be mistreated, used, misused, abused, cheated, bypassed, and taken advantage of; but the

Lord knows, and He is going to abundantly reward the diligent workman. In fact, the reward of the inheritance simply explodes the human mind. It stretches far beyond and above all that we can ask or even think. It includes a new body that will be eternal, a new heavens and earth, and positions of enormous leadership, authority, and service for the Lord Jesus.

"Moreover it is required in stewards, that a man be found faithful" (1 Cor.4:2).

b. Slothful work and idleness will be judged by Christ. Many workmen do wrong on the job. They do wrong by...

- being slothful
- being lazy
- being irresponsible
- being unconcerned
- being unproductive
- being uncaring
- being prejudiced

- cheating
- stealing
- lying
- being careless
- being selfish
- being unfair

The list could go on and on. The point is this: every single person on earth is going to face God for the wrong he has done on the job. He will give an account for his labor and be judged exactly for what he has done. And note: there is no respect of persons. Everyone is going to stand before God—no matter who he is.

"His lord said unto him, Well done, good and faithful servant; thou hast been faithful over a few things, I will make thee ruler over many things: enter thou into the joy of thy lord" (Mt.25:23).

ILLUSTRATION:

Why do we work? It should certainly be for more than the prize of a paycheck. The focus to this question is sharpened by this story:

"Chariots of Fire, the fact-based, Oscar-winning movie, depicts the quest of Harold Abrahams and Eric Liddell to win gold medals in the 1924 Olympics, a feat they both accomplished.

"The difference between Abrahams and Liddell is transparent: Everything Abrahams did was for himself, while everything Liddell did was for the glory of God.

"Eric's sister Jennie mistook her brother's love of running for rebellion against God, and pressed him to return to the mission field in China, where they both were born and their parents lived. One day his sister was upset because he had missed a mission meeting, so Eric decided to have a talk with her. They walked to a grassy spot overlooking the Scottish highlands.

"Clutching her arms, trying to explain his calling to run, he said, 'Jennie, Jennie. You've got to understand. I believe God made me for a purpose—for China. But He also made me fast!--and when I run, I feel His pleasure!'

"That is in sharp contrast to a scene later in the movie, one hour before the final race of Harold Abrahams. While his trainer gave him a rub-down, he lamented to his best friend, 'I'm twenty-four and I've never known contentment. I'm forever in pursuit, and I don't even know what it is I'm chasing.'

"Both men won a gold medal, but one won his medal for himself, while the other won his medal for God. Do you feel God's pleasure in what you do or, like Abrahams, does contentment elude you?"[1]

QUESTIONS:

1. Objectively and honestly, evaluate your work: When you work, do you work as though you were serving the Lord, as diligently as you can? Or do you work as little as you can, getting by with as little work as possible?
2. How does your "boss" feel about your work? That you are a hard worker or that you work only enough to get by?
3. How can you improve your testimony at work? How can you gain the testimony that you are a hard worker?
4. What sort of attitude are you to have when men do not fully appreciate your work? How does trusting God help you in this area?
5. What things can you do to bring Christ to the workplace or into the public? Why do some people tend to think that religion is only for church on Sundays?

2. THE MASTER [EMPLOYER] (v.1).

The employer or manager is to be just and fair (equal) with the employee. There is to be just and fair treatment in...

- wages
- work assignments
- production and goals
- expectations and demands
- promotion

The reason is as clearly stated as it could be: the manager or employer has a Master in heaven. The Lord God sees everything management does, and He holds management accountable for every act.

1. The manager is to do the very same things that are required of the workman. He is to treat the workman just like he expects the workman to treat him. (What a difference this would make in labor-management relations if it were really practiced by both parties!)

The manager or employer must realize that he lives and works...

- to serve both the Lord and the employees with fear and trembling, that is, managing with respect and eager concern (The Amplified New Testament).
- to serve in singleness of heart, managing *as to Christ*.
- to serve not with eye-service, as menpleasers.
- to serve as the servants of Christ, managing and doing the will of Christ from the heart.
- to serve with good will, managing as to the Lord, and not to men.
- to serve knowing that he is to receive a reciprocal reward for how well he managed.

The employer or manager expects at least two things from his workmen: diligence and loyalty. The charge to the employer is the same: be diligent in your management and in your loyalty to the workmen under you. Demonstrate your loyalty with fair wages and job security.

2. The manager is to forbear threats. This does not mean a workman cannot be corrected or released if he is not diligent and loyal. God does not encourage slothfulness, license, nor indulgence. God chastens and disciplines when needed. But note: stern measures are taken only after all other corrective measures have been taken. Every person—no matter how sorry a worker—is worth saving and developing into a conscientious workman if possible. He is a fellow human being who is on earth with the rest of us, and as long as he is on earth, God will continue to reach out to him. Therefore, he is worth reaching if we can. For this reason alone, every step should be taken to reach and train even the most unproductive workman.

The point is this: employers and managers must guard against unwarranted threats, for they too have a Master in heaven, and He has no favorites and shows no favoritism. As employers and managers, we hold every workman accountable to us; so the Lord holds us accountable to Him. Therefore, threats should always be issued courteously and carefully.

> "And, ye masters, do the same things unto them, forbearing threatening: knowing that your Master also is in heaven; neither is there respect of persons with him" (Eph.6:9).

"Woe unto him that buildeth his house by unrighteousness, and his chambers by wrong; that useth his neighbor's service without wages, and giveth him not for his work" (Jer.22:13).

"And I will come near to you to judgment; and I will be a swift witness against the sorcerers, and against the adulterers, and against false swearers, and against those that oppress the hireling [the hired workman] in his wages, the widow, and the fatherless, and that turn aside the stranger from his right, and fear not me, saith the LORD of hosts" (Mal.3:5).

ILLUSTRATION:

Most of us have probably read the classic Charles Dickens short story *A Christmas Carol*. The character, Ebenezer Scrooge, has become the standard when someone thinks about a bad employer. There has never been a more stingy man alive who treated his employees with such disdain. Poor Bob Cratchet—forced to sit in a cold office because Ebenezer refused to let him put sufficient coal in the fireplace. Scrooge paid him less than a pauper's wage, overworked him, and made every attempt to destroy his self-esteem.

As the story progresses, Bob loses his job on Christmas Eve and has to go home to a family that included a sick son, Tiny Tim. With this background, if the story ended here, we could never forgive Dickens or Scrooge. But the story did not end. Scrooge had to face his past in a dream and received a frightening glimpse of his future.

The story closes as Scrooge becomes a new man. He wakes up Christmas morning realizing that his future has been revised. The old Scrooge is gone; and in his place is a fair, giving, and just Scrooge. He brings gifts to Bob's family and rehires him at a great increase of salary.

Do you work for a Scrooge? Are you a Scrooge? Employers have been given a tremendous trust by God for the welfare of their employees and their families. God holds every employer accountable. Dickens' Scrooge saw the light. What will the Scrooge in your life do?

QUESTIONS:

1. What kinds of things is an employer responsible for in the lives of his employees?
2. Contrast the Christian employer with a non-Christian employer. What sort of differences would be noticeable?
3. How do you think God feels when a believer becomes an Ebenezer Scrooge? What can God do to change this sort of person?
4. If you are an employee, how often do you pray for your employer? What do you think your role is in the workplace regarding your Christian witness?
5. If you are an employer, how often do you pray for your employees? What types of barriers do you face as you present Christ in the workplace? How can you make your workplace a little bit of heaven on earth?

SUMMARY:

God has given each Christian worker a fantastic opportunity to be a "Living Bible." Many people that we work with will never set foot in a church. Often, we are the only gospel that they will see or hear. Will you represent Jesus to them?

1. As a slave (employee), you must obey your master (employer).
2. As the master (employer), you must be fair and just with your servants (employees).

PERSONAL JOURNAL NOTES
(Reflection & Response)

1. The most important thing that I learned from this lesson was:

2. The area that I need to work on the most is:

3. I can apply this lesson to my life by:

4. Closing Statement of Commitment:

---

[1] Patrick M. Morley. *The Man in the Mirror* (Dallas, TX: Word Publishing, 1989), p.71-72.

	C. The Believer & His Prayer Life & Witness, 4:2-6	bonds:	intercessor
		4 That I may make it manifest, as I ought to speak.	
1. Pray & continue in prayer	2 Continue in prayer, and watch in the same	5 Walk in wisdom to-ward them that are	**2. Walk wisely before people who are with-out Christ**
a. Persevere in prayer	with thanksgiving;	without, redeeming the time.	
b. Watch in prayer	3 Withal praying also	6 Let your speech be	**3. Speak with grace—**
c. Pray with thanks-giving	for us, that God would open unto us a door of	always with grace, sea-soned with salt, that ye	**answering & sharing what it is that makes**
d. Pray for others, in particular for their ministries—be an	utterance, to speak the mystery of Christ, for which I am also in	may know how ye ought to answer every man.	**your life different**

Section VI
THE RESPONSIBILITIES OF THE BELIEVER
Colossians 3:18-4:6

Study 3:   THE BELIEVER AND HIS PRAYER LIFE AND WITNESS

Text: Colossians 4:2-6

Aim: To live in prayer and be a genuine witness to the world.

Memory Verse:
> "Let your speech be always with grace, seasoned with salt, that ye may know how ye ought to answer every man" (Colossians 4:6).

INTRODUCTION:
Have you ever been accused of praying too much? Probably not. The point is not _how_ much we pray—prayer should be our way of life. From a life of prayer, a genuine and powerful witness impacts the world in which we live.

God never challenges us to a life of shallowness. We are on earth to make a difference. What kind of instructions does God give the Christian believer?

This passage covers two of the most important subjects for the believer—that of his prayer life and his witness.

OUTLINE:
1.   Pray and continue in prayer (v.2-4).
2.   Walk wisely before people who are without Christ (v.5).
3.   Speak with grace—answering and sharing what it is that makes your life different (v.6).

1. PRAY AND CONTINUE IN PRAYER (v.2-4).

Four important instructions are given—instructions that desperately need to be heeded.

1.   First, _continue stedfastly in prayer_. The word "continue" means to be constant, persever-ing, and unwearied in prayer. It means to be in constant and unbroken prayer—to be in constant and unbroken fellowship and communion with God. It means to walk and breathe prayer—to live and move and have our being in prayer. It means to never face a moment when we are not in prayer.

How is this possible? When we have so many duties and affairs that demand our attention, how can we continually walk in unbroken prayer? What Scripture means is that we...

- develop an *attitude of prayer*.
- walk in a *spirit of prayer*.
- take a mental break from our work and spend a moment *in prayer*.
- *pray always* when our minds are not upon some duty.
- *arise early* and pray before daily activities begin. Spend a worship time with God in prayer. Make this a continued practice.
- *pray before going to bed.* Spend an extended time in prayer before going to bed. Make this a continued practice.

In all honesty, the vast majority of us waste minute after minute every hour in useless day-dreaming and wandering thoughts—wasting precious time that could be spent in prayer. If we would learn to captivate these minutes for prayer, we would discover what it is to walk and live in prayer. Note a critical fact: this is the duty of the believer. It is not something God can do for us. We are the ones who have to discipline ourselves to pray. If we do not pray, then prayer never gets done.

Scripture is clear: the believer is to "continue in prayer."

> **"Casting down imaginations, and every high thing that exalteth itself against the knowledge of God, and bringing into captivity <u>every thought</u> to the obedience of Christ" (2 Cor.10:5).**

> **"Ask, and it shall be given you; seek, and ye shall find; knock, and it shall be opened unto you" (Mt.7:7).**

2. Second, *watch in prayer*. The word "watch" means to stay awake, be alert, be sleepless, be active, concentrate. It means to fight against distractions, drowsiness, sluggishness, wandering thoughts, and useless daydreaming. It means to discipline our minds and control our thoughts in prayer. Being very honest, this is a problem that afflicts every believer sometime. Overwork, tiredness, pressure, strain—and an innumerable list of things—can make it very difficult to concentrate in prayer. This is the very reason Paul stresses the need to *watch in prayer*. But note: vigilance in prayer is the duty of the believer. Again, it is not something that God does for us. We are responsible for watching and concentrating. We are the ones who are to discipline our minds and control our thoughts. For this reason, we must never give up in prayer. We must...

- always struggle against drowsiness and wandering thoughts.
- learn to concentrate—to discipline our minds and control our thoughts.
- teach ourselves to watch in prayer.

> **"And he cometh unto the disciples, and findeth them asleep, and saith unto Peter, What, could ye not watch with me one hour? Watch and pray, that ye enter not into temptation: the spirit indeed is willing, but the flesh is weak" (Mt.26:40-41).**

3. Third, *pray with thanksgiving*. When someone does something for us, we thank that person. The One Person who has done more for us than anyone else is God. Therefore, we are to thank Him. In fact, God continues to bless and help us; His hand is constantly upon our lives, looking after and caring for us; therefore, we should continually thank Him. Our praise should be lifted up to Him all through the day as we go about our daily affairs. An hour should never pass when we have not praised and thanked God several times. We should never forget His Son--that He actually took our sins upon Himself, bearing the judgment and punishment of them for us. This alone should continually fill our hearts with thanksgiving and praise.

> **"But thanks be to God, which giveth us the victory through our Lord Jesus Christ" (1 Cor.15:57).**

4. Fourth, *pray for others*, in particular for their ministry. Be an intercessor for God's ministers. Remember Paul was in prison, but note that for which he requested prayer. William Barclay

points out that Paul could have asked that the church pray for his release, for a *not guilty verdict* in his upcoming trial (he was not guilty), or for a peaceful end to his life.[1] But this is not what he requested. He requested prayer for his ministry. He wanted the believers praying that God would give him...

- opportunity for witnessing—for sharing the mystery or salvation of Christ.
- boldness in witnessing (v.4).

We must always remember that prayer is one of the laws of the universe. Prayer is the law by which God works and moves in behalf of men and their world. Granted, it is a law that is denied by most and ignored by others. Even those who understand it to be one of God's laws often neglect it. Nevertheless, God has established the spiritual law that He works in response to prayer. Therefore, if we want the blessings of God upon our lives and ministries—if we want the work of God going forth in power and bearing fruit—we must pray for the ministers of the gospel. We must learn to intercede in prayer.

> **"From whence come wars and fightings among you? come they not hence, even of your lusts that war in your members? Ye lust, and have not: ye kill, and desire to have, and cannot obtain: ye fight and war, yet ye have not, because ye ask not. Ye ask, and receive not, because ye ask amiss, that ye may consume it upon your lusts" (Jas.4:1-3).**

ILLUSTRATION:

Prayer is such a vital part of the believer's life. *God has sovereignly chosen to change and do certain things through those who pray.* Who is counting on your faithful prayers today?

There is a story told about underwater divers who worked during World War II. As fighting raged above the water, they performed their work under the water. While at work, their only connection with the world above was an air line which was hooked up to an air pump. While the underwater divers did their work, a man was stationed next to the pump to make sure it remained operational. If this man left his post, the diver would be at risk if the pump quit pumping air to his lungs.

God has stationed His people in key places. While some go "underwater" and work at bringing down the strongholds of the enemy, others have been assigned to pray for them. Prayer is the life-support system that requires our devotion. All over the world, God's workers are at war with the powers of darkness. Prayer warriors: don't forsake your post. Keep the air coming!

QUESTIONS:
1. God has posted you by the "air pump." Are you a life-saver or are lives at risk in your care?
2. How do you measure up against God's instruction to pray and to continue in prayer? How much do you pray? Are you faithful in praying?
3. What changes do you *need to make* in your prayer life? What changes are you *going to make* in your prayer life?
4. In what ways can you learn how to continue in prayer?
5. What do you think your role is in praying for others and for the work of God?

2. WALK WISELY BEFORE THEM WHO ARE WITHOUT CHRIST (v.5).

Note two significant points.
1. The phrase *"them that are without"* refers to the unbelievers of the world, those who are walking through life without Christ and God. Think what this means: they are walking...
- without hope beyond this life.
- without assurance of life hereafter with God.
- without help in facing the trials and traumas of this life.
- without peace.

- without security.
- without God's care and deliverance.
- without fellowship with God and His family of believers.
- without freedom from guilt—no assurance of forgiveness of sins.
- without light—no freedom from the darkness of death and the grave.

Scripture paints a sharp contrast between unbelievers who are *without Christ* and believers who are *within Christ*.

> **"That at that time ye were without Christ...having no hope, and with-**
> **out God in the world: but now in Christ Jesus ye who sometimes were far**
> **off are made nigh [near] by the blood of Christ" (Eph.4:12-13).**

2.   Believers are to walk in wisdom toward those who are without Christ, redeeming or making the best use of their time. To walk wisely means...

- that we walk thoughtfully, figuring out how to live for Christ before the world.
- that we walk righteously and godly.
- that we walk guarding every step.
- that we walk doing good works.

And note: we redeem the time; that is, we seek to grasp every moment to live for Christ before the lost people of the world. We always look for opportunities to do good and to let our light shine before men. We try to figure out how to make opportunities to bear witness by the way we live.

> **"Therefore we are buried with him by baptism into death: that like**
> **as Christ was raised up from the dead by the glory of the Father, even**
> **so we also should walk in newness of life" (Ro.6:4).**

ILLUSTRATION:

Our days are numbered. Even more important, the days of an unbeliever are also numbered. Every day God gives us opportunities to plant the seed of the gospel into the hearts of the lost.

The Christian believer must be aware of the needs of the lost. The great temptation is to get caught up in our own spiritual accolades and success. Listen to this sobering story.

> *"The Times-Reporter of New Philadelphia, Ohio, reported in September 1985 a celebration at a New Orleans municipal pool. The party around the pool was held to celebrate the first summer in memory without a drowning at any New Orleans city pool. In honor of the occasion, two hundred people gathered, including one hundred certified lifeguards.*
>
> *"As the party was breaking up and the four lifeguards on duty began to clear the pool, they found a fully dressed body in the deep end. They tried to revive Jerome Moody, thirty-one, but it was too late. He had drowned surrounded by lifeguards celebrating their successful season.*
>
> *"I wonder how many visitors and strangers are among us drowning in loneliness, hurt, and doubt, while we, who could help them, don't realize it. We Christians have reason to celebrate, but our mission, as the old hymn says, is to 'rescue the perishing.' And often they are right next to us."[2]*

QUESTIONS:

1.   Do you know at least five people personally who are unbelievers?
2.   What trials and challenges do these unbelievers face in life?
3.   Do you believe you have a role to play in sharing Christ with the lost?
4.   What specific things can you do in order to share Christ with them?
5.   What kinds of barriers are in your life that could confuse an unbeliever in his search for the truth? What practical things can you do to overcome these barriers?

3. SPEAK WITH GRACE—ANSWERING AND SHARING WHAT IT IS THAT MAKES YOUR LIFE DIFFERENT (v.6).

What an expectation God has of us: to be living a life so different and righteous that men ask us what it is that makes us different! How many live a life that is that different? That godly and righteous? Note exactly what is said.

When we are walking among unbelievers, we are to guard our speech and conversation. We are to...

- make sure that we speak with grace, that is, with kindness, courtesy, and graciousness.
- season our conversation with salt; that is, we are to flavor and turn the conversation to tasteful and enjoyable subjects and away from corruptible and tasteless subjects.

What happens when this is done is striking: unbelievers will begin to notice our lives and conversation—that we are different in a good and wholesome way. And some will ask us what it is that gives us such peace and security and assurance in life. We then have a unique opportunity to witness. Then we can reach out to bring in those who are so tragically without Christ, lost and doomed in despair and hopelessness forever.

> "Hold fast the form of sound words, which thou hast heard of me, in faith and love which is in Christ Jesus" (2 Tim.1:13).

ILLUSTRATION:

Does your tongue ever become paralyzed when you are given an opportunity to witness, or when you are confronted with the claims of a false religion? God wants each of us prepared to respond with a strong witness when opportunity arises.

> "Some years ago, Dr. Henrietta Mears visited the Taj Mahal in India. The famed structure is noted for its unusual acoustical qualities. Standing in the center of the white marble mausoleum, the guide said loudly, 'There is no God but Allah and Mohammed is the prophet!'
>
> "His voice reverberated through all the chambers and corridors of the tomb.
>
> "Dr. Mears asked, 'May I say something, too?'
>
> "The guide courteously replied, 'Certainly.' In a clear, distinct voice, Dr. Mears said, 'Jesus Christ. Son of God, is Lord over all!'
>
> "Her voice, too, reverberated from wall to wall and through the corridors of the...shrine, saying, 'Lord over all...over all...over all...over all!'"[3]

How often we are silent when someone gives us an opening to tell what the difference is in our lives. We need to have an answer for every one who does not know and recognize the only living and true God.

QUESTIONS:
1. You can expect certain opportunities to witness, such as dealing with a cult-member who knocks on your door in an attempt to convert you. Do you worry about what you will say?
2. Are you prepared to present the gospel to an unbeliever? What can you do to get prepared?
3. Think of a time when you were put on the spot and had to defend your faith. What thoughts went through your mind as this was happening? What can you do to prepare yourself to defend your faith in Christ?

SUMMARY:

What an exciting day in which to live! God has given us the responsibility to pray for His work and to witness to the world. How are you measuring up to this challenge? Has it been too hard? Do you want just to watch while others do the work? These responsibilities are for all who want to follow the Lord:

1. Pray and continue in prayer.
2. Walk wisely before them who are without Christ.
3. Speak with grace—answering and sharing what it is that makes your life different.

PERSONAL JOURNAL NOTES
(Reflection & Response)

1. The most important thing that I learned from this lesson was:

2. The area that I need to work on the most is:

3. I can apply this lesson to my life by:

4. Closing Statement of Commitment:

---

[1] William Barclay. *The Letters to the Philippians, Colossians, and Thessalonians*, p.198f.
[2] Craig B. Larson, Editor. *Illustrations for Preaching & Teaching*, p.152.
[3] Paul Lee Tan. *Encyclopedia of 7,700 Illustrations: Signs of the Times*, p.1618.

VII. CONCLUSION: THE EXAMPLE OF SOME HEROIC CHRISTIAN BELIEVERS, 4:7-18

1. Tychicus: The believer who served others
2. Onesimus: The believer who sought to correct his past & to make it right
3. Aristarchus: The believer who stood as a companion in trials
4. Mark: The believer who redeemed himself
5. Justus: The Jewish believer who turned from religion to Christ

7 All my state shall Tychicus declare unto you, who is a beloved brother, and a faithful minister and fellowservant in the Lord:
8 Whom I have sent unto you for the same purpose, that he might know your estate, and comfort your hearts;
9 With Onesimus, a faithful and beloved brother, who is one of you. They shall make known unto you all things which are done here.
10 Aristarchus my fellow prisoner saluteth you, and Marcus, sister's son to Barnabas, (touching whom ye received commandments: if he come unto you, receive him;)
11 And Jesus, which is called Justus, who are of the circumcision. These only are my fellowworkers unto the kingdom of God which have been comfort unto me.
12 Epaphras, who is one of you, a servant of Christ, saluteth you, always labouring fervently for you in prayers, that ye may stand perfect and complete in all the will of God.
13 For I bear him record, that he hath a great zeal for you, and them that are in Laodicea, and them in Hierapolis.
14 Luke, the beloved physician, and Demas, greet you.
15 Salute the brethren which are in Laodicea, and Nymphas, and the church which is in his house.
16 And when this epistle is read among you, cause that it be read also in the church of the Laodiceans; and that ye likewise read the epistle from Laodicea.
17 And say to Archippus, Take heed to the ministry which thou hast received in the Lord, that thou fulfil it.
18 The salutation by the hand of me Paul. Remember my bonds. Grace be with you. Amen.

6. Epaphras: The believer who fervently prayed & worked hard for the believers of his church
7. Luke: The beloved physician
8. Demas: The believer who slipped back
9. Nymphas: The believer who kept an open house
10. Archippus: The believer who was given a special task & needed encouragement
11. Paul: The believer who was faithful to the point of suffering imprisonment

---

Section VII
CONCLUSION:
THE EXAMPLE OF SOME HEROIC CHRISTIAN BELIEVERS
Colossians 4:7-18

Study 1:   THE EXAMPLE OF SOME HEROIC CHRISTIAN BELIEVERS

Text: Colossians 4:7-18

Aim: To follow the strong examples of some early Christian believers.

COLOSSIANS 4:7-18

Memory Verse:

"Wherefore seeing we also are compassed about with so great a cloud of witnesses, let us lay aside every weight, and the sin which doth so easily beset us, and let us run with patience the race that is set before us" (Hebrews 12:1).

INTRODUCTION:

If you take a trip to the Baseball Hall of Fame in Cooperstown, New York, you will take a trip back into time. Bronze busts with the likenesses of the hall-of-famers line the walls. On display are old baseballs, bats, gloves, hats, and uniforms which were used by these famous men. As you look at each display, your mind automatically takes you back to that period of time, and history is replayed right there in your mind.

This same experience happens to Christian believers when Biblical characters are studied. As you tour through God's Hall of Fame, you learn from the examples that have been left behind by these hall-of-famers. Instead of seeing bronze busts, baseballs, gloves, bats, hats, and uniforms, we see the outstanding qualities of these people.

This is one of the great lists of God's Hall of Fame, some of the heroic Christian believers of history.

OUTLINE:

1. Tychicus: the believer who served others (v.7-8).
2. Onesimus: the believer who sought to correct his past and to make it right (v.9).
3. Aristarchus: the believer who stood as a companion in trials (v.10).
4. Mark: the believer who redeemed himself (v.10).
5. Justus: the Jewish believer who turned from religion to Christ (v.11).
6. Epaphras: the believer who fervently prayed and worked hard for the believers of his church (v.12-13).
7. Luke: the beloved physician (v.14).
8. Demas: the believer who slipped back (v.14).
9. Nymphas: the believer who kept an open house (v.15-16).
10. Archippus: the believer who was given a special task and needed encouragement (v.17).
11. Paul: the believer who was faithful to the point of suffering imprisonment (v.18).

1. TYCHICUS: THE BELIEVER WHO SERVED OTHERS (v.7-8).

Tychicus was a native of Asia. He was a companion of Paul who often traveled with him (Acts 20:4).

⇒ He was commissioned by Paul as a messenger to various churches (Eph.6:21f; Col.4:7; 2 Tim.4:12; Tit.3:12).

⇒ He was entrusted to deliver the letters of Paul to the Ephesians, Colossians, and Philemon (Eph.6:21-22; Col.4:7-8).

⇒ He was sent on a special mission to Ephesus (2 Tim.4:12).

⇒ He was to be sent to Crete for the purpose of relieving Titus (Tit.3:12).

⇒ He was called not only Paul's beloved brother and faithful minister but also his fellow-slave (Col.4:7).

ILLUSTRATION:

The quality that stood out in Tychicus' life was his willingness to serve others. What qualifies a person to be used by God to serve others?

"Paul has told us, by inspiration, just what they are. D.L. Moody is quoted in the Keswick Calendar as follows:
"Paul sums up five things that God uses: 'the weak things,' 'the foolish things,' 'the

base things,' 'the despised things,' and 'the things which are not.' When we are ready to lay down our strength and our weakness before the Lord, He can use us. "[1]

Apparently, Tychicus had learned this lesson. Can you pass this same test?

QUESTIONS:
1. In what ways are you serving others? Are you comfortable with this level of commitment? Why or why not?
2. We live in a culture that cries out, "Serve Me!" What role do you have in breaking with this way of life?
3. How will an understanding of servanthood by your church leaders make the church relevant in your community?

2. ONESIMUS: THE BELIEVER WHO SOUGHT TO CORRECT HIS PAST AND MAKE IT RIGHT (v.9).

Onesimus was the runaway slave talked about in the Epistle to Philemon. Onesimus had fled from Colosse to Rome. Note what Paul says about him.

1.   He was a faithful and beloved brother. He had been led to the Lord either by Paul or some other believer in Rome. In either case, Paul knew Onesimus and knew him well. Paul was able to declare...

- that Onesimus was faithful to the Lord. He obeyed the Lord and kept His commandments, faithfully walking in Him day by day bearing testimony to His saving grace.

He was also a beloved brother, a brother in the Lord, who was held so dearly by other Christian believers that he was known as a *beloved brother*.

2.   He was so faithful to Christ and so beloved that he was now "one of you." Remember: he was a slave, and some in the Colosse church were wealthy property owners who owned slaves. This is a significant point. There are to be no social distinctions in the Lord's church. The poorest person is to be as welcomed and loved as the richest person.

3.   He was returning to Colosse with Tychicus. Why? Because he had broken the law by running away from his master, Philemon, and he wanted to make things right. He had been converted and God had forgiven him all his sins. He wanted Philemon to forgive him as well. (See The Epistle of Philemon for more discussion.)

> **"Therefore if thou bring thy gift to the altar, and there rememberest that thy brother hath ought against thee; leave there thy gift before the altar, and go thy way; first be reconciled to thy brother, and then come and offer thy gift. Agree with thine adversary quickly, whiles thou art in the way with him; lest at any time the adversary deliver thee to the judge, and the judge deliver thee to the officer, and thou be cast into prison" (Mt.5:23-25).**

QUESTIONS:
1. How hard is it for you to make things right in a broken relationship?
2. What was the source of Onesimus' ability to do the courageous thing? Do you place your trust in that same source?

3. ARISTARCHUS: THE BELIEVER WHO STOOD AS A COMPANION IN TRIALS (v.10).

Scripture says the following about Aristarchus:

⇒   He was a member of the Thessalonian church, a citizen of Thessalonica (Acts 19:29; 20:4).

⇒ He was one of the believers attacked by the violent mob in Ephesus. The citizens were rioting against Christianity because so many people were being converted that it was cutting into the sale of idols made to the goddess Diana. The fact that Aristarchus was one of the believers attacked and dragged before the mob shows that he was a leader and spokesman for Christ (Acts 19:29).

⇒ He went with Paul to minister in Asia (Acts 20:4).

⇒ He is seen traveling with Paul to Rome after Paul had been arrested and was being transferred to Rome as a prisoner (Acts 27:2).

⇒ He is seen as a fellow prisoner with Paul in Rome while Paul was awaiting trial on the charge of treason. Apparently, he too was being charged with the same crime (Col.4:10; Phile.24).

The point is that he was a *real companion*, a companion who stood by the side of his fellow believers through thick and thin. He would never think of deserting his dear friends or the Lord, no matter how difficult the task or terrible the trial. He would face imprisonment and suffer death before he would be a turncoat. He was a good man to have around when facing trials, for he would stand by his friends' side.

"Bear ye one another's burdens, and so fulfil the law of Christ" (Gal.6:2).

QUESTIONS:
1. What qualities do you look for in finding a faithful friend? Do others find these same qualities in you?
2. How do you think God wants you to respond when you have a friend who is undergoing a difficult trial?

4. MARK: THE BELIEVER WHO REDEEMED HIMSELF (v.10).

Mark had earlier deserted Paul and the ministry. But note what Paul says to the Colossian church. He tells the church that they are to receive Mark if he is able to visit them. Apparently, some earlier instructions had been sent to the churches founded by Paul telling them about Mark's desertion. But now the young man had repented and recommitted his life to Christ. He had redeemed himself; therefore, he was to be welcomed.

APPLICATION:
When a believer fails and sins, even if it is desertion of Christ, he is to be welcomed back with open arms once he has repented. We must not hold a person's failure and sin against him. Christ has forgiven us for so much—all of us—therefore, we must forgive and welcome our brothers and sisters back into our hearts and lives.

"Let the wicked forsake his way, and the unrighteous man his thoughts: and let him return unto the LORD, and he will have mercy upon him; and to our God, for he will abundantly pardon" (Is.55:7).

QUESTIONS:
1. Do you think God can redeem any mistake you make? Why or why not?
2. What is the ultimate goal of church discipline or correction? Is this the attitude that your church takes when members sin and then repent?

5. JUSTUS: THE JEWISH BELIEVER WHO TURNED FROM RELIGION TO CHRIST (v.11).

Note the word "circumcision": this means that he was a circumcised Jew who lived in Rome. Jews, of course, were strict religionists. Most of the Jews in Rome rejected Christ and turned a cold shoulder to Paul and his preaching of Christ (cp. Acts 28:17-29). But there were some who turned from religion to Christ (Acts 28:24). Justus was one, and he apparently became so strong in the Lord that he became a close companion of Paul, close enough for Paul to mention him to the Colossians.

Note: Paul says that all believers mentioned so far are Jewish believers, believers who had turned from religion to Christ. They were now working with Paul and other believers—working for the kingdom of God. Note that Paul also says that they had ministered to him personally and were a comfort to him while he was in prison.

APPLICATION:

It is an absolute essential for those who trust religion to turn to Christ. Religion cannot make a person acceptable to God; only Christ can.

> **"For I say unto you, That except your righteousness shall exceed the righteousness of the scribes and Pharisees [religionists], ye shall in no case enter into the kingdom of heaven" (Mt.5:20).**
> **"Not every one that saith unto me, Lord, Lord, shall enter into the kingdom of heaven; but he that doeth the will of my Father which is in heaven" (Mt.7:21).**

ILLUSTRATION:

One of the most difficult things for a lost person to do—a lost person who has been raised in a 'religious family'—is to break free and become born again (converted). Why? Because too many people have substituted religion in the place of a relationship with Jesus Christ. Charles Spurgeon, the great preacher of an earlier generation, had this insight:

> *"Have you ever read 'The Ancient Mariner'? I dare say you thought it one of the strangest imaginations ever put together, especially that part where the old mariner represents the corpses of all the dead men rising up to man the ship,--dead men pulling the rope, dead men steering, dead men spreading sails. I thought what a strange idea that was.*
> *"But do you know, I have lived to see that time. I have gone into churches, and I have seen a dead man in the pulpit, a dead man as deacon, a dead man handling the plate, and dead men sitting to hear."[2]*

Have you made the journey from a life of religion to a relationship which has given you life?

QUESTIONS:
1. Have you ever trusted "religion" to save you?
2. What are some habits or traps you can fall into that tie you to a *religion* but not to Christ?
3. What barriers does religion place in the hearts of people?
4. How does trusting God help you to leave behind a religion and find a personal relationship with Christ?

6. EPAPHRAS: THE BELIEVER WHO FERVENTLY PRAYED AND WORKED HARD FOR THE BELIEVERS OF HIS CHURCH (v.12-13).

⇒ He was the *"minister"* of the Colossian church (Col.1:7).
⇒ He was *"a faithful minister* of Christ" (Col.1:7).
⇒ He was *"a servant of Christ"* (Col.4:12).
⇒ He was a *"fellowservant"* who was held ever so dearly to Paul's heart (Col.1:7).
⇒ He was so committed and dedicated to Christ that Paul called him "my fellowprisoner in Christ Jesus" (Phile.23).
⇒ He was a believer who fervently labored and toiled in prayer for his dear people in Colosse (Col.4:12). He prayed in particular for one thing: that they might be perfect and complete in all the will of God; that is, that they might *know* the complete or full will of God and do it perfectly.

> "Praying always with all prayer and supplication in the Spirit, and watching thereunto with all perseverance and supplication for all saints" (Eph.6:18).

⇒ He was a minister who worked hard for his own church and for all the churches that surrounded him (Col.4:13, Laodicea and Hieropolis). He prayed and prayed much, but he also worked much—so much that his labor was even a testimony to the great minister Paul.

> "Jesus saith unto them, My meat is to do the will of him that sent me, and to finish his work. Say not ye, There are yet four months, and then cometh harvest? behold, I say unto you, Lift up your eyes, and look on the fields; for they are white already to harvest" (Jn.4:34-35).

QUESTIONS:
1. Do you think prayer is work? Explain your answer.
2. Is it sufficient to pray and not work?
3. What is the secret to the life of the church?
4. What commitments to your church need to be renewed in your heart?

7. LUKE: THE BELOVED PHYSICIAN (v.14).

Luke is said to be the *"beloved* physician"—a physician who was endeared to the hearts of believers. Apparently, his medical treatment of believers was diligent, compassionate, warm, and personal. He had an effective ministry for Christ among the believers.

> "A new commandment I give unto you, That ye love one another; as I have loved you, that ye also love one another. By this shall all men know that ye are my disciples, if ye have love one to another" (Jn.13:34-35).
> "And the Lord make you to increase and abound in love one toward another, and toward all men, even as we do toward you" (1 Th.3:12).

QUESTIONS:
1. What do you think makes a person compassionate? Are these qualities a realistic goal for your life? Why or why not?
2. Would anybody call you "beloved"? Explain your answer.

8. DEMAS: THE BELIEVER WHO SLIPPED BACK (v.14).

Demas was a man who turned away from Christ and back to the world. His life is written in tragedy—a life that serves as a warning to other believers—a life that shows the utter necessity of walking in Christ daily. At first, he is seen as a fellow laborer (Phile.24). Later he is just a name, with no commandment at all—perhaps suggesting the detection of some loss of spirit and energy in the work for the Lord (Col.4:14). Finally, he is Demas who "loved this present world" and forsook the Lord's work (2 Tim.4:10).

ILLUSTRATION:
What goes through the mind of a professing believer when he turns away from Christ? How can a person who shows excitement for the things of the Lord suddenly act like none of that meant anything at all? Well, backsliding does not happen "suddenly."

Mike Yaconelli writes in The Wittenburg Door:

> *"I live in a small, rural community. There are lots of cattle ranches around here, and every once in a while a cow wanders off and gets lost....Ask a rancher how a cow gets lost, and chances are he will reply, 'Well, the cow starts nibbling on a tuft of green grass, and when it finishes, it looks ahead to the next tuft of green grass and starts nibbling on that one, and then it nibbles on a tuft of green grass right next to a hole in the fence, so it nibbles on that one and then goes on to the next tuft. The next thing you know the cow has nibbled itself into being lost.'*
>
> *"...[Backsliders] keep moving from one tuft of activity to another, never noticing how far we have gone from home or how far away from the truth we have managed to end up."*[3]

QUESTIONS:
1. Do you ever worry about backsliding? What things have you done to safeguard yourself?
2. What specific things do you think attract potential backsliders?

9. NYMPHAS: THE BELIEVER WHO KEPT AN OPEN HOUSE (v.15).

Note that Nymphas lived in Laodicea, and Paul knew about him and his great testimony for Christ. He was so committed to Christ that he had opened his home to all the believers in the city, allowing them to use his home as the meeting place for the church. Remember: the early church had no buildings; therefore, they met in the homes of believers for joint worship and fellowship.

> **"Distributing to the necessity of saints; given to hospitality" (Ro.12:13).**
>
> **"But a lover of hospitality, a lover of good men, sober, just, holy, temperate" (Tit.1:8).**
>
> **"Be not forgetful to entertain strangers: for thereby some have entertained angels unawares" (Heb.13:2).**
>
> **"Use hospitality one to another without grudging" (1 Pt.4:9).**

QUESTIONS:
1. Who do you know like Nymphas? What qualities does the person have?
2. Where was fellowship centered in the early church? Have we lost any of that intimacy in the modern Church?
3. How can you cultivate and nurture this type of relationship in your own society? In your church?

A CLOSER LOOK: (v.15-16).

What is the letter sent to the Laodiceans?
- Was it a letter that has been lost?
- Was it the *Epistle to Philemon*?
- Was it the *Epistle to the Ephesians*?

No one knows, and opinions vary as to what the letter was. But note Paul's instructions to circulate it and the Colossian letters around and among the churches. This is a striking point: it means that the letters of the New Testament are not just casual letters between friends but are for believers of every generation and for every church. They are the inspired Word of God; and, therefore, are to be available to all believers to study and to live out the Word day by day.

---

10. **ARCHIPPUS: THE BELIEVER WHO WAS GIVEN A SPECIAL TASK AND NEEDED ENCOURAGEMENT (v.17).**

What was the ministry or task assigned to Archippus? We do not know. There is only one other mention of him, and that is where Paul calls him his fellowsoldier (Phile.2). Whatever it was, it must have been a task equal to the thrust of a military patrol. Military commitment and discipline must have been demanded. This is certainly understandable as the minister launches out to carry the gospel to a lost and ungodly world. Whatever the case with Archippus, he needed to be encouraged; he needed to *take heed and complete* his ministry.

APPLICATION:
How many believers quit, never to finish the task and ministry given to them? How many...
- need to "take heed": to keep their eye on God's call and not allow the world and its possessions and attacks to defeat them?
- need to "fulfill": keep on fulfilling and completing the ministry?

QUESTIONS:
1. Who needs your special encouragement today? (Your pastor, a missionary, your Bible teacher, your friend, other?)
2. What sorts of things can be done to encourage God's people when they are doing His work?

11. **PAUL: THE BELIEVER WHO WAS FAITHFUL TO THE POINT OF SUFFERING IMPRISONMENT (v.18).**

Paul signs the letter himself. Remember: his wrists were chained so he had to have a secretary write the letter while he dictated it. He simply closes by saying.
⇒ "Remember my bonds"—imprisonment; that is, pray for me.
⇒ "Grace be with you"—the favor and blessings of God—all of which we do not deserve but which He pours out upon us anyway.

ILLUSTRATION:
How can your faithfulness to Christ be measured? Paul remained faithful—even in the most adverse circumstances.

> "A Baptist pastor from Latvia spoke in Chicago. When his country was taken over by the Communists, many were put to death, and many others were sent to death, and many others were sent to a *living death* in slave-labor camps. The pastor spoke of the horrible persecution which Christians there have suffered. He related the story of a brave boy to whom the Communists had said, 'If you will deny Christianity and Christ, we will let you live!' The brave boy had answered, 'I will not deny my Lord Jesus Christ!' Thinking that they might change his steadfastness, the Communists then said, 'We will give you two hours to think over your fate and change your mind.' Bravely the boy replied, 'I don't need two hours. I know what I will do. I will not deny my Lord Jesus Christ.'
> "He was put to death." [4]

QUESTIONS:
1. What are some sacrifices you have had to make in your faith?
2. In what circumstances would you deny Christ?
3. How do you feel about the possibility of becoming a martyr one day?

SUMMARY:

As you have taken a graphic tour through God's Hall of Fame, what has impressed you the most? Has anything stirred your mind? As you reflect upon all that you have seen, the challenge resounds: *God would have you to be in the Hall of Fame also.* "What?!...Me?...In God's Hall of Fame?!"

Yes, you. God wants you to come to that place in your journey with Him. Impossible? No. Realistic? Yes. Willing? That will be up to you.

1. Tychicus: the believer who served others.
2. Onesimus: the believer who sought to correct his past and to make it right.
3. Aristarchus: the believer who stood as a companion in trials.
4. Mark: the believer who redeemed himself.
5. Justus: the Jewish believer who turned from religion to Christ.
6. Epaphras: the believer who fervently prayed and worked hard for the believers of his church.
7. Luke: the beloved physician.
8. Demas: the believer who slipped back.
9. Nymphas: the believer who kept an open house.
10. Archippus: the believer who was given a special task and needed encouragement.
11. Paul: the believer who was faithful to the point of suffering imprisonment.

PERSONAL JOURNAL NOTES
(Reflection & Response)

1. The most important thing that I learned from this lesson was:

2. The area that I need to work on the most is:

3. I can apply this lesson to my life by:

4. Closing Statement of Commitment:

---

1 Walter B. Knight. *3,000 Illustrations for Christian Service*, p.615.
2 Paul Lee Tan. *Encyclopedia of 7,700 Illustrations: Signs of the Times*, p.1128.
3 Craig B. Larson, Editor. *Illustrations for Preaching & Teaching*, p.230.
4 Walter B. Knight. *Knight's Treasury of 2,000 Illustrations*, p.122.

OUTLINE & SUBJECT INDEX

COLOSSIANS

OUTLINE & SUBJECT INDEX

COLOSSIANS

REMEMBER: When you look up a subject and turn to the Scripture reference, you have not only the Scripture, you have <u>an outline and a discussion</u> (commentary) of the Scripture and subject.

This is one of the <u>GREAT VALUES</u> of the Teacher's Outline & Study Bible. Once you have all the volumes, you will have not only what all other Bible indexes give you, that is, a list of all the subjects and their Scripture references, <u>BUT</u> you will also have...

- An outline of <u>every</u> Scripture and subject in the Bible.
- A discussion (commentary) on every Scripture and subject.
- Every subject supported by other Scriptures or cross references.

<u>DISCOVER THE GREAT VALUE</u> for yourself. Quickly glance below to the very first subject of the Index of Colossians. It is:

AFFECTION, EVIL
Meaning.   Col.3:5-7

Turn to the reference. Glance at the Scripture and outline of the Scripture, then read the commentary. You will immediately see the GREAT VALUE of the INDEX of The Teacher's Outline & Study Bible.

─────────────────

OUTLINE AND SUBJECT INDEX

AFFECTION, EVIL
Meaning.   Col.3:5-7

ALIENATION
Meaning.   Col.1:21-22

ANGELS
Nature. Created.   Col.1:16; cp.
                                                                      Ps.148:2-5
Position in creation. Organized in ranks or orders.   Col.1:16; 2:15
Worship of. False approach to God.   Col.2:18-19

ANGER
Duty. To strip off.   Col.3:8-11

ARCHIPPUS
Discussed.   Col.4:17

ARISTARCHUS
Discussed.   Col.4:10

ASSURANCE
Source - Comes by.
   Discussed.   Col.2:1-7
   Walking in Christ.   Col.2:6-7
Threefold.   Col.2:2

OUTLINE & SUBJECT INDEX

OUTLINE & SUBJECT INDEX

OUTLINE & SUBJECT INDEX

OUTLINE & SUBJECT INDEX

HEAVEN
Fact. Hope is laid up in h.   Col.1:5

HOLY
Meaning.   Col.1:22

HOPE
Basis of.
    Believer's life.   Col.1:5-8
    Faith & love.   Col.1:5-8
Source of h. The gospel or the Word of God.   Col.1:5-8

HUMILITY
Duty. To put on h.   Col.3:12
False h. Caused by. Religion of works.   Col.2:18, 23

HUSBAND
Discussed.   Col.3:19

IMAGE OF GOD
Believers are. Renewed in God's i.   Col.3:10
Christ. Is the i. of God.   Col.1:15

INDWELLING PRESENCE
Is a mystery.   Col.1:26-27
Of Christ. Christ in you. Discussed.   Col.1:26-27
Who dwells within. Christ dwells within.   Col.1:26

INHERITANCE
Of believer. Discussed.   Col.1:12

JESUS CHRIST
Creator. (See **CREATION**, Creator of)
Cross.
    Brings peace.   Col.1:20-23
    Purpose. To reconcile all things to God.   Col.1:20; 1:21-22
    The law was nailed to the cross.   Col.2:14
Death.
    Bore the sins, the guilt & punishment of sin for man.   Col.2:12; 2:20
    Purpose.
    To defeat evil spirits & forces of the universe.   Col.2:15
    To deliver man from sin & death, the law, and evil spirits.   Col.2:13-15
    To reconcile all things to God.   Col.1:20
    Substitutionary.   Col.1:20; 1:21-22
    To bring redemption & forgiveness.   Col.1:14
Deity.
    Embodiment of all wisdom & knowledge.   Col.2:3
    Fulness of God.   Col.1:19; 2:9-10
    Head of all principality & power.   Col.2:9-10
    Ideal, Perfect Man.   Col.2:12; 2:20
    Is the mystery of God.   Col.1:26-27
    Sinless--Perfectly obedient.   Col.1:21-22
    Vs. false teaching.   Col.2:8-23; 2:8-
                                         10; 2:11-12;
                                       2:13-15; 2:16-
                                       19; 2:20-23

OUTLINE & SUBJECT INDEX

OUTLINE & SUBJECT INDEX

OUTLINE & SUBJECT INDEX

OUTLINE & SUBJECT INDEX

OUTLINE & SUBJECT INDEX

WORSHIP

WRATH

SCRIPTURE INDEX

COLOSSIANS

SCRIPTURE INDEX

SCRIPTURE INDEX

(The Scripture Index follows the Order of the Books of the Bible)

SCRIPTURE INDEX

SCRIPTURE INDEX

ILLUSTRATION INDEX

COLOSSIANS

ILLUSTRATION INDEX

ILLUSTRATION INDEX

ILLUSTRATION INDEX

ILLUSTRATION INDEX

ILLUSTRATION INDEX

PURPOSE   STATEMENT

LEADERSHIP MINISTRIES WORLDWIDE

exists to equip ministers, teachers, and laymen in their
understanding, preaching, and teaching of God's Word
by publishing and distributing worldwide
The Preacher's Outline & Sermon Bible®
and related *Outline* Bible materials,
to reach & disciple men, women, boys, and girls for Jesus Christ.

•MISSION STATEMENT•

1. To make the Bible so understandable - its truth so clear and plain - that men
   and women everywhere, whether teacher or student, preacher or hearer,
   can grasp its Message and receive Jesus Christ as Savior; and...
2. To place the Bible in the hands of all who will preach and teach God's Holy
   Word, verse by verse, precept by precept, regardless of the individual's
   ability to purchase it.

The *Outline* Bible materials have been given to LMW for printing and especially
distribution worldwide at/below cost, by those who remain anonymous. One fact,
however, is as true today as it was in the time of Christ:

• The Gospel is free, but the cost of taking it is not •

LMW depends on the generous gifts of Believers with a heart for Him and a love and
burden for the lost. They help pay for the printing, translating, and placing *Outline*
Bible materials in the hands and hearts of those worldwide who will present God's
message with clarity, authority and understanding beyond their own.

LMW was incorporated in the state of Tennessee in July 1992 and received IRS 501(c) 3 nonprofit status in March 1994. LMW is an international, nondenominational mission organization.
All proceeds from USA sales, along with donations from donor partners, go 100% into under-
writing our translation and distribution projects of *Outline* Bible materials to preachers,
church & lay leaders, and Bible students around the world.

8/97   © 1997. Leadership Ministries Worldwide

PO Box 21310 - Chattanooga, TN 37424 • (423) 855-2181 • FAX (423) 855-8616
• E-Mail - outlinebible@compuserve.com — Web site: www.outlinebible.org •

LEADERSHIP MINISTRIES WORLDWIDE

Publisher & Distributor of…

The Preacher's Outline & Sermon Bible

Sharing the OUTLINED BIBLE with the World!

1. **AUTO-PLAN.** Your automatic monthly way to get any/all the volumes, paying as you go.

2. **NEW TESTAMENT.** In 14 volumes. Regular version 3-ring binders. SoftBound Set for church leadership training is compact & affordable for worldwide usage.

3. **OLD TESTAMENT.** In process; 1 volume releases about every 6-8 months, in sequence.

4. **THE MINISTERS HANDBOOK.** Acclaimed as a "must-have" for every minister or Christian worker. Outlines more than 400 verses into topics like Power, Victory, Encouragement, Security, Restoration, etc. Discount for quantities.

5. *THE TEACHER'S OUTLINE & STUDY BIBLE.* Verse-by-verse study & teaching; 45 minute lesson or session. Ideal for study, small groups, classes, even home schooling. Each book also offers a STUDENT JOURNAL for study members.

6. **POSB CD-ROM.** New Testament volumes on NavPress WORD*search*™ CD in STEP. Offers multiple options of Bible study tools; user unlocks and pays for only what they want. Useable with any STEP reader program. Ten Bible text options. **FREE Samples: LMW Web site.**

7. THE OUTLINE. Quarterly newsletter to all users and owners of *POSB.* Complimentary.

8. **LMW AGENT PLAN.** An exciting way any user sells *OUTLINE* materials & earns a second income.

9. **DISTRIBUTION.** Our ultimate mission is to provide *POSB* volumes & materials to preachers, pastors, national church leaders around the world. This is especially for those unable to purchase at U.S. price. USA sales gain goes 100% to provide volumes at affordable prices within the local economy.

10. **TRANSLATIONS.** Korean, Russian, & Spanish are shipping first volumes — a great effort and expense. Next priority: Asian project (1997) with six (6) other languages waiting, as funding allows.

11. **FUNDING PARTNERS.** To cover the cost of all the translations, plus print, publish, and distribute around the world is a multi million dollar project.

    Church-to-Church Partners send *Outline* Bible books to their missionaries, overseas church leaders, Bible Institues and seminaries…at special prices.

12. **REFERRALS.** Literally thousands (perhaps even you!) first heard of *POSB* from a friend. Now Referral Credit pays $16.00 for each new person who orders from a customer's Referral.

13. **CURRICULUM & COPYRIGHT.** Permission may be given to copy specific portions of *POSB* for special group situations. Write/FAX for details. 7/97

For Information about any of the above, kindly FAX, E-Mail, Call, or Write

Please PRAY 1 Minute/Day for LMW!

PO Box 21310, Chattanooga, TN 37424 • (423) 855-2181 • FAX (423) 855-8616
• E-Mail - outlinebible@compuserve.com — www.outlinebible.org •

LEADERSHIP
MINISTRIES
WORLDWIDE

Sharing

The

OUTLINED

BIBLE

With the World!